W9-BHI-109

HISTORY OF ARCHITECTURE

HISTORY OF ARCHITECTURE

FROM ANTIQUITY TO THE PRESENT

Chief Editor: Rolf Toman

Text: Barbara Borngässer

Photographs: Achim Bednorz

Bath · New York · Singapore · Hong Kong · Cologne · Delhi
Melbourne · Amsterdam · Johannesburg · Shenzhen

I. ANTIQUITY   8–39   II. LATE ANTIQUITY: EARLY CHRISTIANITY   40–55
      AND BYZANTIUM

III. ISLAMIC ARCHITECTURE IN EUROPE   56–65   IV. EARLY MIDDLE AGES   66–81

V. ROMANESQUE   82–109   VI. GOTHIC   110–145

VII. RENAISSANCE AND MANNERISM 146–181

VIII. BAROQUE AND ROCOCO 182–225

X. CLASSICISM AND ROMANTICISM 226–247

X. HISTORICISM AND CIVIL ENGINEERING 248–269

PRESENT

Foreword by the Editor

Author and cultural philosopher George Steiner has written an essay in which he proposes an ideal education. The disciplines he rates highest in his plan are mathematics, music, architecture and genetics. He writes that architecture is of particular value because of the extraordinary degree to which it intersects with many other disciplines. Everyone, Steiner maintains, not just young architects, should have at least some basic instruction in the subject: "We find ourselves today, historically speaking, in a magnificent period of architectural achievement. Exceptional public and private buildings, as well as bridges of breathtaking beauty and innovation, are being erected around the globe. The theoretical considerations and technical aspects incorporated in architectural design embrace disciplines ranging from geology, material science, engineering and design to higher mathematics. The realization of an architectural design involves economics and sociology, transportation, urbanization and ecology... ."

Contemporary architecture increasingly relies on computers, so much so

that architecture can be separated into pre- and post-computer ages. Frank Gehry's Guggenheim Museum Bilbao, a very famous building, would not have been possible without computer-assisted holographic modeling. Gehry even joked that the medals he won for its design should go to the computer.

The story of architecture has a decidedly historical dimension, and of course buildings tell us much about the thoughts and lifestyles of people from both the recent and distant past. Archi-

▲ Cape Sounion, Greece, Poseidon Temple, 449 BCE. This marble temple high above the Aegean Sea was rebuilt following the war with Persia.

▼ Michel Virlogeux (structural engineer) and Norman Foster (architect) designed the Viaduc de Millau, which opened in December 2004. Spanning the Tarn River in southern France, it is the tallest cable-stayed bridge in the world with a clearance of 866 feet/270 m.

▶ San Francisco, Transamerica Pyramid, William Pereira, 1969–1972.

tecture does more than tell us about the architects and patrons who built things; it is also a reflection of the people who used them. They might be travelers who admired structures from a distance, or perhaps enemies who sought to attack them. From the very beginning, it has been obvious to patrons and builders everywhere that architecture and aesthetics have a considerable effect on the general public. This is as true of the earliest temples and palaces of antiquity as for the cathedrals and citadels of the Romanesque and Gothic periods. Urban Renaissance palazzos and villas impressed onlookers much as castles and royal abbeys would in the baroque age, just as skyscrapers raised by banks and international corporations, sports arenas and mighty shopping complexes continue to do today.

The history of architecture before you stands out from the many other books available on the subject. This one lets pictures tell the story, with the accompanying text focusing on only the most important issues. This is a survey of architecture that relays what, when, where, by whom and for what purpose. At the same time, because architecture does not exist in isolation, this book looks at each work in its cultural context as a conscious expression of its time. While organized mainly according to the familiar chronological phases common to the disciplines of art and architectural history, there are a few additional consistent points of emphasis. The functional aspects of sacred and secular buildings, together with technological achievements of different eras, are examined in great detail. The social point of view is also brought into focus, particularly with respect to the role of urban planning. Buildings' patrons and architects are named, and architecture as a means of aristocratic and personal self-expression is discussed in context.

Aspects of architectural theory are introduced as a final complement to this wide-ranging survey of architecture from antiquity to the present day. It is the buildings themselves that occupy center stage, rather than their designers. As a result, biographical information about architects is brief, with a few exceptions, as when efforts are made to bring a forgotten architect to the attention of a wider public. We will look at, for example, the works of Marshal Vauban, a seldom-studied baroque period master who devoted his life to the design of purely functional, highly effective fortification systems. The text is concise and written so as to be easy to understand. Technical vocabulary is used only when necessary.

Throughout the course of history, architecture has contributed so much that is beautiful and magnificent to the world. The worth of a great building is apparent even when it is lying in ruins. It is no exaggeration to say that the glorious buildings presented here are foremost among the architectural treasures of humankind.

From the First Huts to the Seven Wonders of the World

The first buildings were constructed after humans adopted a sedentary lifestyle and discovered advantages to permanent housing. Models and materials for the earliest structures were provided by the natural world. Their primary goal was protection: from weather, wild beasts or enemies. Interest in form, style and the acquisition of special skills for creative expression came later, when religious structures—"houses of the gods"— grave monuments, and other buildings expressing social prestige gained cultural importance. These instances of specialized construction can be considered the birth of architecture.

The character, quality and beauty of individual works were already a topic of discussion in Homer's poetry, and by the second century BCE, certain buildings were so famous that books were written about them. The historian Antipater of Sidon wrote descriptions of seven structures, not all of them habitable buildings, in a poem, *The Seven Marvels of the Inhabited World.* Antipater's collected verses testify to the significance of architecture, and are the earliest known example of an architectural canon that compiles and classifies individual monuments. Surveys such as *The Seven Marvels,* which introduce and give detailed commentary on great works, have existed in nearly every era, and cover every variety of architectural style. Similar books—including this one—are still a means of learning about buildings today.

▲ Reconstruction of the Temple of Artemis of Ephesos, 560–440 BCE.

◄ The Chepren (Egyptian = *Khafre*) and Cheops (Egyptian = *Khufu*) Pyramids, ca. 2620–2500 BCE.

▼ Reconstruction of the Mausoleum of Halicarnassos, tomb of the Carian King Mausolos II, 368–350 BCE.

Antipater named seven structures, in part because seven was considered the most cosmologically perfect number. His choice of marvels concentrated on his immediate stomping ground: the Mediterranean and Near East. Antipater's list includes the Hanging Gardens of Babylon; the Colossus of Rhodes; the Pharos (lighthouse) of Alexandria; the Pyramids of Giza; the Temple of Artemis of Ephesos; and the Statue of Zeus at Olympia, one of two colossal sculptures on the list. Only the pyramids have survived.

Over the centuries, there has been no shortage of proposals for expanding or modifying the original list. A recent Internet poll declared seven new Wonders of the World, listing marvels like the Great Wall of China and the Roman Colosseum. More than one million people took part in the survey, confirming that there is as much popular interest in architecture today as ever.

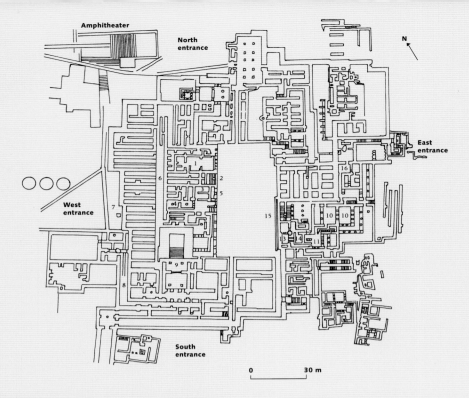

Early Cultures

Long before classical Greek architecture set standards that have guided the art of building ever since, Mesopotamia, the Levant, Egypt and Crete were home to imposing palaces, temples and monumental tombs. Though much less familiar to most than the iconic Egyptian pyramids, of the earliest monumental architecture, the Mesopotamian ziggurats are also worthy of mention. These stepped temple platforms, which tower up to 298 ft (91 m) high, may have functioned as astronomical observatories as well as religious sites. In Egypt, the temple complexes of Karnak, Luxor and Abu Simbel bear witness to the skill of ancient architects. On the island of Crete, the labyrinthine Palace of Knossos was built during the sixteenth and fifteenth centuries BCE. Its complexity, size and elaborate decoration represent the apex of Minoan culture. The Greek

▲ Plan of the Palace of Knossos. The enormous complex included a throne room (1), an elaborate stairway (2), temple storage rooms (3), a pillar shrine (4), a sanctuary (5), magazine-style storage (6), altars (7), a processional way (8), stairway (9), the "Hall of the Double Axes" (10), the "Queen's Megaron" (11), toilets (13), palace storerooms (14), a monumental staircase (15) and a masons' quarter (16).

◀ ▲ ▶ Mycenae, Greece, Lion Gate (l) and the entrance (ctr) and interior (r) of the ca. 1250 BCE tomb called the Treasury of Atreus.

Peloponnesus is the site of what Heinrich Schliemann called the Treasury of Atreus, a Mycenaean tholos tomb. The tomb is roofed by one of the earliest domes, though it not a true dome, but a corbelled one, with each course stepped inward as it rises to the top.

While it is still not clear how close contacts between these early civilizations might have been, it is undisputed that the architecture of earlier, local cultures influenced the course of later Greek architecture. The 600 BCE Hera Temple at Olympia is an example. This rectilinear ante temple has one of the earliest examples of a *peripteros*, rows of columns that enclose a building on all sides. Originally wooden, the columns were replaced one by one by limestone columns in the Doric style. This supports the theory that the structural elements and style of Greek temples derive from local, wooden prototypes.

Another example of later architecture copying earlier monuments comes from the mighty empire of the Persians. Rulers Darius I and Artaxerxes I built the palace city of Persepolis, where construction began in 518 BCE. Like the earlier ziggurats, the palace consists of a series of stepped terraces. The Persian innovation is elaborate figural decoration sculpted in low relief showing the Persian subjects lining up to pay homage.

▲ The palace complex of Persepolis, 518–460 BCE, with relief sculpture on the walls of the stairway leading to the throne room.

▼ Olympia, Temple of Hera, ca. 600 BCE. This view shows the rows of columns constituting the peripteros as well as the cella, the inner cult chamber.

▲ Aegina, Temple of Aphaia, ca. 495 BCE. The Doric-style Temple of Aphaia, built at the transition between the archaic and classical periods, has more elegant proportions than its predecessor on the site. The stone masonry of the building was originally covered in stucco and brightly painted.

The Greek Temple

Greeks and Romans believed their fate lay in the hands of the gods. As a result, their temples and sanctuaries were antiquity's most distinguished works of architecture. Most Greek temples consist of a windowless *cella*, the room housing the cult image, and an *adyton*, a smaller room reserved for priests. Early on, columns were found only in front of the entrance porch (*prostyle*), and later across the rear facade of the building as well (*amphiprostyle*). Still later, a single *peripteros*, or even a double line of columns (*dipteros*), continued around all four sides of the temple. Round temples, called *tholoi*, are a special building type with a rounded cella surrounded by a circular peripteros.

The temple facade consists of a triangular pediment with a flat, often decorated central space called the tympanum. The entablature is beneath the pediment and is supported by the columns. The gabled roof was often decorated with a sculptural *acroterion* of painted stone or terracotta. The famous orders of Greek architecture determine the elements' details, a building's proportions, the style of the column capitals, and the divisions of the architrave. Greek architecture recognized three orders: Doric, Ionic and Corinthian. Doric is considered the oldest and is more robust than the slightly later, slender Ionic order. The elaborate Corinthian order with its characteristic acanthus leaf capital was introduced last, at the turn of the fourth century BCE. Ancient Greek scholars saw these types as natural stylistic developments. Later, Roman author Vitruvius assigned each of the orders a "character." His seminal work, *De architectura*, dedicated to Emperor Augustus, describes column styles in terms of their masculine, feminine or even "maidenly" qualities.

▲ Segesta, Italy, temple, 425–415 BCE. The buildings in this Sicilian sanctuary are fully in the classical style of the 5th century BCE. The Segesta temple is one of the most beautiful examples of Greek art in southern Italy.

▶ Delphi, Greece, Tholos Temple of Athena Pronaia, by Theodoros of Phokaia, ca. 370 BCE.

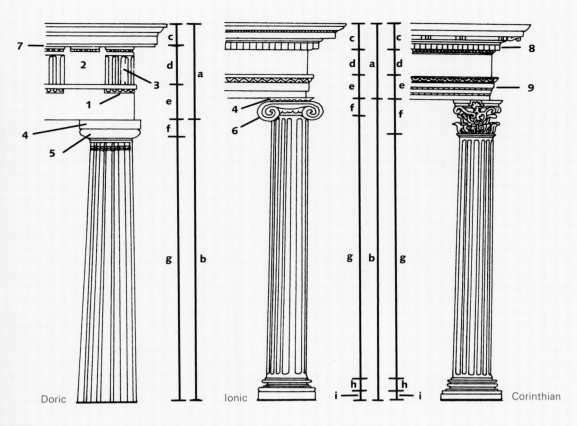

The orders of
classical architecture

a entablature
b column
c cornice
d frieze
e architrave
f capital
g shaft
h base
i plinth or stylobate
1 guttae
2 metope
3 triglyph
4 abacus
5 echinus
6 volute
7 mutule
8 dentils
9 fascia

Doric

Ionic

Corinthian

Stadiums and Theaters

▲ Olympia, entrance to the stadium, 3rd century BCE.

Physical education and intellectual training formed the basis of ancient Greek culture. Victors of the Olympic games held every seven years won fame and glory along with their laurel wreaths, and achieved some measure of social status, as well. Most Greek cities had

several *gymnasia* (sports schools) and *palaestra*, open-air training arenas with tracks and wrestling rings organized around a *peristyle* (columned) court.

Always built into sloping terrain, a Greek theater had rows of seats rising up from the orchestra, a round, flat space like a dance floor. The *skene*, or stage platform, ran along one side. A smaller variation is the *odeion*, which, unlike the theater, was roofed. Due to their better acoustics, odeions were used mainly for musical performances.

The fourth-century-BCE Monument of Lysicrates, dedicated to an important Athenian chorus leader and patron of the arts, is an architectural curiosity. Its opulent styling confirms the high status of ancient Greek theater. It is also one of the earliest Greek structures built completely in the Corinthian order.

▶ The Theater of Epidauros, late 4th and 3rd centuries BCE. The semicircular theater could seat up to 15,000 people. The Greek historian and traveler Pausanias identified Polykleitos the Younger as its architect.

◀ Athens, the Monument of Lysicrates, 335–334 BCE.

Cities and Urban Planning

The Greek *polis* (city) was more than a group of buildings; it was a political and social entity, as well. The polis was organized around an *acropolis*, an upper city often atop a fortified hill, and site of the city's most important sanctuaries. If space allowed, other public buildings might also be there. Most Greek cities had an *agora* (open air marketplace), a *bouleterion* (council hall and court), several *stoa* (columned arcades), a *nymphaeon* (spring house) and a *prytaneon* (city hall). Stadiums, theaters and libraries filled in the urban landscape. Private houses consisted of rooms grouped around a central, peristyle courtyard or, in denser areas, narrow rooms fronted by a columned porch.

As Greek cities expanded, the challenges became more complex, leading to the advent of urban planning. Ancient Greek urban planning culminated in the work of Hippodamos of Miletus, who in 479 BCE devised the standard grid plan known as the Hippodamian system. City planners used its principles well into the twentieth century. Hippodamos designed his grid to make the most efficient use of the unusual shape of the Milesian peninsula. His broad streets, up to 28 ft (8.5 m) wide, cross at right angles, allowing integration of open spaces and plazas. Circulation space could easily be integrated with sanctuaries and public buildings. The Miletus city center of twelve *insulae* (city blocks) could be practically located just south of the agora. Prior to his work at Miletus, Hippodamos had also worked on the city plan for the important Athenian harbor town of Piraeus and had devised an even more advanced system for the challenging, uneven terrain of Priene in Asia Minor.

Urban planning took a different path in the Hellenistic period of the fourth and third centuries BCE: the goal was a visually impressive urban landscape, with the city's practical needs no longer top priority. Planners designed cities that resembled elaborate theatrical sets, with buildings carefully "directed" to dramatic effect. The Great Altar of Pergamon, now in the Pergamon Musuem in Berlin, is best understood in this context. It occupied the highest terrace of Pergamon's upper city, and as its physical location implied, the Pergamon Altar ranks among the highest artistic achievements of that city.

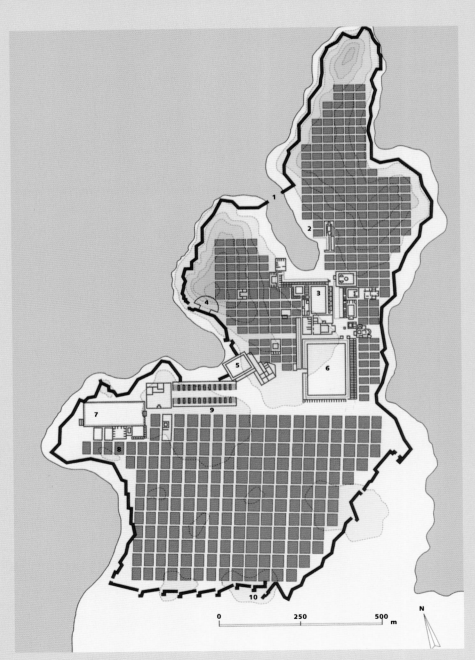

◄ Reconstructed plan of the city of Miletus, Hippodamos of Miletus, 479 BCE.
1. Market gate
2. Roman baths
3. Northern agora
4. Theater
5. Palaestra
6. Southern agora
7. Western agora
8. Athena Temple
9. Stadium
10. Holy gate

0   250   500 m

N

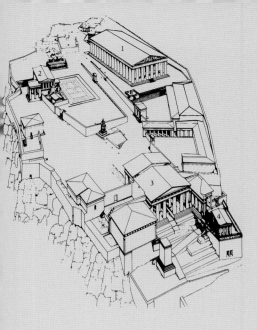

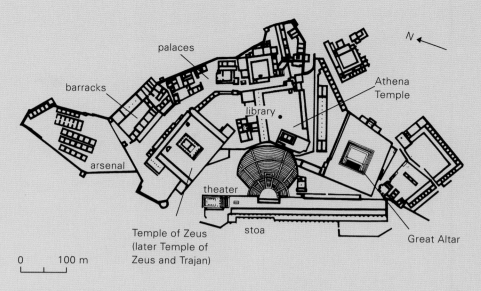

palaces

barracks

Athena
Temple

library

arsenal

N

theater

Temple of Zeus
(later Temple of
Zeus and Trajan)

stoa

Great Altar

0   100 m

▲ Reconstruction of the Athenian Acropolis, late 5th century BCE: 1) Parthenon, 2) Erectheion, 3) Propylaeon, 4) Nike Temple.

▲ Bergama, Turkey, reconstruction of the Pergamon upper city of the 3rd and 2nd centuries BCE.

▼ Berlin, Pergamon Museum with the Great Altar of Zeus, 180–160 BCE.

The Athenian Acropolis

The Acropolis of Athens is by far the most important assemblage of ancient Greek architecture that ever existed. Most of what can be seen today was built in the fifth century BCE, when Athens was the undisputed center of the Hellenic world. The most famous artists of the time, including the sculptor Phidias and architects Iktinos and Kallikrates, were called to work at the Acropolis. The superb Propylaeon complex, designed by Mnesikiles, serves as the gateway to the 512-ft (156-m) high rock plateau and its many sanctuaries. The delicately proportioned Nike Temple is to its right. The higher part of the plateau was occupied by the Chalcotheke, a treasury, along with other buildings, all in service of the cult of the goddess Athena. The monumental statue of Athena Promachus stood in front of her temple: the Parthenon. For reasons of perspective, elements of this Doric order building were deliberately tilted and bowed, using optical

illusions to enhance its magnificence. A colossal gold and ivory statue of Athena stood at one end of the cella. The cella's outer wall had a sculpted frieze showing the Panathenaic procession, the ceremonial finale of the annual festival in Athena's honor. The great altar of the goddess stood at one end of the central axis of the acropolis, with the Erectheion and its famous caryatid

▲ ▶ ▼ Athens, the Acropolis. Southern side of the Erechtheion with caryatid porch (above) and detail of the caryatids (opposite), 421–406 BCE; view of the Acropolis from the southwest showing the Parthenon (below), built 447–432 BCE.

porch to the left. Caryatids, statues of maidens used as columns, would be a favorite decorative device of the classical revival in the nineteenth century.

Roman Architecture

A large part of the Italian peninsula came under Greek influence beginning in the eighth century BCE, circumstances to which numerous large, Greek-style temples in southern Italy and Sicily bear splendid witness. Around the third century BCE, the picture began to change as Rome gained control of not only the Mediterranean, but also of the Atlantic coast as far north as the British Isles. The Roman Empire later added territories as far to the east as the Black Sea. The Roman language, Latin, along with Roman art, spread to the most distant reaches of the new empire, uniting distant peoples and lands. The imprint of Rome on European culture continues to this day.

Roman architecture was at first rather slow to distinguish itself from the overwhelming influence of Greek prototypes. Many Greek buildings were simply copied with little modification, or with the addition of new orders of columns, such as the Tuscan or composite style columns. The new kinds of

▲ Rome, Arch of Constantine in the Forum Romanum, dedicated 315 CE.

columns could appear alone, or with Ionic or Corinthian elements. New techniques, such as the invention of structural concrete and an improved mortar, led to the construction of monumental, domed structures, most prominently baths, basilicas and other

public buildings. Domes in later European architecture were based on Roman models. Roman cities revolved around *fora*, enormous marketplaces and public assembly sites where the emperors erected their monuments. The Roman theater redefined the semicircular Greek variety in a free-standing, round building called the amphitheater. Amphitheaters could be built anywhere, unlike Greek theaters, which had to be built into a hillside. The Romans also developed the podium temple, which had the cella set atop a tall platform like Etruscan prototypes.

The Romans also introduced many completely new building types, such as the triumphal arch. These free-standing monuments, which were raised to honor victorious emperors or generals, are found throughout the Roman Empire. The single-, double- or triple-arched facades would be copied well into the nineteenth century. Villas and palaces, at first simply larger and more elaborate versions of Hellenistic

◄ Timgad, Algeria, view of the theater in the city founded by Trajan around 100 CE.

▲ Rome, round temple in the Forum Boarium, late 2nd century BCE.

▼ Trier, Germany, Aula Palatina, the former throne room of Constantine the Great, ca. 310 CE.

▲ Rome, Trajan's Market, Apollodorus of Damascus, 107–112 CE.

houses, eventually developed into a new kind of private dwelling in which the emphasis was on luxury. The high point of Roman palatial architecture is the Palace of Diocletian in Split, Croatia. Its innovative design elements, such as the "broken pediment," and its sheer scale are an embodiment of the military power and cultural influence of the empire. After Constantine the Great legalized Christianity with the Edict of Milan in 313 CE, ancient, pagan architectural styles and building types were adapted to the new religion. The basilica, with its pillared or columned hall, side naves and large windows, served as the primary prototype for the Early Christian church.

The Throne Room of Constantine the Great, the Aula Palatina in Trier, Germany, is one of the most impressive and best-preserved buildings that has survived from antiquity. While every surface of the interior of the brick-and-mortar structure was originally clad in marble, the brick masonry is all that survives today.

Transportation and Civil Engineering

The Roman Empire, created by war, was maintained by constant military campaigns. An exceptional administrative system and a dense network of transportation and supply routes linked distant provinces and sustained long-range military operations. Roman roads and other civil works built throughout the empire served secondarily as visible proof of Rome's cultural dominance.

The Appian Way, completed in 312 BCE, was one of the world's first long distance highways. It was designed as a military road to connect far-flung, strategically important locations. Many more such roads followed, and they define Europe's transportation routes to the present day. Masters of the vault and arch, the Romans also left behind a number of impressive bridges and, especially, aqueducts that could supply entire cities and regions with water.

The most impressive example of Roman engineering to survive is the Pont du Gard in southern France. Just under 985 ft (300 m) long and up to 164 ft (50 m) high, this beautiful

▶ Nîmes, France, Pont du Gard aqueduct, 19 BCE.

aqueduct with its three levels of arches was completed during the reign of the Emperor Augustus in 19 BCE. Each of its blocks was precisely laid without mortar. There is a similarly elegant aqueduct in Segovia, Spain. Built during the reign of Trajan, it still supplies water to the city today.

Fortification walls with towers and gates surrounded most Roman settlements. The Aurelian Walls encircling Rome were the earliest, completed in 270 CE. By far the most extensive city fortifications in the world at that time, the 12-mile/19-km long walls had 18 gates and 381 towers. Several older, pre-existing buildings were built into them. One of the latest examples of a Roman fortification is the Porta Nigra in Trier, of which only the monumental city gate remains. Like most ancient defense systems, the Trier walls were extensively modified and rebuilt during the medieval period.

Most Roman provincial cities (*colonia*) began as *castra*, or military camps. The camps and the towns were laid out according to a plan based on two major streets crossing at right angles in the city center. The north-south *cardus maximus*, the main commercial and administrative street, and the east-west *decumanus maximus*, which ran between the main entry and exit gates, served as the primary circulation axis. The most important buildings were clustered near the intersection of these two arteries. As befits the military character of both castra and colonia, theaters, baths and other complexes were located on the outer edges of the settlements. The basic Roman city plan is still discernible in many cities today.

◀ Trier, Porta Nigra, late 2nd century BCE.

▶ Rome, Aurelian city walls, ca. 270 CE.

Pompeii and Herculaneum

The 79 BCE eruption of the volcano Vesuvius buried the small towns on its slopes under up to 65 ft (20 m) of lava, ash and mud. The eruption, ash falls and landslides caused great loss of life. For those who study the ancient world, however, the circumstances of the towns' demise could not have been more favorable. Thick volcanic deposits preserved the streets and houses of Pompeii, Herculaneum and Stabiae in their everyday condition, exactly as they were at the moment of their destruction. The first unsystematic excavations began in the mid-eighteenth century and continue today, much more scientifically. There is still a long way to go before all areas of the towns are revealed.

Pompeii and Herculaneum were Oscian cities that had already been occupied variously by Greeks and Etruscans before their conquest by Rome in 89 BCE, after which they were administered as colonies. Several phases of urban development can be read in Pompeii's city plan. The old city, oriented according to two main streets, makes up the southwest quadrant, which includes the forum, baths and theater. The residential quarters follow the Greek Hippodamian system, radiating out from its core in rectilinear insulae. Each insula consisted of a line of houses closed off to the street side, which was instead lined with stores or workshops. Roads were wide, paved, and well-suited for vehicle traffic. Steppingstones were put in place so that pedestrians could easily cross between curbed sidewalks. The last building phase is represented by the Roman palaestra and enormous amphitheater located east of the ring road that encircles the older parts of the city.

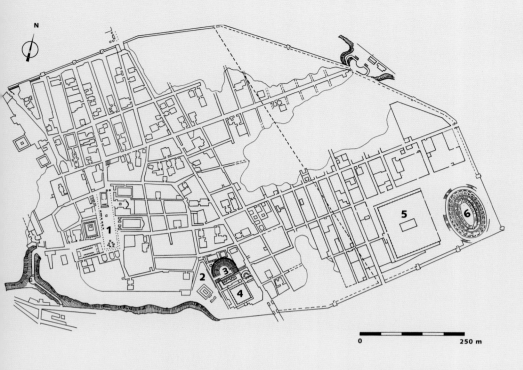

▲ Plan of the city of Pompeii in 79 BCE. The grid plan of the residential quarters is easily recognizable.

1. Forum 2. Forum Triangolare 3. Theater 4. Palaestra 5. Great Palaestra 6. Amphitheater

◀ Pompeii, view of a street with curbed sidewalk and stepping stones.

◄ Pompeii, Villa of the Mysteries, ca. 60 BCE. The frescoes show scenes from a Dionysus cult.

▼ Pompeii, peristyle courtyard of the House of the Dioscuri, 1st century BCE.

The Roman House: Layout and Interior Decoration

The typical Roman house consisted of a series of residential and public rooms organized around an open-air atrium in its center. The larger, most luxurious examples could also have a peristyle courtyard to the rear. The atrium and peristyle might be decorated with fine floor mosaics, while interior walls were plastered and elaborately painted. Brightly colored frescoes were painted with scenes of illusionist architecture set in paradisiacal landscapes. Gods and goddesses gestured from inside painted-on picture frames. Still life paintings, grotesques and imitation marble statues completed the extraordinarily diverse decorative program of the wealthy Roman household.

▲ Herculaneum, Women's Baths, 1st century BCE.

◄ Herculaneum, summer *triclinium* (dining room) with wall mosaic from the House of Neptune and Amphitrite, 1st century BCE.

▲▼ Rome, the Forum Romanum with view of the Temple of Castor and Pollux (above) and Decennial base (below).

▲ Remains of the Temple of Vesta in the Forum Romanum.

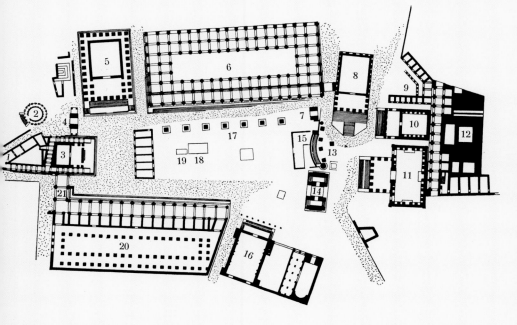

Rome, plan of the Forum Romanum
1. Regia
2. Temple of Vesta
3. Temple of Julius Caesar
4. Arch of Augustus
5. Temple of Castor and Pollux
6. Basilica Julia
7. Arch of Tiberius
8. Temple of Saturn
9. Porticus Deorum Consentium
10. Temple of Vespasian
11. Temple of Concord
12. Tabularium
13. Five-column monument of
   the Tetrarchs
14. Arch of Septimus Severus
15. Rostra
16. Curia
17. Column of Phocas
18. Equestrian statue of Constantine
19. Equestrian statue of Domition
20. Basilica Aemilia
21. Porticus of Gaius and Lucius

Rome: The Forum Romanum and Imperial Fora

The forum is the Roman equivalent of the Greek agora: both are open-air complexes for commercial activity and public assembly. The most important religious and public buildings were built there. Rome had many fora, but the Forum Romanum is the oldest and most important. Located between the Capitoline and Palatine hills, its main axis was the *Via Sacra* (holy street), the route of religious processions, but also of the triumphal parades awarded to victorious generals and emperors. Over the course of the imperial period, Rome grew ever larger, and there was an increasing need for new, more extensive public spaces. Caesar was the first to build his own forum in his name. The Forum Caesaris consists of three columned portico buildings. The emperors Augustus, Nerva and Trajan followed his example, building ever more monumental, increasingly self-referential complexes. The Forum of Augustus introduced the *exedra*, a semicircular, alcove-like space created by bowing the facade of a columned portico. In Augustus' Forum, exedra flank the temple of Mars Ultor, subtly increasing the space available for public assembly. The architect Apollodorus of Damascus used this element to great effect in Trajan's Forum (see p. 23), the largest and most magnificent of them all, built between 107 and 112 CE. Among the many limestone and marble-clad brick buildings in this 660 x 290 ft (200 x 120 m) complex are a covered market building (Trajan's Market) and libraries for both Greek and Latin texts.

◀ The Forum of Augustus, dedicated in 2 BCE, was built in honor of the Battle of Phillippi (42 BCE), in which Octavian, later Augustus, avenged the murder of Julius Caesar. To the right are three columns of the Temple of Mars Ultor.

Temples and Theaters

Roman temples combine Greek architectural elements with traditions native to Italy. The podium temple, a cella and porch elevated on a high platform, was originally an Etruscan type. The earliest example in Rome is the Temple of Portunus in the Forum Boarium, built around 100 BCE, which is at the same time one of the few surviving examples of a Roman Republican temple. The most elegant podium temple, the Maison Carrée in Nîmes, France, dates to the imperial period reign of Emperor Augustus. Later Roman temples were larger with more highly embellished exteriors. The round tholos temple continued to be used throughout the imperial period, when it was dedicated primarily as a cult building for heroes and other more earthbound deities.

The Roman theater was the location of cult activities as well as gladiatorial sports. Unlike Greek theaters, which were semicircular in plan and set against a sloping hillside that supported the seating, Roman theaters were freestanding amphitheaters with rows of seats on all sides. In the process of transformation, the performance area shifted from the *proscenium*, an elevated stage at one end of the theater, to the rounded or elliptical central space of the ground

◀▼ Orange, France, Roman theater, beginning of the 1st century CE. A portrait statue of Augustus is set in the facade (l), and a view of the seating and stage (below).

level orchestra. A tall *scanae* served as an architectonic backdrop. One of the most impressive Roman theaters is the Theater of Mérida in Spain, begun in 18–15 BCE and completed more than a century later during the reigns of emperors Trajan and Hadrian. It could seat an audience of 6,000. Roman amphitheaters were built throughout the Mediterranean and North Africa. The most famous of them all is the Colosseum in Rome.

◄ Nîmes, France, Maison Carrée, 15–12 BCE.

▼ Mérida, Spain, view of the stage and architectonic backdrop of the Roman theater, begun 18–15 BCE.

The Colosseum and the Pantheon

▲ ▼ Rome, Pantheon, 118–125 CE. Interior view showing the cassette structure and central oculus of the great dome (above), and the Pantheon's temple-like porch with 16 monolithic granite columns (below).

Built between 70 and 80 CE, the Colosseum in Rome is the largest amphitheater of the Roman Empire, and is most significant in the history of architecture. With dimensions of 615 x 510 ft (188 x 156 m) and 157 ft (48 m) tall, this massive structure could seat 50,000 people. Due to its weight, the entire amphitheater was built atop foundations providing structural support. Its central arena could be flooded for reenactments of naval battles (*naumachia*). An enormous sunshade (*verlarium*) could be pulled into place to shade the audience from the heat of the sun. The structural engineering of the perimeter walls and arcades would influence architecture well into the modern age. The exterior

facade is divided into three levels, each pierced by eighty arches, and topped by a high attic. Pilasters in the Doric (lowest level), Ionic (middle) and Corinthian orders (upper level) flank each arch.

Built by Hadrian in 118–125 CE, the Pantheon, a temple dedicated to all the gods (*pantheoi*) was also influential. A cylindrical building with a temple-like porch, the Pantheon's roof is a vast, hemispherical dome pierced by a central oculus open to the sky. The concrete dome is supported by barrel vaults and relieving triangles built into the walls. Rectilinear ceiling cutouts (*cassettes*) reduce the dome's great weight and increase its visual appeal. The interior walls are elaborately finished with alternating rounded and rectilinear niches that once held statues of the gods. Today, as then, the enormous dome dominates the space.

▲ ▼ Rome, facade (above) and interior view (below) of the Colosseum, built between 70 and 80 CE. Storage rooms and corridors were located underneath the performance space.

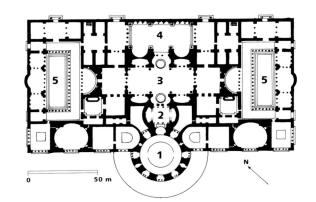

▶ Rome, the Baths
of Caracalla, plan.
1. Caldarium
2. Tepidarium
3. Frigidarium
4. Natatio
5. Palaestra

▼▼ Rome, Baths of Cara-
calla (below), and ruins of
the large, ancient bath complex (bottom), 206–216 CE.

Baths

"A healthy mind in a healthy body." Although the context of the Latin poet Juvenal's famous phrase remains unknown, it documents the value the ancient world placed on physical fitness. The Greeks had already introduced the gymnasium and palaestra as sports and recreation facilities. It was the invention of hypocaust heating systems that made possible the ultimate leisure facility, the Roman bath. Air was heated beneath the floors and then directed into specific rooms and swimming pools, large and small. During the Roman Empire, these comforts reached the height of perfection, with enormous bath complexes found in most Roman cities and provinces. All Roman baths follow a standardized, axial plan that emphasizes symmetry, with few variations other than size. The bath complex began with open-air areas for sports and games, after which visitors entered a series of changing rooms (apodyteria). Next came the sequence of bathing rooms, from the cold bath (frigidarium) to the lukewarm (tepidarium) and the warm (caldarium). There were also swimming pools, steam rooms and pumphouses where refreshments were served. During the reign of Emperor Augustus alone, Rome had a total of 170 public baths. The later Baths of Caracalla (216 CE), built by the emperor of that name, were among the largest and most luxurious. A mighty wall enclosed the enormous complex, which was roofed by a complex system of domes and vaults. As the Roman Empire expanded, these baths became the means by which all of Europe learned to build domes and vaults. The English town of Bath owes its name to the Roman baths that were built there nearly two thousand years ago. They are still in operation.

▶ Bath, England, Roman baths with later modifications, 1st century CE.

Monuments and Commemorative Architecture

Gods were not the only ones honored with cults: Roman emperors, patricians and other important persons also required ceremonial attention. The majority of the personal monuments around Rome were erected during the subject's lifetime or after death to honor their memories. Imperial monuments were built to honor members of the royal family and encourage the growth of personality cults. Obvious examples are the triumphal arches awarded to victorious rulers and generals. It was also possible to erect an arch to oneself. Usually built at important crossroads, these monumental gateways were decorated with relief sculpture illustrating the honoree's heroic deeds. The triumphal arches of Titus, Septimus Severus and Constantine (see p. 22) are among those raised in Rome; many others can be found throughout the Roman provinces.

Emperor Trajan introduced a new kind of monument: the relief-decorated column. Trajan's Column, including its

◀▲ Rome, Trajan's Column, 113 CE (left), and detail of the sculpted scenes from the Dacian Wars (above).

▼ Orange, France, monumental gate located along the main highway out of town, said to celebrate the founding of the city, 26–27 CE.

▲ Rome, near the Porta Ostiensis, pyramid tomb of Gaius Cestius, before 12 BCE.

▲ Rome, Castel Sant'Angelo, mausoleum of Emperor Hadrian, 135–139 CE, rebuilt as part of papal fortifications in the 13th century.

▼ St-Rémy-de-Provence, France, triumphal arch from 20 BCE (r) and what is called the Julian Monument with relief sculpture (l).

▲ Rome, near Porto Maggiore, tomb of the Eurysaces family with decoration proclaiming the family's profession as bakers, 30 BCE.

pedestal, is 125 ft (38 m) high. In celebration of Roman victories in the Dacian Wars, the column was carved to resemble a 656-ft (200-m) long unwinding scroll. Relief sculpture depicts important events and battles. The ashes of Trajan and his wife were entombed in the pedestal. The column was once crowned with a Roman eagle, which Pope Sixtus VI replaced with a statue of St. Peter.

Tombs and mausoleums gained significance in the imperial period. In 135 CE, Emperor Hadrian commissioned the Castel Sant'Angelo in Rome, which was later built into the Aurelian Walls (see p. 24) and used as a fortress. It was designed as a mausoleum for Hadrian and his successors. Among the wide variety of tombs for private citizens or minor officials, many are fantastic and strange. The tomb of the tribune Gaius Cestius is an example. Inspired by the Augustan age's fashion for everything Egyptian, he commissioned a pyramid. More striking still is the tomb of the Eurysaces, a family of bakers who designed their monument to look like a giant oven, proclaiming their profession for all eternity.

The Villa and Palace

The Roman villa began as a simple, rural estate house. Set in the natural landscape, the prototype farmhouse was functional and practical. Over time, the very different *villa suburbana*, an upper class "country" house on the outskirts of the city, became increasingly popular. Like urban houses, villas had an atrium, but also multiple peri-style courtyards, often symmetrically arranged on each side of the residence. Larger villas had multiple wings extending far into the surrounding land, with storage and service rooms. The villa type evolved into a palace with Nero's Golden House, the Domus Aurea. Located between the Forum Romanum and Esquiline Hill, this sprawling dwelling was decorated with expensive materials including gold leaf, frescoes, stucco ceilings and sculptures in niches lining the walls. The most elaborate room was roofed with a dome decorated with frescoes depicting the heavens. Turning a crank made the dome revolve, so that painted stars seemed to move across the night sky. An artificial landscape with lakes, vineyards, meadows and hedges surrounded the palace, turning the otherwise densely populated center of Imperial Rome into a rural fantasy world.

The Villa of Hadrian in nearby Tivoli took the palatial villa even further. Built near the Sabine hills as a rural retreat, it became the emperor's official residence in 188 CE. The complex has over thirty buildings, including theaters, temples and baths. The gardens with their mechanical fountains were particularly wonderful. Hadrian's goal was to create a microcosmos where he could rule, undisturbed, in splendor.

◀▲ Tivoli, Hadrian's Villa, round portico with statues lining the Canopus Grotto (opposite), and the Martime Theater (above), ca. 118 CE.

◀ Eight-cornered domed room in Nero's Domus Aurea (Golden House), 64 CE.

Late Antiquity: Early Christian and Byzantine Architecture

When he legalized Christianity in 313 CE, Constantine the Great legitimized the social and religious changes already spreading through the Roman Empire. A year earlier, Constantine's victory in the Battle of Milvian Bridge was supposedly inspired by a vision of a cross. Thereafter he summoned all Christian bishops in the empire to Rome for a convention in the Lateran Palace. In 324, a basilica at that site was consecrated as St John Lateran, the cathedral church of Rome, the first of all cathedrals. Just a few years later, Constantine commissioned St Peter's Basilica on the site of the apostle Peter's martyrdom.

Christians, for centuries forced to worship in catacombs and other secret places, could finally do so in public. The first Christian religious buildings were decidedly of pagan origin, as Early Christian building masters adapted traditional models to new liturgical requirements. The basilica, a rectilinear, multi-aisled building with a staggered roof above a central nave, was the model for many early churches. In pagan antiquity, most basilicas had been law courts, audience halls or throne rooms. The prototype for smaller Christian churches and mausoleums was the round tholos temple. Many of the earliest Christian buildings are known to us only in modified form due to their pagan origins. The ideological

▲ Milan, San Lorenzo, third quarter of the 4th century, interior.

and aesthetic associations of pagan architecture became less tolerable over time. Until at least the fourteenth century, nothing "ancient" would be considered acceptable. Exceptions were made for the churches in the Holy Land, which were perceived more as sacred relics than as buildings, and were therefore left largely intact. In contrast, St John Lateran and St Peter's were rebuilt, renovated and rebuilt anew in spectacular fashion over the course of several centuries.

By the fourth century CE, Rome had all but lost its power. A new center developed in the east, leading to the division of the empire into two unequal parts in 395. The Eastern Roman Empire flourished around its capital, Constantinople, formerly the Greek and Roman city of Byzantium. The Western Roman Empire, battered by barbarian

◄ Rome, Early Christian catacomb under the Via Latina, 4th century.

▲ Ravenna, Italy, San Vitale, 526–547, exterior.

▼ Rome, Basilica of Maxentius, 306–312. Constantine the Great's rival, Maxentius, commissioned this impressive building in the Forum Romanum. After Maxentius was defeated at the Battle of Milvian Bridge, Constantine ordered the building completed.

invasions, was ruled primarily from Ravenna, Italy, a small, fortified town that was made its capital in 404.

Ravenna has survived as a magnificent witness to the ambition of Early Christian and Byzantine architecture, and in particular the skillful use of mosaic decoration. Its enormous basilicas with their complex decorative mosaics survived to enchant visitors well into the medieval period. The eight-cornered, central-plan church of San Vitale, influenced by Eastern Roman models, was said to have been the inspiration for Charlemagne's Palantine Chapel in Aachen (see p.75).

Early Christian Architecture in Rome

Between 323 and 326, Constantine the Great commissioned "Old" St Peter's, the first church over the grave of Peter the apostle. Almost 300 ft (90 m) long and nearly 200 ft (60 m) wide, the new basilica at the foot of Vatican Hill dwarfed all other churches in the city. Old St Peter's was a five-aisled basilica with a central nave supported by marble columns. A spacious transept accommodated many worshipers. The focal point was the site of Peter's grave, beneath the high altar apse. In front of the church was an atrium lined with columns and vaulted arcades. Old St Peter's was gradually demolished after 1506 to allow for construction of the new St Peter's, a Renaissance masterpiece.

Constantine's daughter Constantina commissioned another famous Early Christian work. Santa Costanza is the mausoleum she built just outside Rome

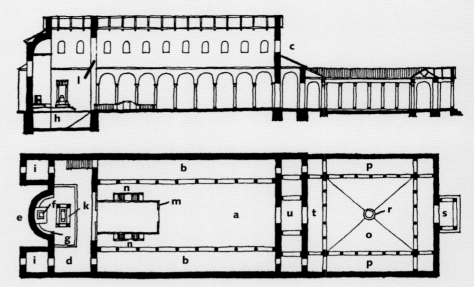

▲ Plan and elevation of an Early Christian basilica: a) nave, b) aisles, c) clerestory, d) sanctuary or transept, e) apse, f) cathedra, g) presbytery, h) crypt, i) pastophorien, k) altar, l) triumphal arch, m) chancel, n) ambo, o) atrium, p) peristyle, r) cantharus, s) narthex.

▶ Rome, Santa Costanza, Mausoleum of Constantina, 4th century.

▶▶ ▼ Rome, Santa Sabina, 422–432, exterior and interior views.

for the mortal remains of herself and her sister, Helena. The brick building has one of the loveliest interiors of late antiquity, clad entirely in marble and superb mosaics. Elegant, double-shafted granite columns support a vaulted arcade (*ambulatory*), which defines the inner sanctum with the sarcophagus at its center. A columned portico, no longer standing, encircled the building.

Among many buildings in Rome, Santa Sabina, recently completely restored, may provide the most accurate picture of typical Early Christian sacred architecture. Built early in the fifth century, the three-aisled church has no transept and no apse mosaic. Twenty Corinthian columns supporting the nave roof are spoil from an ancient building. Most Early Christian architecture, even Old St Peter's, freely incorporated elements from Rome's enormous store of ruins. Large, bowed windows in the long walls of Santa Sabina light the interior, which has a simple, flat, wooden roof.

◀ Rome, Old St Peter's, ca. 323–326. Cross section facing west from a 17th-century painting, based on an earlier drawing.

Religious Sites in the Holy Land

In late antiquity, Jewish, Christian and eventually Islamic traditions overlapped to the extent that a building type originating in one religion could be adapted for the rituals of another. Synagogues and central-plan churches are the best examples. Constantine the Great founded the earliest Christian sacred buildings in the Holy Land, basing their design on Roman prototypes. Buildings at holy sites in Jerusalem and Bethlehem became models for Christian, Jewish and Islamic architecture around the world.

The Church of the Holy Sepulcher, begun in 326, has a complex plan designed to efficiently guide crowds of pilgrims through the sacred sites. A rectilinear atrium led to a five-aisled basilica, which led to a second peristyle courtyard connected to Calvary, the traditional site of the crucifixion. Further along is the Rotunda of the Anastasis, which has an ambulatory, sculpted pilasters and domed roof. The Rotunda is the only part of Constantine's original church that

▲ Jerusalem, Church of the Holy Sepulcher, ca. 326.

◄ Jerusalem, Dome of the Rock (*Qubbat as-Sakhrah*), late 7th century.

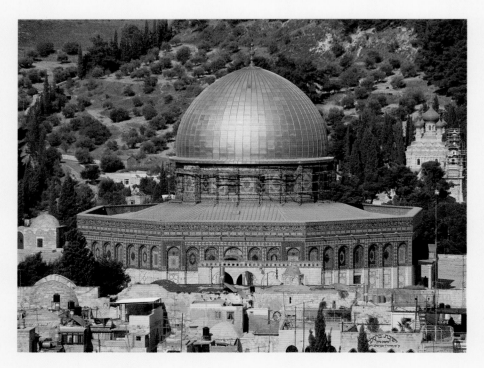

remains (in a slightly altered form). The Church of the Nativity in Bethlehem combines elements of the longitudinal basilica and the central-plan church. A five-aisled basilica terminates in a central-plan octagonal "chapel," where one can descend into the Grotto of the Nativity, a cave in which a silver star marks the spot where Jesus was born.

The relationship between churches and saints' burial places had significant influence on Early Christian architecture, as did the need to direct worshippers along a route through the cult site. An ideal pilgrimage began in the atrium,

a space also open to the unbaptized. It continued through the church, ending at the sanctuary with its promise of salvation. Memorials and cults dedicated to saints often determined the plan of early monasteries. In 438, St Sabbas lived as a hermit on the slopes of the Valley of Kidron near Jerusalem. His grave became the focal point of one of the most important monasteries in

▲ Qalaat Seman, Syria, Monastery of Simeon, 5th-century octagon around the column of St Simeon Stylites.

Palestine. The North Syrian site of Qalaat Seman, a significant pilgrimage destination of late antiquity, was organized around a column. It was the pillar atop which the ascetic St Simeon Stylites (in Greek, *style* = pillar) had lived for thirty-seven years. Here as well, a central-plan octagon was chosen for the innermost sanctuary, with four three-aisled basilicas extending symmetrically from the central room. Early Islamic sacred buildings in Jerusalem also used a central plan. The Dome of the Rock (in Arabic, *Qubbat as-Sakhrah*), is a central-plan octagon. It was commissioned by the caliph Abd'al-Malik in the late seventh century.

◄ Sabbas Monastery on the slopes of the Valley of Kidron near Jerusalem, 6th century.

◀ Ravenna, Mausoleum of Galla Placidia, ca. 425–430, view of interior mosaics.

▶ Ravenna, San Vitale, 526–547, interior view of the central octagon.

Ravenna

It was Emperor Honorius who made the harbor town of Ravenna the capital of the Western Roman Empire. Theodoric, king of the Ostrogoths, conquered the city a century later in 494. He declared Ravenna, by then adorned with magnificent buildings, his principal residence.

In Ravenna, Early Christian and Byzantine period architecture and mosaic decoration has survived to testify to the glories of the age. The basilicas of Sant' Apollinare Nuovo and Sant' Apollinare in Classe, with their gleaming interior mosaics, cast their glow far into the medieval period. Funerary monuments, like the famous late Roman mausoleum of Empress Galla Placidia, still charm today. Completed around 430, and thus fully within the imperial period, the cruciform, central-plan mausoleum consists of a low, four-cornered vaulted room with short, barrel-vaulted halls extending from each side. The modest brickwork of the exterior belies the uniquely magnificent mosaics of the interior, which are famous for their use of Roman iconography reimagined as Christian symbolism.

▶ Ravenna, Mausoleum of Theodoric, ca. 420, exterior.

Among Byzantine central-plan buildings, Ravenna's San Vitale occupies a special position. This octagonal brick church was begun in 526 under the patronage of the banker Julianus Argentarius. It was built in roughly the same time period as the much larger church of Hagia Sophia in Constantinople. Both San Vitale and Hagia Sophia are influenced by central-plan buildings, have two stories of ambulatories, and employ curving lines of columns set between pillars supporting a central dome. Although not particularly large, San Vitale's arched arcades seem to soar to a great height. Light streaming in the eight windows at the base of the dome draws the eye upward from the deep shadows below. San Vitale's elaborately carved columns and capitals were imported from Constantinople workshops.

Theodoric erected a majestic mausoleum just outside Ravenna's gates. A massive, monolithic dome roofs this ten-cornered building. As is typical for Ostrogoth architecture, the exterior of the dome is decorated with an ornamental frieze.

▲ Istanbul, Church of Sts Sergius and Bacchus, begun ca. 526. The interior decoration stems from a 19th-century renovation.

▼ Istanbul, Kariye Camii, formerly St Savior in Chora, mosaic of Christ Pantocrator in the south dome of the inner narthex.

Byzantine Architecture

The division of the Roman Empire into East and West ensured the continued rise of Constantinople, and the entire eastern Mediterranean region. The city on the Bosporus now called Istanbul began as the Greek city of Byzantion, later Latinized to Byzantium. In 330, Constantine the Great declared it capital of the Roman Empire, fittingly naming it "New Rome." The empire would endure for over a thousand years; the Byzantine Empire came to an end only with Ottoman Turks' conquest of Constantinople in 1453.

Byzantine art has deep roots in the classical and late antique periods, and it lives on yet in the traditional architecture of the Greek Orthodox Church. Monumental art and architecture were closely bound to the person of the emperor. Identified by the Eastern Church as Christ's representative on earth, the emperor's highest priority

was constructing sacred buildings. Domed basilicas and Greek cruciform, centrally planned buildings with hierarchically ordered interior spaces were typical of the Byzantine style. Illusionist mosaic decoration on a gold background was the rule, its lack of realism enhancing the otherworldliness of the cosmic realms depicted. In contrast, Byzantine exteriors were plain brickwork. The relative lack of exterior decoration is a remnant of the modest facades of late antiquity. A few centuries later, some buildings, such as the Blachernae Palace, were subtly embellished with molded terracotta or decorative brick.

The reign of Justinian I (527–565) is considered the golden age of Byzantine art and architecture. He commissioned a host of churches in his capital, including Sts Sergius and Bacchus and the masterpiece of Byzantine architecture, Hagia Sophia. Over the following centuries, variations on the basic elements of these early Byzantine buildings would appear again and again in both secular and sacred architecture.

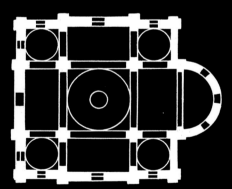

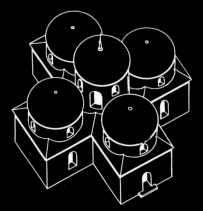

◀ Schematic drawing and plan of a Byzantine central-plan building. Four wings radiate from the central unit, forming in plan a Greek (equidistant) cross.

▲ Mount Athos, Chilandariou Monastery, early 13th century, apsidal arms of the cruciform building and the west side porch.

Constantinople

Constantinople experienced a golden age from the fourth through seventh centuries. Its population quintupled within a few years after being named the new capital of the Roman Empire. Its fortifications were first built by Constantine, but were strengthened and expanded by Theodosius II in the fifth century to accommodate the city's growth. Large sections of the Theodosian walls are still standing today. Two immense cisterns, roofed with arches supported by hundreds of columns, bear further witness to Byzantine skill in civil architecture and engineering. The indisputable masterpiece of Byzantine ecclesiastical architecture is the church of Hagia Sophia. Begun in 532, it replaced an earlier version that had been destroyed during a rebellion. The architects Isidore of Miletus and Anthemius of Tralles designed a building that bridged the typological categories of basilica and central-plan building. Completed in just five years, Justinian is said to have proclaimed when he saw it, "Solomon, I have surpassed thee!" The emperor's contention that the new church was at least comparable to the biblical Solomon's temple is entirely borne out by this stunning building. Contemporary witnesses looked up at the enormous main dome supported by four massive pillars and found themselves at a loss for words. What they saw before them was simply inex-

pressible. The gold of the mosaics in combination with the immense open space of the main room illuminated by light streaming through windows in the base of the dome continues to cast a spell on visitors today. Part of that amazing dome had already collapsed by 558, after which it was redesigned and rebuilt.

▲ Istanbul, Theodosian land walls, 408–450, square tower.

▼ Istanbul, Basilica Cistern, begun in 475 and reconstructed following a fire in 532 by order of Justinian I.

◄ ▼ Istanbul, Hagia Sophia, Isidore of Miletus and Anthemius of Tralles, 532–537, interior view (l) and plan (below).

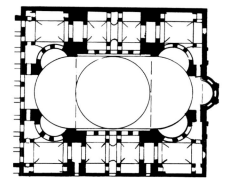

Later Byzantine Architecture

Despite endless border wars, the Byzantine Empire was able to expand for varying periods of time into the Balkans, Italy and North Africa. Russia fell under Byzantine influence during the tenth and eleventh centuries as Byzantine missionaries carried the Orthodox faith into every conquered territory. Cultural influences went hand in hand with religious conversion. Byzantine masons and mosaic artists found their talents greatly valued by wealthy patrons dwelling on the edge of the empire.

Venice remained in close cultural contact with Constantinople even after Byzantine rule there came to an end. San Marco in Venice, built in 1063 and completed in 1094, represents a synthesis of Byzantine and Venetian architectural and decorative styles.

Modeled on the Justinian Church of the Apostles in Constantinople, San Marco has a cruciform plan and a five-domed roof. It is decorated with gold mosaics everywhere, inside and out. Work on the decorative program, which also included marble and bronze sculptures, continued well into the thirteenth century, making San Marco a veritable mélange of artistic styles.

The central-plan, domed building lived on in monastery churches such as

◀ ▲ Greece, Hosios Loukas Monastery, interior view of the Katholikon (l, consecrated 1011); and the Panagia Church, 10th century (above).

▶ Venice, San Marco, begun 1063, view of the choir decorated with late 12th-century mosaics.

those at Hosios Loukas in Greece. St Sophia's Cathedral in Kiev (begun 1037) is one of Eastern Europe's most important religious buildings. Later examples of Byzantine style include the interior mosaics of Kariye Camii in Istanbul, now a mosque, but once the Church of the Savior in Chora (interiors, mid-fourteenth century), and the Church of the Apostles in Thessaloniki (1310–1314).

Islamic Architecture in Europe

Islamic architecture began modestly. The first mosque was part of the Prophet Mohammed's house. After his death, religious and secular architecture developed in several directions. The gilded Dome of the Rock (*Qubbat as-Sakhrah*, see p. 46) in Jerusalem, the splendid Ummayad mosques in Damascus and Córdoba, the luxurious Alhambra palace in Spain, and magnificent multi-domed buildings of the Ottoman master architect Sinan bear witness to the sophisticated Islamic aesthetic. The fairy-tale mausoleum known as the Taj Mahal is also an Islamic building, as are the high-tech mosques of today.

Over almost 1400 years, Islamic architecture has maintained a certain continuity despite differences in government and topography encountered as the religion spread. The basic elements of the essential Islamic building types, modeled on late antique and Jewish predecessors, were established by the

▲ Near Castile, Spain, detail of Gómaz Castle, 756.

▲ Seville, Spain, Torre del Oro, a military watchtower, early 13th century.

seventh and eighth centuries. By the eighth century, the traditional elements of a mosque were in place, including the *mihrab*—a niche in the prayer wall indicating the direction of Mecca—an arcaded courtyard and minarets. Minarets

were originally massive towers, first used for the call to prayer in the fourteenth century. The mosque was part of a larger complex that could include a Koran school (*madrasa*), hospital, lodging for travelers (*caravanserai*) and baths

Important Islamic Buildings in Europe

Málaga: *Alcazaba* (citadel)
Almería: *Alcazaba, Medina* (old city)
Córdoba: *Ummayad Great Mosque, Madinat az-Zahra* (palace city)
Toledo: *Mosque of Bab-al-Mardum (Mezquita de Cristo de la Luz), Santa María la Blanca* (synagogue) *Puerta del Sol*
Zaragoza: *Aljafería* (castle)
Seville: *Torre del Oro, Patio de los Naranjos* (palace), *La Giralda*
Niebla: *City wall*
Granada: *Alhambra* and *Generalife* (palaces), *El Albaicín* (old city)
Istanbul: *Beyazit, Suleimaniye, Sultanahmet ("Blue") and Sehzade ("Prince's") Mosques, Topkapi Palace*
Palermo (Islamic influenced): *San Cataldo, Palermo Cathedral, Zisa* (palace)

▲ Areas under Islamic control (Al-Andalus) on the Iberian Peninsula.

hammam). Islamic architecture is also famous for massive fortifications and desert palaces, the latter boasting efficient, ingenious water supply systems.

The architectural achievements of the Arab world enriched all of Europe during the eight centuries of Islamic rule in much of the Iberian Peninsula. The Ummayed dynasty brought an early golden age to Córdoba and Toledo. After the fall of the Córdoba caliphate in 1031, al-Andalus was divided into smaller Islamic states called *taifas*. Luxurious royal courts in Seville, Zaragoza and Málaga became places where cultures of the East and West exchanged information as well as goods. The height of Islamic culture in Europe arrived just before its end, with the Nasrid dynasty in Granada and its uniquely fascinating palace complex: the Alhambra. Outside of Iberia, a mixed Norman-Arab culture developed during the twelfth century in the Sicilian city of Palermo. The superb mosques of Sinan, master architect of the Ottoman sultan Suleiman the Magnificent, adorned sixteenth century Istanbul, and survive to astonish today.

ler version common in buildings of the Visigoths (see p. 70), their predecessors in Spain. A uniquely Islamic architectural detail is *muqarnas*, a three-dimensional plaster decoration resembling honeycombs or stalactites used to embellish domes, vaults and niches.

▲ Istanbul, aerial view of the Suleimaniye complex designed by Sinan, 16th century.

▼ Granada, Spain, wall decoration from the Hall of the Two Sisters in the Alhambra Palace.

Decorative Systems

Ornament and elaborate interior decoration are integral to Islamic architecture. The greatest achievements of Islamic art are found indoors, where painted plaster, tile and mosaic completely cover the walls and ceilings, much like the carpets and prayer rugs on the tile floors. The decorative motifs consist of elaborate, dense, intertwining, infinitely repeating vegetative, geometric and calligraphic elements. The overwhelming preference for nonfigural art derives from the Islamic religion, which is strictly nonrepresentational in mosques and other sacred spaces, though figural representation is usually tolerated in a secular context. Islamic architecture is also responsible for the use of the horseshoe arch, adapted from a much simp-

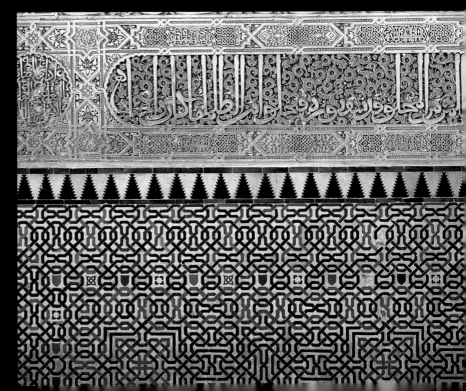

Córdoba: The Mezquita

In 756, Abd er-Rahman I made Córdoba the capital of his emirate. In 785, he began construction of a great mosque that would later be called *Mezquita*, a Spanish transcription of the Arabic word for mosque (*masjid*). After 200 years of renovations and additions by later emirs, the Córdoba mosque had become one of the largest and most elaborate religious buildings in the world. Its interior elevations are nothing short of spectacular, with two stories of arches supporting the structure's massive weight. Horseshoe arches of alternating red and white stone blocks are supported by 110 columns. Massive pillars atop the column capitals support a second level of arches, which in turn hold the domed and vaulted roof. Seemingly endless repetition of form, delightful views through the forest of columns, and the dramatic play of light on stone make entering the prayer hall an overwhelming experience.

Between 833 and 848, the mosque was expanded by eight bays to the south; twelve more were added in 961. In 987, Caliph al-Mansur expanded the entire prayer hall to the east, bringing it

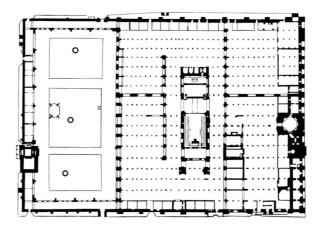

◄ Córdoba, Great Mosque (Mezquita), 795–988. The ground plan shows the entire complex as it survives today. The *maqsura* and *mihrab* were located underneath the baroque sacristy on the east side. The Christian cathedral added in the 16th century can be seen in the center.

Glossary: The Mosque

Mosque: Islamic religious building
Mezquita: Spanish word for mosque
Medrese or Madrasa: Koran school
Minaret: Tower from which the
 muezzin sings the call to prayer
Masjid: mosque
Camii masjid: Friday mosque
Haram: sanctuary
Imam: prayer leader
Maqsura: rulers' area of a prayer hall
Mihrab: wall niche pointing to Mecca
Minbar: speaker's podium
Qibla: direction of prayers to Mecca
Riwaq: arched arcade or portico
Sahn: mosque courtyard

▲ Ribbed dome in front of the mihrab, 961.

◄ ▼ Views of the interior (left) and exterior of the Mezquita.

Madinat az-Zahra

The "city of flowers," built between 936 and 976, was one of the finest palace citadels in the Arab world. Travelers from all over the globe were awed by the enormous size of the residence built by the caliphs Abd ar-Rahman III and al-Hakam II.

Located just outside Córdoba, this well planned, nearly perfectly rectangular palace city occupies three functionally diverse terraces. The caliph's palace occupies the highest ground. Government and administrative buildings are on the middle terrace, including Salón Rico (see pp. 56–57), where important guests of the caliph were housed. Mosques and residential quarters took up most of the lowest terrace. The palace declined after the vizier al-Mansur seized control from the caliph. Madinat az-Zahra was destroyed in a raid a few years later in 1010. The complex was plundered for its rich building materials for the greater part of a millennium. Large parts of the ruins of this mighty complex remain unexcavated today.

◀ Córdoba, Mezquita, facade of the mihrab.

▶ Madinat az-Zahra, view of the middle terrace of the former palace city, 936–976. The beautiful Salón Rico was located on this terrace (see pp. 56–57).

to its current size. The interior decor was completed sometime after 961 under Caliph Hakam II. The part of the complex leading into the center aisle, now called the Capilla de Villaviciosa, was completed during that period. Its two stories of interlocking arches supporting a massive dome are the artistic high point of the mosque. The filigree decor of the mihrab and *maqsura*, the part of the prayer hall closest to the qibla wall that would be reserved for the ruler, are simply beyond compare.

Granada: The Alhambra

The varied history of the Islamic kingdoms in Europe came to an end with the Nasirid dynasty of Granada (1232–1492), but also reached a glittering architectural zenith in the Alhambra palace. Mohammed I chose this well-defended city on the edge of the Sierra Nevada as his residence in 1237. Over the next century, Granada blossomed into magnificence. The legendary Alhambra that visitors see today dates mainly to the reigns of Yusuf I (1333–1354) and Mohammed II (1354–1391). Alhambra means "the red one" in Arabic, a reference to the local stone and red clay of which it is made, as well as to the surrounding red sandstone mountains. The palace came to stand for the epitome of Arab culture and refinement; the nineteenth-century Romantic poets made it a focal point for their exotic, orientalist dreams.

The palatial citadel rising against a backdrop of red hills incorporates a unique range of Islamic and Christian elements, reflecting its historical development and the input of a number of rulers. It is particular good luck that Emperor Charles V did not destroy this

▲ View of the sculpted alabaster fountain supported by 12 stone lions in the Court of the Lions. It is divided into four parts, each with a water channel, symbolizing the four rivers of Paradise.

▲ A muqarnas dome with a honey-combed and stalactite decorated plaster surface, second half of the 14th century.

remnant of Islamic rule. Instead, he added a large Christian-Habsburg building in the mannerist style more suited to his own style of living. He used the rest of the Alhambra complex for official receptions and administrative functions.

The beguiling magnificence of the Alhambra is evident as soon as one crosses the mighty walls of the *alcazaba*, massive fortifications leading to the palace, and the first pavilion, the *mexuar*, which may have been used as an audience hall. Here visitors find delicate painted plaster moldings, ornaments and calligraphic decoration of unsurpassed sophistication and beauty, all under an intricately carved hardwood ceiling. The next room is the *cuarto dorado*, or Golden Room, distinguished by its gilded, sculpted plaster walls and ceilings. The Comares Palace, thought to be the residential rooms of the Nasirid rulers, was organized around the famous Court of the Myrtles, which had a central reflecting pool. The most private part of the palace was probably the harem around the Court of the Lions, named for its famous sculpted fountain. The Alhambra also had a prayer hall, steam baths, flush toilets, and even hot and cold running water.

◄ View of the Alhambra against the backdrop of the Sierra Nevada.

▶ *Cuarto dorado* and facade of Comares Palace, second half of the 14th century.

The Mixing of Cultures

Islamic, Jewish and Christian traditions all met in the Iberian Peninsula. Evidence of this can be seen in Spanish architecture despite the bitter battles of the *reconquista* (reconquest) taking place throughout the most fruitful period of cultural interaction. Christian nobles greatly appreciated the beauty and comfort of Moorish residences. They also readily converted Moslem and Jewish religious buildings into Christian churches without extensively altering their substance or decorative elements. After the final defeat of the last Islamic kingdom, a stylistic fusion, known as Mudéjar style, heavily influenced by Islamic buildings, became the preferred style of the new Christian rulers. Toledo, which was under Moslem rule for "only" 373 years (712–1085), is a prime example. Eastern and Western cultures met there to trade and exchange cultural information until the Arabs' final expulsion in 1610.

▶ Seville, Spain, arcaded ambulatory around the courtyard of Casa de Pilatos, ca. 1500. This urban palace is famous for its mixture of Renaissance and Islamic decor.

The Aljafería in Zaragoza, built in the early eleventh century by the Banu Hud dynasty, became the residence of the Christian kings of Aragon in 1118. They left the Moorish palace essentially intact. Today it is considered one of the most important, best-preserved buildings of the Taifa period of Islamic Spain.

In Seville, an enormous cathedral was built over the Almohad mosque, elegantly integrating the pre-existing Islamic elements into a functionally

◀ Seville Cathedral, 15th and 16th centuries. The late 12th-century Patio de los Naranjos (Courtyard of the Oranges) is also visible.

▼ Toledo, Spain, San Cristo de Luz, built in 999 as a mosque near Bab al-Mardum gate, expanded into a Christian church in 1187.

Alcalá de Henares, paranito (assembly room) of the university, 1516.

Teruel, Spain, Santa Maria Cathedral, 1257–1258, bell tower.

Burgos, Spain, cathedral, view of the cimborio (lantern tower), 1567.

Mudéjar Architecture

The Arabic word *mudayyan* means "the submissive" in the sense that all Moslems are submissive to Islam. The Spanish word *mudéjar* is a corruption of *mudayyan*, used by the Spanish to indicate the submissive tax status of Moslems living under Christian rule. The *mudéjares* played a significant role in society from the thirteenth through fifteenth centuries, until their final expulsion from the Iberian Peninsula in 1610.

Islamic decorative forms, including continuous, interlocking geometrical and calligraphic motifs and elaborate, textile-like decoration of important facades, were all easily integrated into Christian architecture. Islamic building techniques, such as the mastery of brick masonry (*ladrillo*) and construction of elaborate decorated ceilings (*artesonado*), influenced Spanish architecture for centuries. The use of ceramic moldings (*azulejos*) with wooden (*carpintería*) and plaster (*yeserias*) details are characteristic of Mediterranean architecture's ongoing interest in surface decoration.

Mudejarism was formulated as a stylistic category in 1859 by art historian Amador de los Rios. Several scholars now consider it the earliest expression of Spanish culture.

Christian design. The mosque's massive minaret was refitted as a Christian bell tower, Seville's famous Giralda. The forecourt of the mosque, its palms replaced by orange trees, became the well-known Patio de los Naranjos.

Seville's Alcazar, its royal palace, is a seamless blend of an Islamic original with additions by Christian rulers. The Casa de Pilatos, built by the first Marqués de Tarifa, mixes Renaissance architecture with a essentially Islamic repertoire of formal and decorative elements.

Toledo, Spain, interior of Santa Maria La Bianca, a synagogue transformed into a Christian church, ca. 1250.

Zaragoza, Aljafería, Spain, second half of the 11th century, east facade of the former Moslem fort rebuilt as a royal residence.

IV. Early Middle Ages

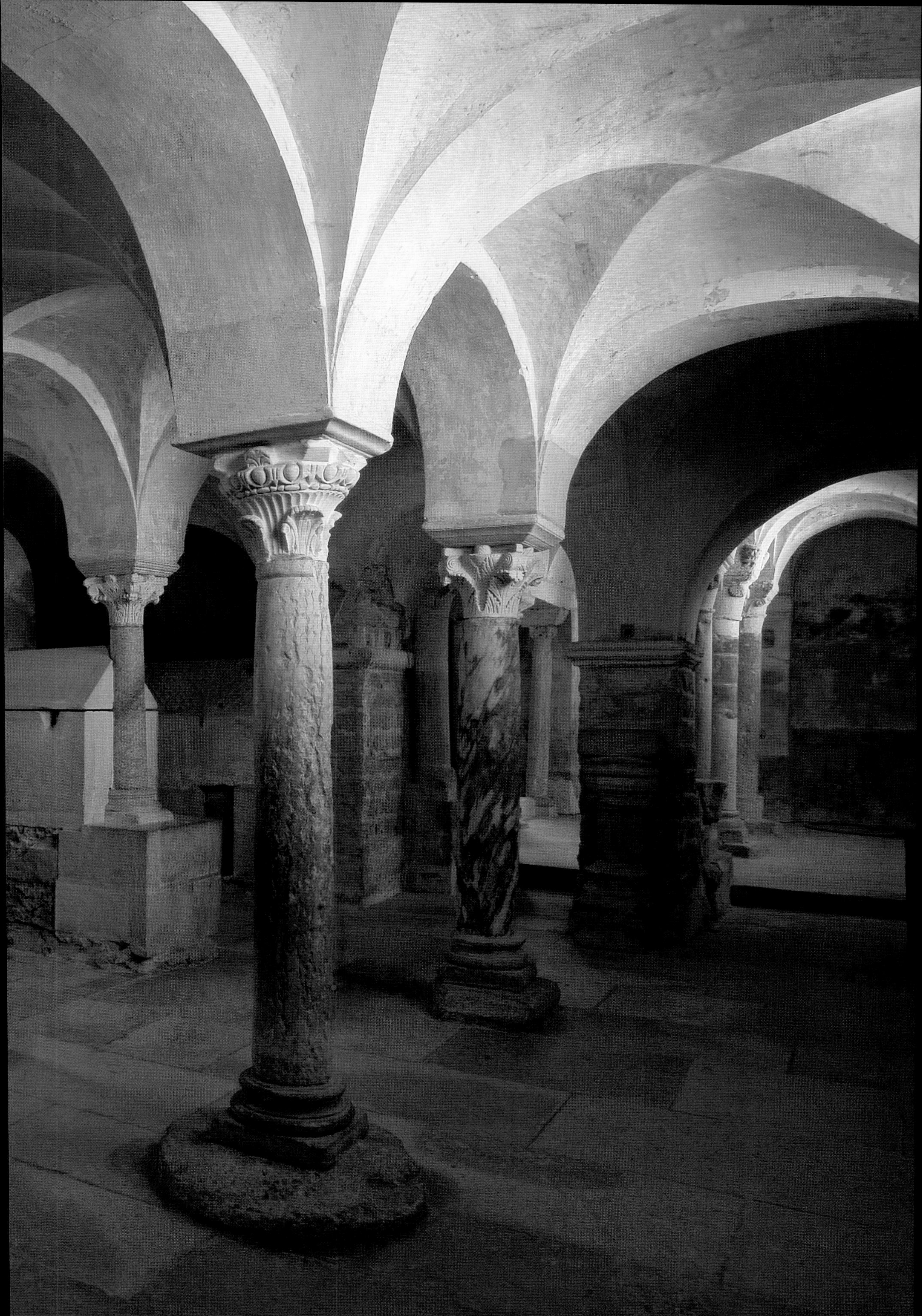

◀ Poitiers, Baptistère St-Jean (Baptistery of St John), 6th to 7th century, facade.

Early Middle Ages

The period of time between late antiquity and the high Middle Ages was long known as the Dark Ages and, in the past, art produced between the Roman and Romanesque periods was often stigmatized as barbarian. Today scholars recognize that the centuries that elapsed between the fall of the Roman Empire and the realignment of Europe after the turn of the millennium represent an extremely fruitful era. What was once considered an interim period is now seen as an era of historical continuity and the foundation of the medieval world. Only a few enduring monuments were produced during the migration period, as the epoch between the fifth and seventh centuries is often called. Nevertheless, even these rare examples attest to the fact that a fundamental reformulation of traditional architectural forms was taking place. The major centers of this

▶ Germigny-des-Prés, oratory of Bishop Theodulf of Orléans, after 806, interior.

development were the Iberian Peninsula, Merovingian Gaul and the British Isles; however, the evidence from these regions has been preserved primarily in the form of illuminated manuscripts.

The architecture of the Visigoths in Spain deliberately continued in the late antique tradition. Its typical characteristics include polished ashlar block construction; opulent sculpted ornamentation in the form of rosettes, crosses and scrollwork; and stilted horseshoe arches, which were thus in common use even before the arrival of the Arabs. Visigoth and Islamic motifs overlap one another in Mozarabic art, the most important example of which is the abbey church of San Miguel de Escalada. In contrast, the stately palaces of the Asturian kingdom signalize the beginning of the *Reconquista*—the Christian return to power on the Iberian Peninsula.

A prime example of Merovingian architecture is the baptistery in Poitiers. Built on top of an Early Christian construction, its facades display the typical combination of natural stone and brick; cornices and niches, columns and arches enliven the walls. Byzantine influences are evident in the chapel of Santa Maria della Valle in Cividale. Its slender stucco figures are among the oldest examples of medieval monumental sculpture in existence.

Under Carolingian rule, sacred architecture became a political symbol. It was no accident that Charlemagne had himself crowned by Pope Leo III on December 25, 800. Now cathedrals and monasteries, parish churches and palace chapels, swore an allegiance between the Church and the Empire. Aachen's palatine chapel represents the grandiose beginning of a new artistic era, in which the architectural and decorative ideals of antiquity and Early Christianity were resurrected (see p. 75). Imposing abbey churches such as those in Lorsch and Corvey (both in Germany) were also symbols of regal entitlement. Their fortified westworks and crypts set standards that would become effectively obligatory throughout the coming centuries. In Germigny-des-Prés, Bishop Theodulf of Orléans had his oratory near Fleury built on a central plan and dominated by a massive square crossing tower.

From the time of its formation in 529, the Benedictine Order—the first monastic order of the Western Church—played a decisive role in the political as well as the cultural structure of the developing Western world.

One unique testament to its complex organization is the plan for an ideal church kept at St Gall, Switzerland, which provides us with precise information about the layout and structure of an ideal Carolingian monastery. Whether it was intended to be interpreted as a concrete design or as an ideal plan remains an enigma to this day; what is certain is that the plan set the precedent for medieval monastery construction.

Following the collapse of the Carolingian empire, the Salian, Ottonian and Hohenstaufen rulers drew on the architectural style of the ninth century. The construction of the abbey church of St Michael in Hildesheim, Germany was an important step in the process of hierarchically organizing the interior space of the church. Its modular system, which derives the key unit for its architectural plan from the crossing square, established the system for the structural principles of Romanesque architecture.

▲ Cividale, Italy, Santa Maria della Valle, pre-774, western wall with stucco figures.

◄ Ottmarsheim, Alsace, former monastic church, ca. 1020, interior of the octagon.

The degree to which Carolingian architecture maintained its influence, even as late as the eleventh century, is evident from the former monastic church of Ottmarsheim in Alsace, whose design makes clear reference to the palatine chapel in Aachen. The single—but not insubstantial—difference between this church and its 220-year older prototype is the absence of any decorative elements from the earlier period.

Early Medieval Architecture in Spain

The Iberian Peninsula is rich in early medieval architecture. The oldest structures were built between the late sixth century and early eighth century under the rule of the Visigoths, who governed large parts of what is now Spain from their residence in Toledo. When the Arab encroachment that began in 711 brought their empire to an end, the focus of Christian culture moved to the Kingdom of Asturias, which thus became the starting point for the *Reconquista*—the recapture of Christian power. In the ninth century, in particular, elaborate structures were built in this region that drew on Visigoth tradition. The tenth century was the heyday of Mozarabic art (*musta'rib* = "arabicized"), which combines elements of the late antique, Visigothic and Islamic cultures. The Mozabic style was able to blossom thanks to the lively exchange of both intellectual and technical knowledge that existed between the Islamic and Christian regions.

In general, the Visigoth church buildings feature a blocky basilical structure. The choir is usually divided into three parts and closed off in a straight line. The outer walls are made of large ashlars. In contrast to the buildings' simple, unadorned architecture, greater attention was paid to the decoration. This can be seen in the scrollwork friezes of Quintanilla de las Viñas or San Pedro de la Nave, as well as in the church of Santa Cristina de Lena, which dates from as early as the Asturian period. Its richly decorated iconostasis—the only choir screen in existence that dates from the pre-

▲ Monte Naranco near Oviedo, palace pavilion, pre-848.

▼ San Miguel de Escalada near León, dedicated in 913.

▲ Santa Cristina de Lena, mid-9th century, interior with iconostas (enclosure).

Romanesque era (some scholars even attribute it to the Visigoth period)—bears a Latin inscription.

The most important works of Asturian architecture, however, are the two buildings located at Monte Naranco near Oviedo: San Miguel de Liño (Lillo) and the Belvedere, a two-story palace hall that was later converted into the church of Santa María de Naranco. Both structures were part of the palace of King Ramiro I, who commissioned them around 848. The palace hall is a box-shaped structure with elegant open loggias at each end of its upper floor. A double outdoor staircase connected the lower and upper levels, providing access to the central naves, which are both enclosed under barrel vaults. The columns and capitals are covered with delicate ornamentation.

San Miguel de Liño (Lillo) was actually just the western section of a much larger palace chapel that collapsed in the thirteenth century. This blocky structure is remarkable for its unusual height. Its bold, solid construction could be attributed to the court architects of Ramiro I, who also experimented with vaulted stone construction in other buildings, such as San Salvador de Valdediós. Its capitals, columns and pilasters display reliefs of ornamental plants and highly stylized figurative scenes.

The abbey church of San Miguel de Escalada, dedicated in 913, is considered to be the most important surviving example of Mozarabic architecture, although it contains many overlapping elements of Visigothic and oriental design. Particularly striking is the use of the Islamic horseshoe-shaped arch, which reappears in the ground plan of the three apses as well as in the arches of the long side portico.

Monastic Building in the Early Middle Ages

The history of monastic building in the Western world began in 529, when Benedict of Nursia conferred a simple but memorable set of statutes on the monastery of Monte Cassino, which he founded. The well-known Rule of St Benedict clearly established the structural organization of the monastic community, setting down its theological, scientific and ethical goals as well as the monks' communal lifestyle. It served as a model for nearly every monastic order that was founded after it.

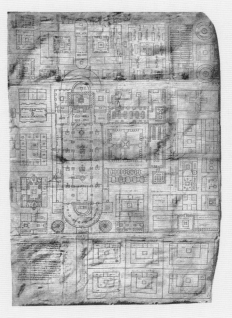

The architectural consequence of this statute was the development of an ideal plan that—with very few exceptions—served as a guideline for the construction of monasteries throughout the medieval period. Nevertheless, it was quite often the most powerful abbeys from which innovative structures or new aesthetic ideas arose.

The St Gall plan is a unique witness to cultural history that provides us with insight not only into the physical structure of an early medieval monastery, but also into the organization of daily monastic life. The 30.5 x 44 in (77 x 112 cm) sheet of parchment is one of the earliest surviving medieval architectural drawings. In addition to

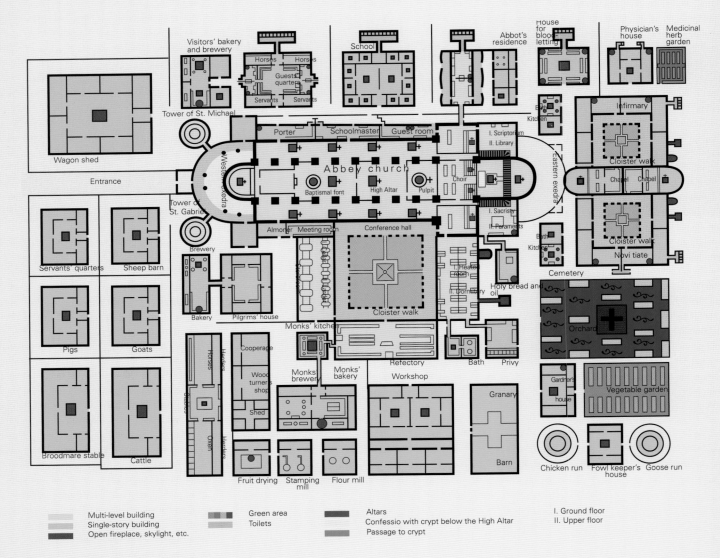

the floor plans of the buildings, the parchment contains over 300 written specifications. It is the very model of an ideal: it was presented to Gozbert, the abbot of St Gall, not as a blueprint for a specific construction, but as a guideline to follow.

Drafted around 830, the plan provides detailed information about the layout of a monastic complex (perhaps on the island of Reichenau on Lake Constance). It was intended to be a reflection of cosmic order. At its center is the double-choired abbey church, which incorporates a sacristy and library, set over an underground crypt. To the south, a covered walkway connects the church to a refectory and kitchen, dormitory, storerooms, heated rooms and washrooms; this walkway defines the cloister, the monks' enclosed area. The plan lacks a chapter house, a feature that would later become common. To the north of the church is the more formal area of the monastery, containing the abbot's residence and rooms for important guests; these are balanced by the pilgrims' house on the south side of the church. Behind the eastern apse are the hospital, the cemetery and the novitiate, which contains its own chapel. Utility rooms such as a bakery and brewery are set south of the cloister. Gardens, stables and barns are grouped around the outer periphery of the complex, as well as additional production areas and workshops.

The creator of the St Gall plan is believed to have been Abbot Hatto I of Reichenau. It is an interesting coincidence that after 890, the abbey church of St Georg of Oberzell was founded above his cell; the church would later contain one of the most important fresco cycles of the tenth century. The nave, with its arcaded side aisles and

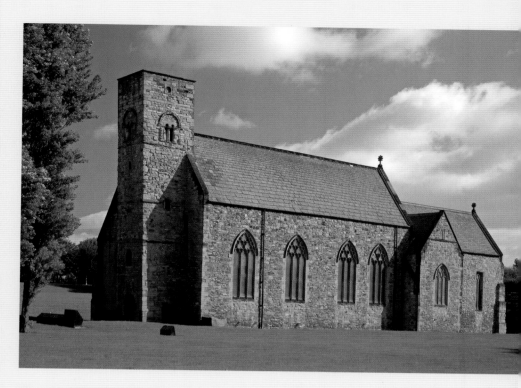

▲ Monkwearmouth, England, abbey church, tower and narthex, late 7th century.

▼ Reichenau, Oberzell, abbey church of St Georg, 890–896; frescoes date from the late 10th century.

flat roof, is typical for the interior of a Carolingian abbey church. As the St Gall prototype suggests, the western end of the church is flanked by two towers. In this case, they contain altars dedicated to the archangels Michael and Gabriel.

The north English abbey church of Monkwearmouth, founded as early as the seventh century, also features an imposing western tower.

▲ Müstair, Switzerland, Benedictine convent of St John, ca. 800, southeastern view with late Gothic bell tower and abbess's tower.

▼ Lorsch, gatehouse to the atrium of the (destroyed) abbey church of St Nazarius, dedicated 774.

Aachen and Carolingian Architecture

Two cultural strands come together in Carolingian architecture: the heritage of the migration period and the revival of antique and late antique culture. The reference to Rome was part of a political program. The Frankish king, Charlemagne, who had himself crowned emperor in the Eternal City in the year 800, and had his palatinate in Aachen rendered as a *Nova Roma*, used antique culture to underscore his political legitimacy. Architecture was now obliged to take on a demonstrative role: palace, parish and abbey churches—not to mention cathedrals—became testaments to an empire which understood itself to be the legitimate heir of the *Imperium Romanum*. Massive stone *more romano* (in the Roman manner) construction became the imperial style. The palatine chapel at Aachen is the embodiment of this Carolingian "renaissance," and became the model for countless centrally planned medieval buildings. Its core element is a domed octagon, encircled by a sixteen-sided, two-story gallery.

The Gatehouse of Lorsch, once part of the atrium of the abbey church of St Nazarius, is reminiscent of Roman triumphal arches. The arrangement of its facade, with its columns and pilasters, reveals a knowledge of classical orders.

The Early Christian basilica with its longitudinal alignment, the central plan with ambulatory, and the crypt—all influenced by the architecture of the Roman Empire—were adapted to fit new liturgical demands and differentiated spatially. One striking example of this design is the Benedictine Convent of St John in Müstair (Grisons, Switzerland), which is thought to have been founded by Charlemagne.

▶ Aachen, cathedral, former palatine chapel, dedicated 800; view into the octagon.

Westwork and Crypt

Both the growing cult of the saints and the imperial ritual of the Carolingian period called for a redefinition of church space. The former led to the further development of the crypt, which had evolved from the late antique confessio—an accessible martyrs' tomb located beneath the high altar of a church. St Peter's in Rome, containing the grave of the prince of the apostles, served as the model for this extremely significant aspect of medieval architecture. During the

▼ Fulda, Germany, church of St Michael, crypt, 820–822.

Carolingian period, crypts were constructed in either a tunnel or a ring shape, allowing for an ever-growing number of the faithful to visit the tomb of the saint in question. The crypt of the church of St Michael in Fulda, Germany is a well-known example of the centralized type. Originally a two-story mortuary chapel, the crypt was modeled after the anastasis rotunda in the Church of the Holy Sepulcher in Jerusalem. In the period that followed, vast hall crypts were built—often containing several aisles and imposing arrangements of columns—which could accommodate even more pilgrims.

The monumental westwork flanked by two towers was thought to be another Carolingian innovation. Recent research, however, has suggested that this theory is nineteenth-century wishful thinking. Nonetheless, it remains certain that the monumental fortress-like tower fronts, which pre-date Carolingian building, represent a new and completely non-antique form of architecture, although their function remains open to debate. Interpretations range from fortification to martyrium, from imperial gallery to a specific type of St Michael's chapel.

The earliest example of this kind of westwork is probably the structure at St Riquier in Centula, France, with its dominating group of towers. The most impressive example that has been preserved is the former abbey church of Corvey, where the foundation stone

for the westwork was laid in 873. In
this case, it is a blocky, multi-level
structure containing a porch and side
towers and originally also a central
spire. The interior consists of an
entrance hall, called a *quadrum* or
crypt, above which is a chapel with
a surrounding gallery. It was impressively decorated with sculpture and
frescoes.

Whatever its purpose, the westwork was a structural element that
lived on in Ottonian and Romanesque
architecture.

▼ ▶ Corvey, Germany, former abbey
church, westwork, 873–985; chapel with
surrounding gallery; facade; ground plan
(reconstruction).

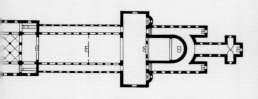

Ottonian and Salian Church Building

The coronation of Emperor Otto I in 936 and the subsequent reign of the Saxon Ottonians sparked a massive surge in prosperity that also had an impact on building construction from the second half of the tenth century. Carolingian architectural elements were developed and further differentiated. In addition to the building of monasteries, diocesan churches or cathedrals also took on primary importance.

A western annex modeled after the palatine chapel in Aachen was added to

▼ ▶ Hildesheim, former Benedictine monastery of St Michael, 1010–1033; renovated 1162–1186 after a fire; interior view and exterior view from the southwest.

the Essen cathedral, and construction began on the eastern sections of the cathedral in Mainz. The Benedictine abbey church of St Pantaleon in Cologne was given a new westwork: its structure—including stair towers, rounded arch friezes, cornices and pilasters—is much more complex than that of the abbey church in Corvey. Like Charlemagne, Otto the Great also imported *spolia* from antique buildings and had them integrated into "his" church structures. At Magdeburg Cathedral, they were even incorporated into the new Gothic section and presented in regal splendor.

The collegiate church of St Cyriacus in Gernrode, in the Harz mountain region of Germany, is one of the best-preserved monuments from the Ottonian period. Originally a convent church founded in 961, it was a seminal work

▲ Cologne, St Pantaleon, westwork, 984–ca. 1000, reconstructed after many changes.

▲ Gernrode, former Convent Church of St Cyriacus, last third of the 10th century, interior.

in Romanesque architecture. The nave is lined with galleries—an unusual feature for a church in Germany at that time, which can probably be attributed to its intended function as a convent. Another novel characteristic is the accentuated subdivision of the building through the alternating use of columns and piers, as well as the segregated crossing, which places an architectural emphasis on the crossing point between the nave and the transept.

The structural experiments suggested at Gernrode were perfected just a short time later, at the church of the Benedictine monastery of St Michael in Hildesheim. Founded by the artistically minded Bishop Bernward, it is highly consistent throughout its structure. The modular system of the floor plan is based on the size of the crossing square, a unit that reappears in the spans of the nave and the two transepts. The crossing is framed on all sides by large archways, thus emphasizing it visually as the liturgical area. The corners of the square units are accentuated by piers, and aligned between each of these are two more slender columns, a pattern known as the Saxon alternating system, which subsequently became widespread. Despite many changes, the systematic structure of the building is also evident from the exterior. The major units— nave, transepts, choir, crossing tower and flanking towers—are clearly differentiated from one another, and the building is recognizable as a consistently structured, harmonious whole.

St Michael's church in Hildesheim represents the establishment of a type that set the tone for the sacred architecture of the Romanesque period. Thus, with regard to developments in the neighboring countries of the Holy Roman Empire, as well, one often speaks in terms of the proto Romanesque and early Romanesque periods.

Early Romanesque Architecture in Catalonia

In the eighth and ninth centuries, the Pyrenees were the scene of climactic events in world history because they formed a buffer zone between the Christian and Islamic worlds. Following the recapture of Catalonia in 801, Charlemagne established the *Marca Hispanica* (or Spanish March), which served as the starting point for the later phases of the *Reconquista*.

The monastery of St Pere de Rodes was evidently founded for strategic reasons. There is evidence that an abbey existed here as early as the eighth century—perhaps even during the time of the Arab occupation. The surviving structure was probably begun

▲ St Pere de Rodes, former Benedictine monastery, begun in the 9th century, dedicated 1022.

▶ Cardona, castle church of St Vicenç, 1029–1040, view into the narrow nave.

in the ninth century, although the church was not dedicated until 1022. Now in ruins, it closely resembles the more or less contemporary abbey church of St-Michel-de-Cuxa in southern France. At 121 ft (37 m), it is uncommonly long for the period. The three aisles of the high, barrel-vaulted nave are separated by T-sectioned piers with unusually high plinths; these open onto a broad transept with lateral apses. There is a ring crypt located directly beneath the ambulatory of the main choir. It is difficult to imagine how such an architectural model would have reached Rodes, since it did not become typical for that region until significantly later. Almost equally puzzling is the

motif of applied columns on the piers in the nave.

The castle church of St Vicenç in Cardona is a striking and immensely important example from this period in architectural history. Founded by Viscount Beremund and constructed between 1029 and 1040, it is an extraordinary relic of the early Romanesque movement in Catalonia. Its elevations and ground plan display a previously unseen degree of clarity and regularity. Behind the narthex, the nave contains three wide, rectangular bays, each of which is flanked in turn by three smaller bays in the side aisles. The choir, main apse and two minor apses are joined to the deep transept.

Romanesque Architecture

The span between the mid-eleventh century and the early thirteenth century is commonly called the Romanesque period. The term was coined in the early nineteenth century, when scholars noted that a number of its formal elements were borrowed from Roman artistic tradition. The development of Romanesque architecture is intimately connected to the Holy Roman Empire, whose rulers saw themselves as agents of spiritual and worldly power in equal measure. This close tie between clerical and secular proved to be extremely productive for the development of both sacred and profane architecture, but it also provoked opposition: at the Burgundian monastery of Cluny, a movement grew among those who insisted that the pope should be recognized as the sole spiritual authority.

quick succession by the monks at Cluny (see p. 90) exerted a lasting French influence on the European sacred architecture that followed: for example, the barrel vault—and, closely associated with it, the restructuring of wall designs. The pilgrimage churches that lined the route to Santiago de Compostela also experimented with the forms developed at Cluny. In the twelfth century, it was the Cistercians—and the ideal of austerity that they promoted—that brought new impulses to medieval architecture.

At the same time, a wide variety of other developments were taking place: for example, the knightly orders of Spain modeled their buildings on historical sites in the Holy Land. The *cimborrios* (pierced domes) in the cathedrals of Zamora, Salamanca and Toro established a specifically Spanish dome tradition. Byzantine forms came to the west via Venice; in Tuscany, the preferred styles were marble facings and classicizing motifs. The Normans developed their own monumental architectural style which could be seen from Normandy to as far away as England and Sicily. Architects in western France experimented with different forms of vaults and domes; classicizing portals could be found in the south.

Architectural sculpture moved beyond its role as a purely decorative feature, as well. Around the year 1000, the first apotropaic carvings (images intended to ward off evil) appeared on capitals. With the building of the third church at Cluny, a complex program of images was developed which covered the exterior portals, capitals and corbels as well as the interior. This trend reached a magnificent climax in the abbey church of Vézelay in Burgundy. A boom in technical craftsmanship

▲ Worms, Germany, cathedral of St Peter, western choir, late 12th–early 13th centuries, integrating older architectural elements.

▲ Arles, St-Trophîme, portal, ca. 1190–1200. In the tympanum: Christ in Majesty, surrounded by the symbols of the Evangelists.

◀ St-Savin-sur-Gartempe, former priory church, 1065–1080 and 1095–1115, nave with arcade of colossal columns and barrel vault.

went hand in hand with the advanced differentiation of architecture and sculptural ornamentation. Stonemasons and sculptors sometimes traveled across Europe to hire themselves out to prestigious master builders.

In general, we can distinguish three stylistic phases of the Romanesque period. The early Romanesque architecture of the eleventh century formulated the basic structures of sacred architecture, especially. Over a period of just a few decades, thousands of monasteries and churches were built all across the Western world—which, despite regional idiosyncrasies, display an astonishing uniformity of appearance and are clearly distinguishable from the architecture of the Carolingian and Ottonian periods.

The replacement of wood buildings by more enduring and prestigious stone construction was only a superficial indicator of this change. The truly seminal development of this period was the increased demand for monu-

▲ Zamora, Spain, cathedral, 1151–1171, view into crossing dome (*cimborrio*).

▲ Vézelay, former abbey church of Ste-Madeleine, main portal with tympanum depicting the Pentecost miracle, 1125–30.

▲ Tomar, Portugal, Templar church, late 12th century.

mentality, the clear organization of architectural elements, and the rhythmic composition of wall surfaces.

The high Romanesque period, which began around 1100, saw the introduction of continuously vaulted interiors in place of the older wooden-roofed constructions, as well as more heavily sculpted building designs. Both the interior and exterior walls were divided into several tiers; previously solid walls were dissolved into clerestories, triforia and arcades. Then, in the first half of the thirteenth century—when French architects were already experimenting with the "Gothic" system—the great, distinctively tiered and richly decorated Romanesque cathedrals of the Rhineland were being built. Due to the skillful merging and progression of their architectural elements, their characteristic groups of towers and their decorative sculptural ornamentation, they came to be the embodiment of the *Reichskirche*—the imperial church of the Holy Roman Empire.

Regional Developments in France

The emergence of Romanesque architecture was not a simple, linear process. Rather, during the tenth and eleventh centuries, the region that is now France served as a fertile experimental ground. The separate regions exhibited tendencies toward different architectural forms, and their sacred as well as secular institutions also pursued a variety of goals in their building policies.

The architecture of Normandy is worthy of particular attention. Under Norman rule, a stable political structure had developed in this region, which engaged in constant exchanges with other areas. The Normans' dynastic relationships extended as far as Sicily, which developed a Norman culture of its own. The Normans' contact with England—which they conquered at the Battle of Hastings in 1066—was particularly close. In terms of architecture, therefore, one can justifiably speak of an Anglo-Norman style, which is characterized by twin-towered facades, galleries and double-shelled walls.

The vaulting of the nave and transept with groin vaults established the basis for Gothic vaulting techniques. The abbey church of Jumièges (in Normandy), on the other hand, which is today a ruin, set a precedent for the articulation of nave walls. Each pair of bays was connected by a wall shaft, creating a rhythmic, vertical pattern from which the overall structure of the interior could be derived.

A completely different, but no less impressive interior originated in

▲ Tournus, former abbey church of St-Philibert, 10th century to 1120, interior.

◄ ▲ Jumièges, former abbey church of Nôtre-Dame, 1040–1067, view from the south and facade.

Tournus, in Burgundy: the nave of the abbey church of St-Philibert is astonishing for its height and vastness. Massive, round stone pillars support freestanding arches across which transverse barrels have been laid—a vault construction that was most likely added after the church was built, and which created a grandiose effect.

Aquitaine and Poitou were home to many hall churches with barrel or groin vaults, but even more popular were domed churches in which the bays of the nave were vaulted with a series of pendentive domes. The vaulted group is exemplified by the former abbey church of St-Savin-sur-Gartempe, the nave of which was

▼ St-Nectaire, former abbey church of St-Nectaire, begun ca. 1080.

▲ Périgueux, St-Front, begun ca. 1120, view from the south.

constructed between 1095 and 1115 (see p. 84). In this church the aisles are separated by a colossal arcade. The barrel vault extends the length of the nave with no transverse arches (the church is lit indirectly from the side aisles).

The cathedrals of Angoulême and Périgueux represent the domed type of church. Built on a Latin cross, Angloulême has four domes over its nave, while Périgueux was built on a Greek cross and has five domes. In both churches, the domes rest on pendentives (curving spandrels linking the base of the dome to the piers). It is possible that this type of vaulted roof was inspired by Early Christian or Byzantine examples.

Other visions clearly inspired the block-like exterior of the pilgrimage church of St-Nectaire in Auvergne. Here, the clerestory was omitted in favor of a barrel vault, and the architectural elements progress from the low-ceilinged chapels to the aisles, to the pitched roofs and the facade towers all the way to the looming crossing tower.

From Normandy to England

The former abbey church of St-Étienne in Caen, Normandy, was seminal for sacred Romanesque architecture in France and England alike. Behind its imposing twin-towered facade, the nave reveals a three-tier wall construction consisting of arcade, triforium and double-walled clerestory. Sexpartite rib vaults were added at the beginning of the twelfth century.

One of the most impressive examples of this Anglo-Norman architectural style is Durham Cathedral. Like their counterparts on the French mainland, builders here also experimented with stone vaulting. When construction began in 1093, this technique had apparently already been planned for the choir; the rib vaulting used for the entire nave—thought to be the earliest of its kind—was built in a second phase of construction that began ca. 1120. The elevation of the nave is determined by the pronounced alternation of

▲ Caen, abbey church of St-Étienne, ca. 1065–1081, vaulted ceiling ca. 1120, choir ca. 1200, interior.

▲ Durham Cathedral, 1093–1133, interior.

▶ Ely Cathedral, begun 1083, western facade, late 12th century.

compound piers and massive elaborately patterned drum piers.

The history of the Benedictine abbey of Ely goes back to the seventh century. The present church was begun in 1083 and was elevated to the status of cathedral in 1109. The enormous western transept with its soaring middle tower dates from the late twelfth century.

As was true everywhere else in Europe, the Cistercian abbeys in England were modeled on the ideals that evolved under Bernard of Clairvaux (see pp. 90–91). Nevertheless, the architecture was adjusted to comply with local conditions, for example, as far as the choice of building materials was concerned. Unfortunately, most of the Cistercian abbeys in England were destroyed—as at Fountains and

Rievaulx, which survive today as picturesque ruins. Of the original abbey of Bury St Edmunds, only the massive, four-story gateway tower survives.

◀ Rievaulx Abbey, former Cistercian church, founded 1132.

▶ Bury St Edmunds, former abbey, begun after 1081, tower over entrance hall.

▲ Paray-le-Monial, priory church, ca. 1100.

▼ Autun, cathedral of St-Lazare, 1120 to mid-12th century, nave elevation.

The Reformation of the Monasteries

In 910, William of Aquitaine founded a Benedictine monastery in the Burgundian town of Cluny which came to epitomize monastic autarchy: the Cluniac monks recognized papal authority alone, and not that of any secular ruler. Their ideas met with widespread approval, and their architecture was equally influential: in particular, the second (955–981) and third (1088–1130) abbey churches, which were built in quick succession, set new architectural standards. Since Cluny III was destroyed in 1790, we can only guess at its size and splendor based on our knowledge of the buildings it inspired. The priory church of Paray-le-Monial, for example, with its narthex, pointed barrel vaults, and choir with ambulatory and chapels, is thought to be a miniature copy of the earlier structure. Even the cathedral of St-Lazare in Autun followed this pattern.

In the early twelfth century, discontent reappeared in the monasteries of France, this time over the expansion of Cluniac wealth and power. The unrest culminated in 1098 in the founding of the Cistercian order—a movement to return to the original rules established by St Benedict. Mystical piety, labor and austerity were the values stipulated by the most famous Cistercian abbot, Bernard of Clairvaux. Their architecture was intended to embody these ideals. The abbey of Cîteaux was the first monastery Bernard founded; it was followed by La Ferté, Pontigny, Morimond and Clairvaux. These monasteries in turn founded daughter houses within a short period of time. All Cistercian monasteries followed the same ideal plan, which specified the overall layout of the abbey as well as the details of its furnishings. The renunciation of luxury was their highest commandment.

Of the early Cistercian monasteries, only Fontenay has preserved its original appearance—most likely dictated by Bernard himself. The interior of the church, built between 1139 and 1147, is notable for its sublime austerity: the exquisite masonry work is the church's sole decoration.

▼ Cluny, model of the third abbey church, 1088–1130, southeastern view.

▼ Cistercian abbey of Fontenay, 1139–1147, interior.

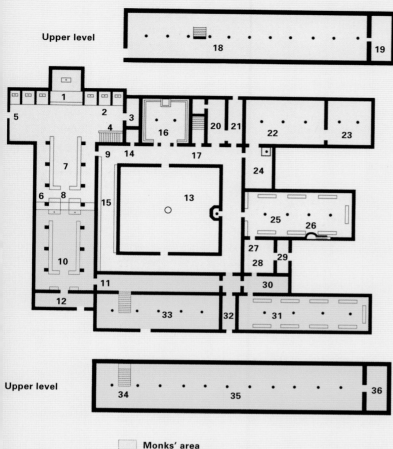

Upper level

18   19

1
2
5
3
4
16   20   21   22   23
9   14   17
7   24
6   8   15   13
25   26
10   27
11   28   29
12   30
33   32   31

Upper level

34   35   36

Monks' area
Lay brothers' area

Ideal plan for a Cistercian abbey

1. Sanctuary and High Altar
2. Side altars
3. Sacristies
4. Night stairs
5. Cemetery door
6. Choir screen
7. Monks' choir
8. Invalids' choir
9. Monks' door to cloister
10. Lay brothers' choir
11. Lay brothers' door
12. Narthex
13. Pump in cloister yard
14. Armarium (library)
15. Cloister passage (collation area)
16. Chapter house
17. Day stair to 18
18. Monks' dormitory
19. Latrines
20. Monks' speaking room
21. Passageway
22. Scriptorium (monks' hall)
23. Novices' hall
24. Calefactorium (warming room)
25. Monks' refectory
26. Reader's seat
27. Hatch
28. Kitchen
29. Larders
30. Lay brothers' speaking room
31. Lay brothers' refectory
32. Lay brothers' passageway
33. Cellar
34. Lay brothers' stairway
35. Lay brothers' dormitory
36. Latrines

▼ Fontenay, view of monastery grounds. As a result of extensive restoration carried out in the first third of the 20th century, Fontenay Abbey, founded in 1118 by Bernard of Clairvaux, is one of the best-preserved Cistercian monasteries in Europe. It very closely resembles the ideal plan depicted above.

The Cloister

The central point of a monastery is the cloister, which is usually adjacent to the church on the south side. This square courtyard, bordered by galleries, derives its English name from the Latin word *claustrum*, which means a secluded area). The form of the cloister was probably inspired by the peristylum (see pp. 16, 27), a columned courtyard found in ancient Roman houses.

As we have already seen in the ideal plan of St Gall from the early ninth century (see p. 72), the cloister passageway enclosed the more secluded areas of the monastery, those that were not open to the public. These included the chapter house, the parlatorium (the room where the monks were allowed to speak), refectory (dining hall), kitchen and storeroom, warming rooms and library. On the upper level were the dormitory and, later, the monks' cells. Originally located in the center of the cloister and later on the side closest to the refectory was the pump house, which was primarily used for ritual washing.

In addition to its role as the focal point of communal monastic life, the cloister could also function as a burial area at times. Abbots and other especially honored persons were interred within its walls, where elaborate tombs were built for them. Even today, many cloisters continue to serve as places of contemplation and retreat. In some cases, cloisters were also added to cathedrals and other sacred buildings.

▲ Catalonia, Santa Maria de Poblet, Cistercian cloister, pump house, 12th century.

In every era, the decoration of the cloister was a supremely important task, one that involved the combined contributions of each aspect of the arts. The architectural focus was the design of the colonnades and vaults in the cloister yard itself, as well as the embellishment of the adjoining rooms. As the order's assembly room, the chapter house had the most formal design. In the dining halls and dormitories—which were vast, elongated spaces—the challenge was to span extremely large areas and, if possible, to vault them. Architects found a number of innovative solutions to this challenge, which were later also applied to secular constructions.

The most important element, however, was sculpture, which brought three-dimensional life into the cloister. A graphic encyclopedia of medieval thought in the context of the salvation narrative unfolds in column reliefs, capitals and corbels.

▼ Moissac, France, former abbey church of St-Pierre, view into cloister, 1100.

Capital Sculpture

The capital, the crowning member of a column and the connecting point between the supporting and supported sections of a structure, took on a fundamentally new design function in Romanesque architecture. The stylized foliage patterns of classical and Byzantine architecture and the solidly geometrical forms of the

▲ Cologne, St Maria im Kapitol, plain cushion capital, mid-11th century.

▲ Quedlinburg, Germany, former convent church of St Servatius, cushion capital with figures, before 1129.

▲ Provence, France, Le Thoronet, former Cistercian abbey, crocket capital in the chapter house, mid-12th century.

▼ Santo Domingo de Silos, Spain, double cloister capitals, mid-12th century (see also pp. 82–83).

▲ Serrabone, former priory church of Nôtre-Dame, double capital on the singers' rostrum, second half of the 12th century.

Ottonian period made way for fully three-dimensional representations of people, animals and mythical creatures. In this way, the Romanesque capital became a bearer of images: stories from both the Old and New Testaments, myths, as well as everyday scenes were intended to move and instruct the viewer. Beginning in Burgundy and southern and western France, the use of figurative capitals spread throughout Europe in the twelfth century. The Cistercian monasteries, however, were an exception: here, where any type of figurative representation was undesirable, the crocket capital had a heyday.

The Pilgrims' Way

In the eleventh and twelfth centuries, the pilgrimage to Santiago de Compostela became a mass movement. Following any of four branching routes, streams of pilgrims surged through France and Spain to be united at the supposed grave of the Apostle James. The popularity of the saint—who, as a *matamoros* (= killer of the Moors), was thought to have led the reconquest of the Moorish territories—knew no bounds; it competed only with that of pilgrimages to Rome.

Countless churches, chapels, hospices and hospitals were founded along the pilgrimage route, a building boom that could only be accomplished through the operation of supraregional stonemasons' and builders' lodges. The result was an astonishing degree of similarity in building designs and forms. In their need to provide space for a huge host of the faithful, pilgrim-

▼ Santiago de Compostela, cathedral, Pórtico de la Gloria by Master Mateo, 1168–1188.

▲ Conques, France, church of Ste-Foy, begun ca.1050, view from the east.

age churches developed a distinctive form characterized by an extended transept with supplementary apses and a choir ambulatory with apsidioles (minor apses). Examples survive at St-Sernin in Toulouse or at Ste-Foy-de-Conques. With its five aisles and eleven bays, the nave of St-Sernin is immense. The abbey of Ste-Foy in Conques was initially built in a more modest, antiquated style. As the influx of pilgrims to the martyr's relics

increased, however, a more spacious apse was built, modeled on that of St-Sernin. The nave was covered with a barrel vault, whose thrust was absorbed by triforia. Like all the churches along the Way of St James, Ste-Foy is richly sculpted. The tympanum on the western portal shows the Last Judgment. With twelve figures, it is the most complex element of this kind that survives from the Romanesque period.

▼ The pilgrims' way to Santiago de Compostela: the four major routes leading through France.

▲ Conques, Sainte-Foy, tympanum on the western portal, second quarter of the 12th century.

▼ Toulouse, St-Sernin, 1080 to mid-12th century, nave elevation.

Toulouse, St-Sernin   Conques, Ste-Foy

The culmination of the pilgrimage was, of course, the cathedral of Santiago de Compostela, whose new Romanesque construction was begun in 1075. It became one of the greatest churches of its era. The highlight of its design is the elaborate triple portal, the Pórtico de la Gloria, a masterpiece of sculpture created by Master Mateo in the twelfth century. On its trumeau is the apostle James; above him Christ in Majesty presides over the Last Judgment.

The Imperial Cathedrals

In 1025, immediately after the first Salian king, Conrad II, was elected, construction began at Limburg an der Haardt on the first German church to embody the new—Romanesque— ideas of spatial design. Just five years later, Conrad ordered the cornerstone to be laid for Speyer Cathedral. Intended as a mausoleum for the German emperors, the cathedral was vaulted during the rule of Henry IV. The three-aisled basilica plan was preserved, with its imposing western section, extended transept and elevated round-ended choir. Beneath the eastern bays lie the graves of the emperors, directly adjoining the spacious hall crypt, whose pillars are topped with massive cushion capitals. The distinctive features of Romanesque building are clearly visible in the building's design: the windows and arcades are integrated within a colossal order; the wall is a skeletal structure of supports and non-weight-bearing retaining walls.

▼ ▶ Mainz, Germany, cathedral of St Martin and St Stephen, begun 1081, eastern view and detail of the dwarf gallery on the eastern apse.

The dwarf gallery encircling the apse is considered a Lombard element. The multi-tiered clusters of towers underscore the extraordinary importance of this imperial church.

With its enormous proportions and imposing vaults, Speyer Cathedral became a model for other imperial buildings, such as the cathedrals of Mainz and Worms. Mainz Cathedral, which had been destroyed by fire in 1081, was rebuilt at the behest of Emperor Henry IV and completed around 1137. The similarities to the slightly older Speyer Cathedral are particularly clear in the eastern section. Worms Cathedral (see p. 84) was rebuilt at the turn of the twelfth century over the old Ottonian ground plan. Its western choir is composed of the familiar sandstone blocks; however, the workmanship is far more elaborate than that of the earlier construction.

◀ ▲ ▶ Speyer, Germany, cathedral of St Mary and St Stephen, begun ca. 1030, eastern view, crypt and view into the nave.

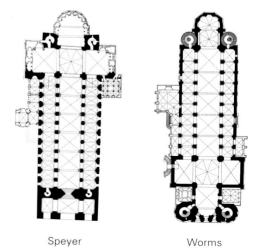

Speyer   Worms

Cologne and the Rhineland

Under the Ottonian rulers, the focus of German building activity had been in Saxony. Under the Salians, the focus shifted to their home territory of the Rhineland. Speyer Cathedral, a mausoleum for kings and emperors, set the standard for sacred architecture from that time on. In its train, countless churches were built exemplifying the high quality and unity of the early Romanesque movement in Germany—such as St Aposteln (Church of the Holy Apostles) and St Maria im Kapitol in Cologne, the western section of the minster in Essen, as well as the cathedrals of Bamberg, Mainz and Trier. However, in the course of the following century, all of these churches were "renovated"—an indication of their status and of the desire for a more "up-to-date" style.

St Maria im Kapitol displays a feature unique to the sacred architecture of Cologne: the cloverleaf or triconch form, presumably inspired

▶ Maria Laach, Benedictine abbey church, founded 1093; choir completed ca. 1170, western view with paradise, 1230–1240.

◀ Schwarzrheindorf, double chapel (now St Mary and St Clement), begun 1151, interior.

by late antique architecture. It lends a central concentration to the eastern section of the structure. The abbey church of Maria Laach, dedicated in 1093, was completely vaulted in the early twelfth century. This double-choired complex, with its staggered, far-reaching clusters of buildings, is united externally through the use of structural elements such as pilaster strips, round arches and blind arcades. Its late Hohenstaufen atrium, the

assembly area for worshipers who were not yet baptized, is reminiscent of Early Christian churches. The double chapel of Schwarzrheindorf near Bonn originally served as the private chapel of the archbishop of Cologne, Arnold von Wied. Built on a cross-shaped plan and topped with a tower, the upper and lower floors are connected by an internal opening.

From about 1200, the Rhineland again became a major building center: new choirs were added to St Aposteln and Gross St Martin (Great St Martin's Church), modeled on that of St Maria im Kapitol. The first pointed rib vaults also appeared during this period. The imperial cathedrals of the Salian period were reworked and certain technical and stylistic aspects were updated—with vaulting, for example, and more strongly articulated exteriors.

▲ Cologne, St Aposteln, 1020–1030, tower cluster.

◀ Cologne, St Maria im Kapitol, dedicated 1065, external view of the triconch.

Colors and Materials

Medieval architecture was anything but colorless; builders consciously made use of colorful mountings or varied materials to structure and decorate their work. Of course, the various types of marble that could be found in Italy were not readily available in central, western and northern Europe. In these regions, designers had to make do with quarry stones, brick, stucco or glazes. Limburg Cathedral is a vivid example of the way in which color was used in building design. A turning point between German late Romanesque architecture and the new, early Gothic movement imported from France, the church creates a picturesque view rising over the rocky banks of the Lahn River. Visible from far away, the red accents of the building's sculpted sections contribute greatly to its impressive appearance.

Owing to a shortage of natural stone in northern Germany and throughout the Baltic region, brick building had a heyday that lasted throughout the Middle Ages. Brick and necessity became the mother of invention. The structural properties of bricks, which are fired and set in layers, are completely different from those of quarry stones, so the use of this material generated a separate and

▲ Jericho, former Premonstratensian church of St Mary and St Nicholas, begun ca. 1144.

▲ Ratzeburg, Germany, cathedral of St Mary and St John, begun ca. 1160–1170; narthex 1215–1220.

▶ Limburg an der Lahn, Germany, cathedral, former abbey church of St George and St Nicholas, 1215–1235.

extremely delicate kind of formal expression. This can be seen as early as the Premonstratensian church in Jericho, which dispenses completely with sculptural decoration. Nevertheless, the interplay of the red bricks with the unadorned, archaic forms creates an aesthetic of its own.

Romanesque brick architecture reached an apogee with Ratzeburg Cathedral, in northern Germany, where the church's facades captivate viewers with their contrasting colors and rich decoration. The cornices, pilaster strips and lace-like friezes create an extraordinarily lively surface. All surfaces are richly decorated in the narthex, where glazed bricks create colorful accents. The Vor Frue Kirke (Church of Our Lady) in Kalundborg, Denmark, constitutes a typological anomaly: the central section of the once-fortified church rises from the cross-shaped ground plan; towering above it are five strongly jutting octagonal towers.

In Scandinavia, wood was the preferred building material. In Norway, some thirty stave churches still stand and bear witness to the virtuosity of medieval carvers and carpenters. The most impressive is the church in Borgund, which dates from the mid-twelfth century. Its walls are constructed of posts, forming a wooden skeleton; its roofs overlap one another in tiers. The portals and gables are decorated with beast heads and there is runic graffiti.

▲ Kalundborg, Denmark, Vor Frue Kirke, 1170–1190, exterior of the former fortified church.

◀▲ Borgund, Norway, stave church, ca. 1150, exterior; interior view.

Florence and Pisa

The development of Romanesque architecture followed a different course in Italy than in central Europe. As early as the eleventh century, master builders in Tuscany were modeling their designs after the architecture of antiquity: thus, balanced proportions, the clear arrangement of surfaces and the use of classical orders became the particular trademarks of central Italian Romanesque architecture. Narrow bands of light and dark (greenish) marble form geometric patterns and enliven the surfaces. This elaborate "encrustation" or inlay style endured well into the fifteenth century and had a decisive influence on the architecture of the early Renaissance.

A number of these highly decorative monuments can be found in Florence: the baptistery of St John is a compact, octagonal structure whose facades are festively decorated with different colored strips of marble. Here, the design shows a clear differentiation between structural and decorative elements, between the actual wall mass and the artistic arrangement. Classical motifs such as the orders of columns and pilasters on the two main levels or the fluted pilasters on the parapet help

▲ Florence, Baptistery of St John, ca. 1060–1150, exterior.

▼ Florence, San Miniato al Monte, ca. 1070–1150, interior.

explain why, in the fifteenth century, this was widely believed to be an antique building.

The church of San Miniato al Monte, situated high above the city, is a further example of this "Tuscan proto-Renaissance". Inside, the continuous arcades typical of Early Christian basilicas are combined with Romanesque principles of organization.

The Campo dei Miracoli (the "Field of Miracles") in Pisa contains no less than four representative works of the Italian Romanesque period: the cathedral, founded in 1063 after the Pisan victory over the Saracens; the baptistery (begun ca. 1152); the "Leaning

Tower" or campanile, founded in 1173, and the camposanto (the thirteenth-century cemetery). Although these buildings were constructed over the course of several centuries, the monumental grouping appears to be a harmonious ensemble of structures with elegantly decorated facades of marble inlay and blind arcades carefully designed to complement one another. The marble facade of the cathedral became the prototype for countless other buildings, from Tuscany to as far away as Sardinia: delicately clad in a web-like arrangement of arcades and columned galleries, it nevertheless preserves its structural clarity.

▲ Pistoia, San Giovanni Fuorcivitas, mid-12th century, detail of the facade.

▼ Pisa, Campo dei Miracoli: in the foreground is the cathedral, begun by mason Buscheto in 1063.

▲ Milan, San Ambrogio,
9th–12th centuries, atrium.

▲ Modena, San Geminiano Cathedral, begun
1099, dedicated 1184; facade with sculpture
by Master Wiligelmo, early 12th century.

Northern Italy

The culture of Lombardy and the Veneto evolved directly from the antique and Early Christian heritage. Lombard master builders, who were skilled in both Roman and Byzantine construction techniques, contributed to the spread of northern Italian stylistic elements.

The primarily Romanesque church of San Ambrogio in Milan is a key building of its time. New work on the basilica was begun in the ninth century, although its present appearance dates from the period between 1088 and 1128. The atrium draws on an Early Christian architectural style: the fore-court, lined with columned halls, was a gathering place for pilgrims who came to be symbolically cleansed of their sin.

No fewer than five sanctuaries were erected over the grave of the mir-acle worker St Zeno, bishop and later patron saint of Verona, before work was begun in 1118 on the present Romanesque church. The majestic building is built in tuff and marble; inside, massive compound piers alter-nate with slender columns. At the

eastern end of the nave, a partially sunken crypt extends across the entire width of the structure.

Rebuilding of Modena Cathedral was begun in 1099 under the direction of Countess Matilda of Tuscany. The three-aisled church with its superb sil-houette is one of the most important sacred buildings of the Emilia Romagna—not least because so much informa-tion has been preserved about the artists involved in its construction. Master Lanfranco designed the archi-tecture and Master Wiligelmo created the sculptures on the facade.

Southern Italy

The southern Italian province of Apulia is home to some unique examples of Romanesque architecture. The region owes its cultural wealth to the Nor-mans, who campaigned against the Byzantine and Arab hegemonies there. With the foundation of the church of San Nicola in Bari, a uniquely Apulian architectural style was created which was copied in numerous churches along the Adriatic coast. One of the

▼ Verona, San Zeno Maggiore, 1118–
1138, interior, view toward the east
including the crypt and raised choir.

▼ Monreale, cathedral, cloister,
ca. 1200.

most impressive of these is Trani Cathedral. The hallmarks of this group of buildings include the blocky, continuous transept and the height of the nave, which looms high above the side aisles and often has a large rose window on its facade.

Sicily has been a meeting point for various cultures from time immemorial. Its architecture—and above all, its magnificent mosaic cycles—bear eloquent witness to this merging of cultures. In Monreale Cathedral, Byzantine mosaics, Arabic floor designs, bronze doors from

▲ Trani, San Nicola Pellegrino, late 11th century.

Pisa, and the cloister with its fantastically carved capitals constitute a unique conglomerate of eastern and western art.

City Complexes and Municipal Buildings

In contrast to sacred buildings, examples of secular Romanesque architecture are rare. Fortifications as well as city palaces and residential buildings were subject to constant change—whether for defensive purposes or for the sake of prestige. Yet another reason for the scarcity of surviving monuments has to do with the building material: most were made of wood, which provided fuel for countless conflagrations. Nevertheless, in many places throughout Europe, we can still get a sense of the layout of a medieval city complex. The structure of the cities that grew up around cathedrals, bishops' residences, castles and centers of trade has often been preserved.

City walls protected the citizens from enemy incursions. One of the most beautiful and best-preserved circular walls dating from the Romanesque period is in the Spanish city of Ávila: it is over 1.5 miles (2.5 km) long, has an average height of 39 ft (12 m) and it encompasses ninety towers and nine gates. But danger lurked inside the cities, too —a fact attested by the patrician towers of northern and central Italy, many of which can still be admired in the Tuscan city of San Gimignano. Aristocratic families, who were in constant dispute with rival clans or parties, retreated into these nearly impenetrable residential towers, which could be up to 164 ft (50 m) high. Despite the constant neighborhood feuds and severe political conflicts, an enormous boom in city building work took place at the

▲ Milan, Italy, Palazzo della Ragione (Broletto Nuovo), completed in 1233.

▼ Ávila, Spain, circular wall enclosing the city; it contains 90 towers and 9 gates.

► San Gimignano, Italy, view of the city with medieval patrician towers.

▼ St-Antonin, France, city mansion of the Granolhet family, mid-12th century.

beginning of the twelfth century. Municipal constructions such as city halls, market halls and hospitals developed into independent building projects. The town houses of the patricians began to compete with those of the nobility. The oldest city halls in Italy—known as *broletti* (*brolo* = self-contained district)—were built as early as the eleventh and twelfth centuries. However, those that survive date primarily from the thirteenth century. Examples include the broletti in Pavia, Viterbo and Orvieto, or the Palazzo della Ragione in Milan. The city homes of the nobility soon became similarly elaborate: in St-Antonin in southern France, the Granolhet family mansion is flanked by an imposing tower. The ground floor includes majestic arcades, and the main level houses a vast ballroom.

▲ Gelnhausen, Germany, imperial palace, great hall, second half of the 12th century.

▲ Goslar, Germany, reconstruction of the imperial palace begun in the 11th century.

▼ Ribeauvillé, Alsace, Château St-Ulrich, early 12th to 13th centuries.

Castles, Palaces and Bridges

In the turbulent periods of the Middle Ages, castles served as well-fortified residences as well as highly visible expressions of territorial power. By the end of the fifteenth century, there may have been as many as 40,000 fortified building complexes in France alone. Located on top of a hill or surrounded by moats, builders took advantage of local geography. Reinforced walls with towers, gates and drawbridges made up the outer circle of defense, in the midst of which stood the great hall or palace, the residence, and/or a tower-like, freestanding keep. In case of an assault on the castle, a keep served as a last refuge for its residents. Called the *Bergfried* in Germany or the *donjon* in France, it contained only modest, single rooms. The great hall, on the other hand, was elegantly furnished. In addition to rooms for the nobility, it contained a single or double chapel as well as a festival hall (knights' hall) for formal receptions and celebrations.

▲ Huesca, Spain, Loarre Castle, 11th–12th centuries.

Loarre Castle is a magnificent fortification, hierarchically organized both architecturally and functionally. It marks the boundary between the reconquered Christian section and the Moorish region of Aragón, Spain.

A variation on the castle form is the *Pfalz* or palace. Scattered throughout the empire, palaces served as temporary residences for the German emperors and kings; there was no permanent seat of government at that time. In addition to the palace in Aachen and the (reconstructed) imperial palace in Goslar, the ruins of an extraordinarily complex palace site have been preserved in Gelnhausen that still displays elaborate sculptural ornamentation.

Bridges served an extremely important strategic function, as well as an economic one. Stone bridges, especially, were based on Roman building techniques. One example is the bridge near Besalú in Catalonia, which was erected at the crossing of two highways and has undergone numerous renovations.

◀ Besalú, Catalonia, medieval stone bridge over the Fluvià River.

Gothic Architecture

Italian art theorists of the fifteenth and sixteenth centuries described everything that they considered to be barbaric and uncouth as *maniera dei goti* (in the Gothic style). Those who wanted to revive the classical legacy considered medieval northern European art, in particular, inferior to that of their compatriots. Only when the Romantic movement rediscovered pre-Renaissance architecture, at the end of the eighteenth and the beginning of the nineteenth centuries, was this era positively valued.

Today, the art of the late Middle Ages, that is, between the second half of the twelfth and the beginning of the sixteenth centuries, is called Gothic, although the course of its development varied from one region to another.

▲ Pontigny, former Cistercian abbey church, begun 1145, choir 1186–1210.

Gothic architectural style first appeared in France around 1140 CE, but the transition from late Romanesque to early Gothic did not take place in Germany until the thirteenth century. However, the design of the Cologne Cathedral (which was not finally completed until the nineteenth century) represented the ideal of Gothic cathedral architecture. The same problem of definition arises at the close of the era: while Michelangelo brought Renaissance architecture into full bloom in Italy, bold late Gothic hall churches were being built in other countries.

The definition of the term Gothic is therefore based less on assigning dates than upon such details of construction as pointed arches and rib vaults. These are but one component of the overall aesthetic concept, the goal of which was to dissolve walls and to saturate interior space with

light. This dematerialization is not merely a matter of form: it is the realization of mystical ideas that had evolved in contemporary literature and philosophy. In France, the onset of Gothic architecture was linked with the consolidation of the monarchy. The cathedrals that spread this new style throughout French territory

◀ Paris, cathedral of Nôtre-Dame (1163 to ca. 1245), nave wall.

▶ Paris, La Sainte Chapelle, palace chapel of the old Palais de la Cité, begun 1241, consecrated 1248, view of the upper chapel with it sumptuous stained glass panels.

▲ Castel del Monte, Italy, begun
ca. 1240.

Through that structure, the thrust of the ribbed masonry vault and its pressure on the walls, which were now perforated with numerous large windows, is conducted outward by means of flying buttresses and pier buttresses. The interior becomes a glass shrine, bound only by the filigreed textures of the structural elements. Serving as decoration were tracery, windows, architectural ornamentation derived from basic geometric shapes and, later on, articulated wall surfaces. By the late Gothic period, relatively simple shapes had developed into a dizzying web of lines. The same is true of fifteenth- and sixteenth-century vaults, which became fields on which to experiment with bold, extravagant designs.

Naturally, secular architecture also benefited from the new technological developments. Castel del Monte in Apulia, Italy, is an octagonal castle commissioned in 1240 by Emperor Frederick II, and is an outstanding example of castle building in the Staufer period. It is a unique blend of ancient Roman, Islamic and Gothic elements. Structural clarity and technical perfection lend it timeless beauty.

◀ Cologne Cathedral, cornerstone laid 1248, construction begun 1560, completed in the 19th century; interior view of the choir, dedicated 1322.

▶ Burg Eltz, Germany, also called Ringhausburg, begun 13th century.

St-Denis and the Origins of Gothic Style

In fact, Gothic architecture was not "invented" at St-Denis, but this Benedictine abbey near the gates of Paris surely counts as a milestone in architectural history. Both the western section of the abbey church (ca. 1130–1140) and the choir ambulatory (1140–1144) set new standards. Tradition and innovation went hand-in-hand here: the western section readopted the form of the Carolingian westwork, with a massiveness reminiscent of Norman facades. But the powerful vertical emphasis of the piers and the sculptural articulation of the walls are quite new. While the pointed arches of the choir and the ribbed vaulting are not new inventions, in St-Denis they are

▲ Noyon, France, cathedral of Nôtre-Dame, begun mid-12th century, exterior view of the choir.

▲ Soissons, France, cathedral of St-Gervais-et-Protais, ca. 1180–1190, south transept arm.

more successfully fused, to create an open space. The wall surface of the choir's double ambulatory is barely discernable anymore. Long windows extend practically to the floor and lend the space a festive brightness, exactly as intended by Abbot Suger, who ascribed metaphorical meaning to light.

Within a few decades, these new architectural forms took hold throughout the Île-de-France region. The cathedrals of Sens, Noyon, Senlis, Laon, Paris and Soissons, to name only the most important, experimented with the positioning of columns and piers, various wall elevations and types of vaults, as well as the design of the choir and its ambulatory. The exterior of Laon Cathedral, with its strong projections and deep shadows, shows just how creative the early Gothic period was. Yet it is also clearly related to the interior of the church, which opens into three aisles behind the facade.

◄ Laon, cathedral of Nôtre-Dame, facade, begun by 1200.

▶ St-Denis near Paris, former Benedictine abbey church, choir ambulatory, 1140–1144.

Chartres and Reims

The diversity of forms and structures continued into the thirteenth century, but a new aesthetic also gradually entered the picture, one whose stimulus was drawn from systemic unification, structural clarity and monumentality. This phase continued through the early fourteenth century and is called high Gothic. The cathedrals of Chartres and Reims are its consummate legacy.

Chartres owes its popularity to a unique relic, the tunic of the Blessed Virgin Mary, which was given to the cathedral as a gift by Charles the Bald in 876. Since then, the little town has been the destination for a seemingly endless stream of pilgrims, which has resulted in constant renovations and additions to the cathedral. Construction of the present cathedral began 1194, following a fire in the old Romanesque church, and was completed within a relatively short period, around 1220. Older sections were incorporated into the new structure.

The majestic and picturesque hilltop cathedral with its asymmetrical towers and massive buttresses is visible long before one actually arrives at Chartres. The interior, which is also uncommonly delicate and well proportioned, makes an immediate and indelible impression, an effect that is due to the new, three-tiered elevation (arcade, triforium, clerestory) and the drum piers articulated with half or three-quarter columns. Both elements were definitive of high Gothic architecture. The wide-open transept and spacious double choir ambulatory with chapels were able to accommodate a large number of the faithful.

▲ ▶ Chartres, cathedral of Nôtre-Dame, 1194–ca. 1220, southeastern view of the exterior; interior.

Design Books and Architectural Drawings

The architectural upheavals of the thirteenth century were the result of technical, logistical and communications advances. A lively exchange of ideas and know-how commenced between building owners and master builders, carpenters and stonemasons, in which architectural drawings and design books played a major role. Their contents ran the gamut from initial sketches to detailed blueprints.

Some of these drafts, several feet high and drawn on parchment, have been preserved. The most important among them is the plan drawing for the facade of the Strasbourg Münster. The facade of the Cologne Cathedral was not built until the nineteenth century, but it is almost identical to the spectacular original design (Cologne Plan F). Books like the famous sketchbook by Villard de Honnecourt found their way into architects' travel gear. On study trips or while employed at various construction sites, they copied down new and unusual floor plans and vertical sections, which they were able to present or use elsewhere. Artists were extraordinarily mobile: Parisian architects were consulted for the construction of Uppsala Cathedral, and others shuttled between the Île-de-France and Catalonia.

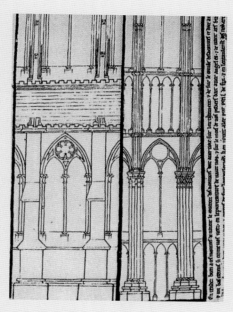

▲ Villard de Honnecourt's sketchbook, Paris, Bibliotheque Nationale, ms. fr. 19093, fol. 31v, vertical section of the nave in Reims.

▲ Sketch of the west facade of Strasbourg Münster (detail), 1365–1385, parchment, height 157.5 in (400 cm), Strasbourg.

negation of loads and weight. Nonetheless, despite these supremely successful, state-of-the-art features, Bourges had almost no successors in France, and thus remains quite unique in architectural history.

The cathedral of Amiens was designed to surpass the size and splendor of Chartres and Reims. Amiens owes its delicate, light-suffused structure to architect Robert de Luzarches and his successors, who managed to complete work on the church between 1220 and 1288 in an astoundingly uniform way. Amiens signifies the beginning of the rayonnant Gothic style in France. The interior space is characterized by high arcades that occupy half of the three-tiered elevation, along with the light-infused choir triforium, where glass windows are featured in lieu of a dark rear wall. The facade, which is reminiscent of a gossamer web, transports the observer into another world.

Some limits remained to be overcome, however. The Cathedral of St-Pierre in Beauvais became a warning against architectural hubris: the choir of this structure, at an unimaginable height at the time of 157 ft (48 m), collapsed just twelve years after it was consecrated.

▶ Beauvais, St-Pierre Cathedral, exterior view of the choir, begun 1225, renovated after collapse 1284.

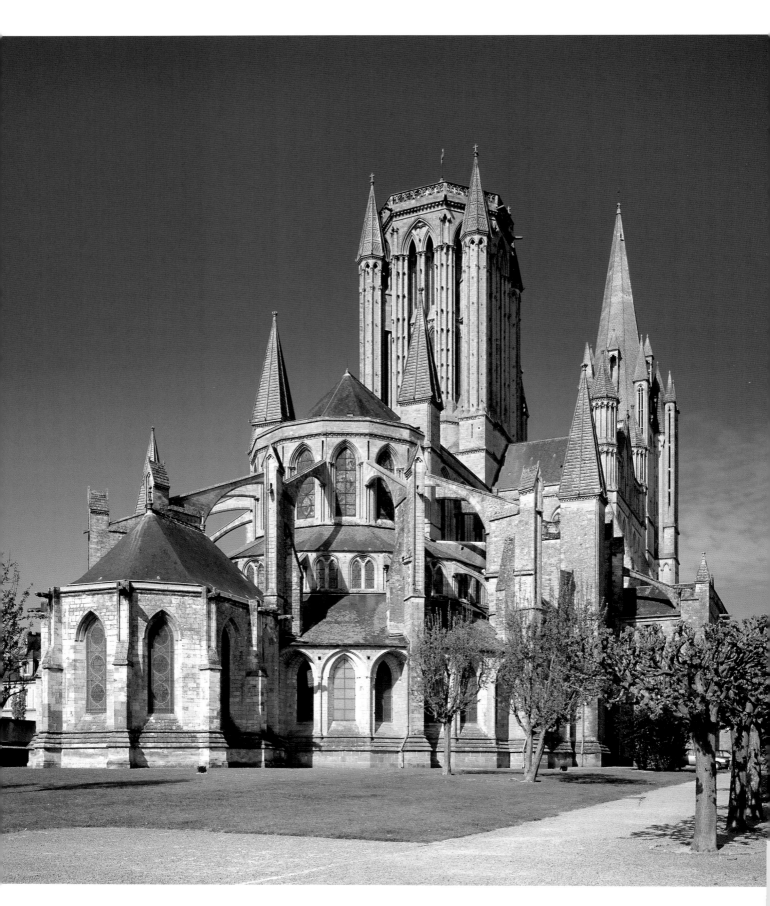

Gothic in the French Provinces

Distinctive solutions were sometimes found outside the mainstream of Gothic architecture. Thus, the Cathedral of Coutances in Normandy is exceptional in architectural history: this erstwhile Romanesque structure did not burn down, as was often the case elsewhere, but underwent step-by-step renovations from west to east. As a result, it allows us to track the course of technical progress and stylistic development in Gothic architecture. While the Romanesque walls were preserved in the facade and nave, the choir is a completely new construction in the High Gothic style. The delicate, octagonal crossing tower towering above the choir is a Norman architectural form brought to the highest level of refinement.

Work on the new Auxerre Cathedral dragged on into the sixteenth century, chiefly because of structural problems in the choir area. Yet, in spite of the many renovations and reinforcements, this cathedral is impressive in its elegance and delicacy. The building's exterior reflects its long architectural history: thus, the facade belongs to the late Gothic, flamboyant style, and the south tower was never built. "Classic" Gothic cathedrals were unable to gain a foothold in Western France. For this reason, St Pierre in Poitiers was built as a hall church in Romanesque style with dome-shaped vaults.

◀ Coutances, Nôtre-Dame Cathedral, renovated begun 1180, exterior view of the choir, ca. 1220.

▲ Auxerre, St-Étienne Cathedral, exterior view, new construction begun 1215.

▼ Poitiers, St-Pierre Cathedral, begun mid-12th century, view of the interior.

England

Early English, the first of three phases into which English Gothic architecture is generally divided, spans the years from approximately 1170 to 1240. In this period, ideas from early French Gothic, which were primarily imparted by the Cistercians, were incorporated into English building projects. In fact, in the case of Canterbury Cathedral, the Frenchman William of Sens won an architectural competition that had been announced by the monks.

In Wells Cathedral, in western England, French architectural forms were realized according to a uniquely English method. The linear tiers of the arcades and triforia are extremely fine. The crossing piers, required because of structural problems, interconnect in a striking manner to create a bold, large-scale construction.

▲ Wells Cathedral, west facade, ca. 1230–1240.

▼ Salisbury Cathedral, 1220–1266, view of the exterior from the northeast.

◀ Lincoln Cathedral, Angel Choir,
between 1256 and 1280.

English cathedrals often stand at
the outskirts of the oldest part of a city
in an open, grassy cathedral area called
the close or precinct. Instead of the
twin-towered facades traditional in
France and Germany, English cathedrals have spreading screen facades,
which were superimposed on the
naves without structural logic. The
facade of Wells Cathedral may be the
most beautiful of its kind. It is covered
with a delicate network of blind
arcades, whose niches once displayed
the whole history of salvation in
sculpture and relief.

Westminster Abbey in London
was the trailblazer for the Decorated
Style (1240–1330), which was
dedicated primarily to decorative
experiment. One motif introduced
there, the glazing of the typically
English flat eastern choir wall, was
further developed in the well-known
Angel Choir at Lincoln, where the
windows were greatly enlarged and
elaborately traceried.

The predominantly vertical and
horizontal lines of the Perpendicular
Style (beginning 1330) can be seen as
a reaction to the excessive variety of
the Decorated Style. In it, narrow
panels form a latticework that overlies
and unifies the surfaces. In the fifteenth century, much artistic innovation came from the colleges. Those
most heavily endowed by the monarchy were very splendidly decorated,
and their chapels served as royal burial
places. King's College Chapel in
Cambridge, with gossamer tracery
between filigreed piers and breathtaking fan vaults, may well count
among the most beautiful sacred
spaces of all time.

◀ King's College Chapel, Cambridge,
1416–1515, view of the interior.

Spain

French Gothic cathedrals did not catch on in Spain until the second decade of the thirteenth century. Mauricio, the bishop of Burgos, played a key role in this process, having been in a position to follow the progress of architecture in Paris during his studies there. In 1221 he laid the cornerstone for the construction of a new cathedral in Burgos. Just nine years later, services were already being held in the choir, whose ambulatory was closely modeled on that of Bourges Cathedral.

With five aisles, a double ambulatory and an annulus that originally included fifteen chapels, the Toledo Cathedral is the largest structure built in Spain in the thirteenth century. As the seat of the archbishop and primate of Spain, it enjoyed high status among the cathedrals of the Iberian Peninsula. Begun in approximately 1222–1223, this church is also modeled on the Bourges Cathedral. Another synthesis of French rayonnant

architectural elements is found at León Cathedral. Within it can also be found traces of the coronation church of Reims, the royal mausoleum at St-Denis, as well as the palace chapel of the old imperial palace in Paris, the Sainte Chapelle.

The exterior of the pilgrimage church of Santa Maria del Mar in Barcelona is utterly plain and gives casual observers little indication that one of

▶ Barcelona, Santa Maria del Mar, Berenguer de Montagut, Ramon Despuig, 1329–1383, interior view toward the east.

◀ Girona, Santa Maria Cathedral, Henri and Jacques de Fauran, Guillem Bofill, 1312–1604 (begun 1417), view into nave.

the most grandiose of Gothic spaces lies hidden behind its facade. The simple floor plan follows Catalonian and Provencal tradition: a three-aisled nave with a truncated transept, the side aisles and the chapels, which are placed between the buttresses, all wind around the choir. The span of the central aisle's four bays is unusual and, at nearly 46 ft (14 m), created a sensation. It was surpassed only by the vaulting of Girona Cathedral, begun in 1312, where a lengthy technical and aesthetic debate preceded its construction. In the end, Guillem Bofill persevered and in 1416 began building the most expansive Gothic vault in the world, over 111 ft (34 m) high and nearly 75 ft (23 m) wide.

▲ Toledo Cathedral, begun 1222–1223, view toward the choir ambulatory.

▶ León Cathedral, begun 1255, panoramic view.

The Holy Roman Empire

The Liebfrauenkirche (Church of Our Dear Lady) in Trier is seen as the harbinger of the classic Gothic period in Germany. Begun by 1235, the structure essentially incorporates French motifs (especially from Reims Cathedral)—including compound piers, tracery windows and ribbed vaulting, here set on a two-story construction—but it places these elements in a new relationship to one another. Unlike its prototypes, the Liebfrauenkirche is a central-plan building consisting of two short, three-aisled lateral arms with radial chapels in the corners. The eastern arm was slightly lengthened for the choir. This layout is unusual for a parish church, and can presumably be traced back to a previous structure from late antiquity.

▲ Strasbourg Münster, begun ca. 1180, nave (begun ca. 1240).

▼ Trier, former Liebfrauenkirche (Church of Our Dear Lady), begun by 1235, eastern view.

▲ Marburg, former hospital and pilgrimage church of St Elisabeth, begun 1235, interior toward the northwest.

Brick Gothic

The Gothic style spread to the North Sea and Baltic Sea regions in the late thirteenth century and "mastered" an essentially brittle material: brick. The starting point for this development was the Marienkirche (St Mary's) in Lübeck, Germany, which was redesigned in direct imitation of French cathedrals. From that point on, the basilical elevation (the recently completed nave had been adapted to match) and the choir, whose chapel vaults are fused with those of the ambulatory, served as models for numerous other parish churches and cathedrals in northern Germany, Scandinavia and Poland. St Mary's Church in Gdánsk, where construction was not completed until the sixteenth century, is a masterpiece of brick Gothic architecture.

The realization of Gothic ornamental forms presented a special challenge for architects and artisans. Cut stone was relatively easy to chisel into tracery, capitals and friezes, while working with fragile brick imposed restraints on craftsmanship. Necessity is the mother of invention, however, and the facades of brick churches are thus characterized by a unique, emphatically structural, decorative style that often includes the offsetting of glazed bricks and lends a colorful accent to the wall.

▲ Lübeck, Marienkirche, ca. 1260–1265 to 1351, view of the choir.

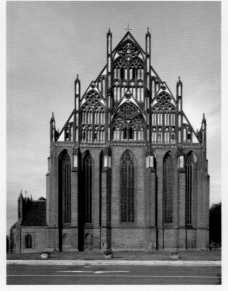

▲ Prenzlau, Marienkirche, begun after 1325, facade.

▲ Chorin, former Cistercian abbey church, 1273–1334, facade.

The style of the hospital and pilgrimage church of St Elisabeth in Marburg is closely related to that of the Liebfrauenkirche in Trier and may even predate it. The structure was built above the grave of St Elisabeth of Thuringia, beginning in 1235, and therefore had two functions. The hall of the nave offered space for crowds of the faithful to worship, while the triconch of the choir (a markedly Rhenish Romanesque architectural form) was reserved for the clergy.

Work began around 1240 on the new nave of the Strasbourg Münster, even though the choir and transept had been only just been completed in a late Romanesque style. The structure that emerged by 1275 ranked as one of the most modern in France, and within the borders of the Roman Empire, as well. The new abbey church of St-Denis near Paris seems to have served as a model, because here again there are piers with applied column shafts continuing unbroken up to the spring of the vault, plus a glazed, box-like triforium and windows decorated with tracery. Immediately following the completion of the nave at Strasbourg, the cornerstone for the grandiose west facade was laid, probably by its designer, the famous master builder Erwin von Steinbach.

The "sum total" of French Gothic architecture was expressed in the Cologne Cathedral, although it would remain incomplete for many years. The cathedrals of Amiens and Reims, the abbey church of St-Denis and, finally, the main aisle portions of the spectacular but never finished Beauvais Cathedral were the decisive models for the design of the Cologne ideal (see p. 113).

Sacred Buildings in Italy

The Gothic era in Italy took hold through the architecture of the mendicant orders. Work on the double church in Assisi, built above the grave of St Francis, began in 1228. The stone building embodies the ideal of the order's founder, which is humility, and the upper church would become the model for all Italian sacred structures. The wide, two-story nave is clearly structured and flooded with light; narrow clustered columns support the ribs of the square bay. San Fortunato, in Todi, is another church that is suffused with light. Wide ribbed vaulting spans its almost directionless space.

The Dominican church of Santa Maria Novella in Florence set new standards: the Latin cross of the nearly 329-ft (100-m) long church is more articulated than divided by slender piers with classically authentic half-columns. The two-tone, accented arches are a special feature. The Franciscans also started to build a spectacular new structure in this city on the Arno in 1294: Santa Croce was intended to surpass the Dominican church in height and length.

Siena Cathedral is an example of the ambition of local authorities. However, the plan to erect a new cathedral at a right angle to the existing Romanesque one (which would then be integrated with the new church as a transept) failed, owing to serious instability. Arnolfo di Cambio delivered the first plans for the new cathedral in Florence, but died in 1234. Following his death, Giotto took the position of *capomaestro* (master builder) but dedicated himself solely to the construction of the campanile (bell tower).

▼ Florence, Santa Maria Novella, begun 1246, interior view.

▲ Assisi, San Francesco, 1228–1253, interior of the upper church.

◄ Todi, San Fortunato, 1292–1328, interior.

▲ Florence, campanile, begun 1334 by Giotto di Bondone, completed by Andrea Pisano and Francesco Talenti.

▲ Siena Cathedral, begun mid-12th century, renovated in the 13th and 14th centuries.

▼ Pisa, Santa Maria della Spina, 1323–1333, view of the exterior.

Work on the cathedral itself did not resume until 1357, based this time on plans by Francesco Talenti, who decided on a rib-vaulted nave of colossal proportions and an even more gigantic dome above the crossing. The nave was completed in 1378 and the crossing piers in 1398. In 1420, Filippo Brunelleschi was entrusted with the construction of this unique dome, which ushered in a new era.

By contrast, the Church of Santa Maria della Spina in Pisa gives the delicate impression of a reliquary: this oratory does, in fact, house a splinter from Christ's crown of thorns. The architecture clearly harks back to the Sainte Chapelle in Paris, where the entire crown was enshrined.

Municipal Palaces

As with their sacred buildings, Italian cities also competed over the magnificence of their city halls. The feuding rival cities of Siena and Florence began to build imposing structures nearly simultaneously. These were integrated into representative city squares, and the local authorities issued strict requirements for their construction.

The Palazzo Pubblico in Siena was built as a three-winged complex starting in 1297. The Palazzo, with its raised center section and narrow campanile, dominates the semicircle of the *campo*, the city's central square, like a grandiose theatrical backdrop. Arcades on the ground floor and elegant triforium windows lend it an open, inviting character.

By contrast, the Palazzo Vecchio in Florence, begun just two years later, seems closed off and forbidding. The fortress-like block is crowned with a

◀ Florence, Palazzo Vecchio, 1299 to ca. 1320–1330, view from the Piazza della Signoria.

▲ Siena, the Campo with the Palazzo Pubblico, begun 1297.

▼ Venice, Doges Palace, begun ca. 1340, facade toward the Piazetta.

projecting parapet walk and battlement. Even the campanile, rising asymmetrically above the top floor and resting on the remains of an older defense tower, appears indomitable and menacing.

The interiors of both palaces were splendidly furnished. Their great halls were decorated with historic or allegorical frescoes that were intended to instruct and to exhort the council members who met there to virtue. The most important artists of the day collaborated on the decoration of these rooms.

The Palazzo Ducale in Venice is also representative of a typical city palace. The picturesque double loggia in front and the colorful brick pattern of the main floor fall within the tradition of Venetian palaces, many of which have facades that overlook the water, with complex arcades and filigreed lancet windows. On the other hand, the purely decorative battlement of the Palazzo Ducale is a play on Islamic motifs.

Castles and Fortresses

While the building of Romanesque castles first and foremost served strategic demands, aesthetic and representative motifs came to the fore in the thirteenth century. The movement toward artistic cambering and differentiated spatial organization was already apparent in the southern Italian castles built by the Staufer emperors, of which Castel del Monte is the shining example (see p. 113). Ceremonial developments and the need for courtly social intercourse required nuancing and the rearrangement of the entire fortification.

A castle belonging to the noble della Scala family, whose members ruled over the city of Verona for more than a hundred years, sprang up on the picturesque southern bank of Lago di Garda (Garda Lake). This family proclaimed its imperial allegiance— Italy was at the time sharply divided between the Ghibellines, who were mainly loyal to the Holy Roman emperor, and the Guelfs, who supported the pope—through the form of the merlons (battlements), which resembled swallowtails.

Bellver Castle is an unusual complex. Dominating the Bay of Palma de Mallorca, it served as both a fortress and a royal residence. But this dual function does not explain why the living areas were arranged in a ring around the inner courtyard, which opens up into elegant, two-storied arcades. At the same time, the exterior remained defensive: three supporting towers and a freestanding donjon or keep (Torre de l'Homenatge, or Tower of Homage) provided the necessary protection. There is no clear reason for this original floor plan, but it may be related to that of Castel del Monte, which is some fifty years older. Incidentally, when Emperor Charles V commissioned his new palace in the Alhambra in the sixteenth century, he may have used this building as a model.

When the Roman popes resided in Avignon from 1309 to 1376, they also had a colossal palace built to the highest contemporary standards. French master builders Pierre Poisson and Jean de Louvres were commissioned to execute the project. The ascetic, fortress-like Old Palace went up between 1334 and 1342. The New Palace, constructed from 1342 to 1352, clearly displays refined, decorative late Gothic taste. The interior is furnished with utmost pomp: chapels, vestries, and sleeping and eating quarters satisfied the pontiff's spiritual and worldly needs alike. The opulent, decorative frescoes were painted primarily by Italian artists, including Simone Martini.

▼ Sirmione, Italy, Scaliger Castle, late 13th century.

▲ Palma de Mallorca, Bellver Castle, Pere Salvà, 1309–1314, inner courtyard.

▼ Avignon, Papal Palace, 1334–1352, entrance facade.

Late Gothic

For a long time, late Gothic architecture was considered decadent, with nothing new to contribute to the achievements of thirteenth-century high Gothic architecture. Indeed, the "classic cathedrals" would continue to be definitive for quite some time. Nonetheless, incredible works that are every bit as impressive as their predecessors did come into being during the period. Time and again, master builders on the cutting edge showed surprising ingenuity, moving away from trusted motifs toward new self-awareness. These masters demonstrated their virtuosity and pushed structural load capacity to the very limit with their buildings.

An early example of this venturesome, imaginative architecture is the "palm tree" in the Dominican (Jacobin) church in Toulouse. As the eastern column of the double-aisled church

▲ Toulouse, Dominican church (Jacobin church), umbrella vault ("the palm tree"), completed 1385.

space, it merges with the star-shaped apse vault. By the fifteenth century, sacred spaces were entirely "dematerialized," becoming glass shrines through which light flowed almost unobstructed. In southern Germany, especially, where members of the Parler family (three generations of architects) were active, overwhelming, nearly weightless church spaces came into being. The Parlers produced a variety of hall churches in which the nave and side aisles were the same height and shared a common roof. Since many town churches followed this architectural model, it is tempting (but untenable) to see the hall church as a middle-class architectural form.

Tracery developed into a dizzying web of lines derived from the most complex geometric shapes. Distinctive of the flamboyant style, these decorations could cover the entire surface, as at the chapel of Sant Jordi in

Barcelona, for example. The delicate architecture of the Arras Town Hall is even reminiscent of goldsmithery. At the same time, interlacing tendril patterns suggested the invasion of nature into inanimate building, and blurred the boundary between architecture and sculpture.

◄ Arras, Town Hall, ca. 1450–1572.

▶ Freiberg Cathedral, pulpit ("Tulip Pulpit"), Hans Witten, 1508–1510.

Vaults became experimental fields for bold, artful structures. Diamond (cellular), star and net vaults, fan vaults and highly complex lierne vaults seemed to defy reality and opened up to master builders possibilities that had previously been undreamed of.

Only Italy, where the early Renaissance began to take hold around 1420, managed to avoid the overly extravagant architectural excesses of the late Gothic period. In every other European country, and even in the New World, they would survive into the sixteenth century. Regional variants were cultivated, such as the flamboyant style in France and western Europe, the decorated and perpendicular styles in England, and the florido, flamigero, or hispano-flamenco styles in Spain. Thus, late Gothic architectural and decorative methods did not constitute a stylistic period that would eventually become obsolete, but were instead options that carried over into the Renaissance. In many places, the dialogue concerned which style was more appropriate for a particular architectural task or monument. Thus, Gothic forms were preferred in church architecture up through the seventeenth century, because they had so long been intertwined with western spirituality. In Portugal, the Manueline style associated late Gothic decorative forms with Renaissance ornamentation. At burial sites and in representative buildings, these made a foil for heraldic and emblematic motifs. In Portugal, work continued on the Dominican convent of Batalha until well into the sixteenth century. It was begun in 1388 when Alfonso Domingues delivered the plans for the entire complex (he successfully completed the three-aisled church); and Master Huguet, an architect who may have been of English extraction, took over the work in 1402.

▲ Barcelona, Palau de la Generalitat, facade of the chapel of Sant Jordi, Marc Safont, 1434.

▼ Batalha, Portugal, Monastery of Santa Maria da Vitória, 1388–1533, overall view.

Buildings in Cities

The rise of cities resulted in the construction of secular buildings that stood in visible competition with sacred structures. The Netherlands led the way with the construction of monumental town halls, cloth halls, warehouses and hospitals that advertised the wealth and power of the municipalities. It was no coincidence that they were graced with high towers and decorated with tracery. The town hall in Leuven, Belgium, built around the middle of the fifteenth century, looks like a sumptuous reliquary shrine. Although its niche figures are somewhat more recent, it is still representative of late Gothic town halls with magnificent facades. Merchants expressed their pride through monumental market halls and bourses, among which the Llotja in Palma de Mallorca is an outstanding example. The wide interior is supported by six twisted columns, while the exterior with its corner towers looks more like a fortress.

Teaching, moral education and health care, tasks that had been generally assumed by the monasteries, now began to receive financial support from patricians and the nobility—not solely for charitable reasons, but also for the sake of the donors' own salvation. Thus Nicolas Rolin, chancellor to the dukes of Burgundy, founded a hospital in Beaune, the Hôtel-Dieu, which, thanks to its vineyards, was one of the wealthiest institutions of its time. This three-winged complex extends around an inner courtyard. The large hospital room has a wooden barrel vaulted ceiling. The famous Altar of the Last Judgment by Rogier van der Weyden once stood in the west chapel.

◄ Leuven, Belgium, Town Hall, Sulpitius van Vorst and Matheus de Layens, 1448–1459.

▲ Beaune, Hôtel-Dieu, Jean Rateau, 1443–1452, interior of the hospital.

▼ Palma de Mallorca, Llotja (bourse), Guillem Sagrera, 1426, facade.

Building and Decoration

An unprecedented building boom took place in the late Middle Ages. The expansion of cities, the differentiation of construction tasks and the bourgeoisie's increasing demand for representation affected the number and organization of building sites, and had a concomitant effect on architecture. Individuality and a multiplicity of design solutions became inherently worthy assets with which master builders achieved high artistic status. The number of sources in which the architect or architects are mentioned by name multiplies exponentially in this period. Craftsmanship also improved:

stonecutting, for example, reached a level of precision and delicacy almost comparable with goldsmithery.

Vault design became an architectural topos. It may be a matter of debate whether or not vaults were seen in metaphorical terms, e.g., as symbols of the firmament of heaven or paradise. But it is certain that a delight in creating abstract patterns and mastering technical challenges was the main stimulus behind the diversity and craftsmanship of the new decorative vaults, whose ribbing represents both geometric patterns and plant forms. Peter Parler's vaults in Prague Cathedral produced a sort of catalogue of potential forms. The structural and decorative designs used in Prague were subsequently recorded in

▼ Salamanca, New Cathedral, Juan de Álava und Rodrigo Gil de Hontañón, begun 1520, view toward the crossing.

▲ Gdánsk, St Mary's Church, cellular vault by Heinrich Hetzel, 1498–1502.

▼ Belem (near Lisbon), Jerónimos Monastery, Diogo Boytac and João de Castilho, 1517, interior of the church and vault.

fifteenth-century pattern books. Southern Germany and Bohemia became centers of late Gothic vault architecture, but Saxony was also prominent owing to a record economic boom produced by ore mining. St Anne's Church in Annaberg has one of the most beautiful interiors in all of Germany, thanks to Jakob Heilmann's ribbonwork star vaults. The cellular vaults in St Mary's Church in Gdánsk are a masterful achievement, both aesthetically and in terms of design.

Master builders all over Europe competed in designing spectacular vaults. The complex lierne vault above the nave of the Jerónimos Monastery in Belém near Lisbon is supported on six octagonal columns, 82 ft (25 m) high and completely covered with

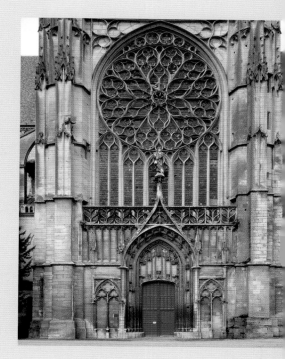

▲ Salem, Germany, former Cistercian abbey church, consecrated 1414, tracery window.

▼ Annaberg, St Anna, Konrad Pflüger, Peter Ulrich and Jacob Heilmann, 1499–1525, interior view facing east.

▲ Sens Cathedral, Marin Chambiges, 1490–1512, south transept facade.

Renaissance decoration. The similar vault over the transept spans its entire width. The New Cathedral of Salamanca, Spain, also has rich, sixteenth-century fan and lierne vaults. The walls and facade, are decorated with stone lace, as well. Even the Cistercians could not resist decorative tracery, and the abbey church in Salem, in southern Germany near the Lake of Constance, is laden with it.

The longevity of high Gothic and late Gothic facades in France is unique. Following the end of the Hundred Years War in 1453, building continued on quite a number of unfinished churches, including the Cathedral of Sens, to which a flamboyant transept facade was added between 1490 and 1512. Often the building masters in charge of these projects reverted to older models, which were then modernized with new forms of tracery.

Late Gothic Sacred Architecture in Germany

The growth of cities also influenced sacred architecture. Parish churches began to appear in large numbers and were the driving force behind architectural innovation. This is especially noticeable in Swabia and Bavaria, where people experimented with various types of hall churches.

In a hall church, the nave and side aisles are the same height, and they share a common roof. In this way, the wide, unified spaces accommodated the aesthetic tastes of the late Middle Ages. The Heiligkreuzkirche (Church of the Holy Cross) in Schwäbisch-Gmünd is a milestone in late Gothic sacred architecture, the work of the Parler family of master builders. It is the earliest hall church in Swabia. Slender drum piers support the ornate lierne vaults of the nave. The spatial independence of the main choir is an innovation and was ascribed to Peter Parler's father, Heinrich.

As a type, the Gmünd choir continued to exert an influence through the second half of the fifteenth century. St Lorenz in Nuremberg echoed the choir hall, but also introduced a horizontal accent with a continuous gallery with tracery balustrades.

Impressive late Gothic hall churches also went up in the royal residences of the Wittelsbach dynasty, the majority of which were built of brick. St Martin in Landshut is the greatest oeuvre of Hans von Burghausen, founder of the fifteenth-century Bavarian architectural school. Here, an overwhelmingly wide space opens up to the visitor. Slender octagonal piers support a decorative, 95-ft (29-m) high lierne vault; at about 3 ft (1 m) in diameter, they would

▲ Landshut, St Martin, Hans von Burghausen, begun 1380, interior view.

▶ Schwäbisch-Gmünd, Heiligkreuzkirche, view of the interior; nave: 1310–1315, choir: 1351–1380, consecrated 1410, vaulting between 1491 and 1521.

appear to be more like narrow poles than load-bearing supports.

The Frauenkirche (Church of Our Lady) in Munich completes the circle of great Gothic hall churches. Its distinctive onion domes (or Swiss bonnets) still distinguish the skyline of the city today. Although closely modeled on Landshut, the interior makes a distinctly cooler impression: the columns are more massive and stand closer together. As in Bavaria, hall churches were prevalent in Saxony.

Towers

A fierce competition over the height and originality of church towers erupted. Towers had always been a symbol of lordliness, but now, with the availability of new technical possibilities, tower construction became a veritable exhibition. As far back as the late thirteenth century, when construction on the west tower of Freiburg Münster began, contemporaries considered it the "most beautiful tower in Christendom." Without prominent antecedents, it would be nearly impossible to explain its audacious construction or its sophisticated design language. In fact, its direct prototypes are the west facade of Strasbourg Cathedral and Cologne Cathedral's Plan F (see p. 119). About a hundred years later, in 1392, the city of Ulm summoned Ulrich of Ensingen, a gifted master builder who was concurrently overseeing building sites in Strasbourg and Esslingen. It was he who created the grandiose, 528-ft (161-m) high tower that dominates Ulm Münster, the parish church of this city on the Danube. His venturesome construction rivaled all contemporary cathedrals in appearance. Finally, part of the Basel Münster, St George's Tower, was also completed according to Ulrich of Ensingen's design.

▲ Basel Münster, St George's Tower, completed ca. 1430.

▼ Vienna, Maria am Gestade, Michael Knab, 1394–1427, pyramidal tower roof.

▲ Freiburg Münster, West Tower, second half 13th century–1320, interior view of the steeple.

▼ Ulm Münster, planned 1392.

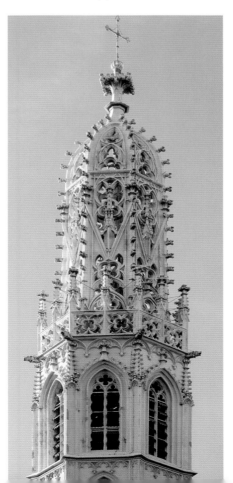

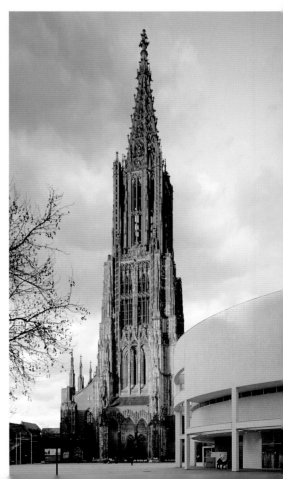

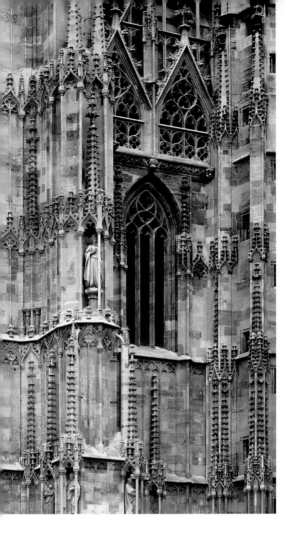

▲ Vienna, St Stephen's Cathedral, detail of the North or Eagle's Tower, after 1450.

▲ Vienna, St Stephan's Cathedral, Anton Pilgram, 1514–1515, pulpit.

▶ Prague, St Vitus Cathedral, Matthias von Arras and Peter Parler, interior view of the choir, after 1352.

Prague and Vienna

Prague, one of the most prosperous cities in the Holy Roman Empire, became an archbishopric 1344. Construction on St Vitus Cathedral began immediately under the leadership of Matthias of Arras. By the time of his death in 1352, he had been able to build the choir ambulatory and the arcades of the main choir in the southern French Gothic style, thus establishing the main features of this colossal work. His successor was Peter Parler, who had previously been active in Schwäbisch-Gmünd. Parler ushered in decisive innovations: he dispensed with the transverse arches that separated the nave bays and created an optically continuous vault, articulated only with diagonal ribs. His second seminal innovation concerned the triforium, whose windows formed a single continuous plain with the clerestory, which is thus pushed back from the triforium colonnade. The resultant staggered wall surface, linked with the alternating projection and recession of the triforium canopy, create an especially striking design. The busts in the triforium, which portray the two master builders of the cathedral, the family of Emperor Charles IV and the archbishops of Prague, demonstrate that Parler was well aware of his creative powers.

The appearance of St Stephen's Cathedral in Vienna was altered by constant renovations and new construction, client interventions and numerous fires.

The Giant's Door in the heart of the Romanesque western section is one of the oldest parts of the building. The consecration of today's cathedral took place in 1263, and work on the three-aisled hall-type choir began in 1304. Then came the new layout of the remaining parts of the church, including the towers. Architectural ornamentation and sculpture, such as Anton Pilgram's magnificent pulpit, mark the transition from the late Gothic to the Renaissance.

Architecture and Status Symbols

The dazzling skill of the best master builders, the audacious vaults and artistic details that they were able to integrate into late Gothic structures, charmed the clergy and feudal patrons alike. The delight in sheer opulence, and in experimentation with materials and technology, was immense. Initiating a building project was no longer simply a matter of owning a more splendid and comfortable palace than that of one's neighbor; above all, the architecture had to be unique, deeply impressive and surprising. Among the most highly prized status symbols was the *Wendelstein*, or massive, stone spiral staircase, which rested elegantly against the outer wall of a castle or palace. Popular in the late Gothic and Renaissance (although not in Italy), marvelous examples have been

▼ Bourges, France, Palais Jacques-Coeur, 1443–1453, inner courtyard facade.

▼ Meissen, Germany, Albrechtsburg, Arnold von Westfalen, begun 1471, grand staircase.

▲ Bourg-en-Bresse, France, Brou monastic church, 1513–1532, rood screen.

◄ Prague, Vladislav Hall in Prague Castle, Benedikt Ried, 1493–1520.

preserved in Meissen and Torgau in Germany and Blois and Chambord in France. The structural engineering of these staircases is still astonishing today. They could be single or double barreled, they might wind around a balluster or a hollow space, or they could be conceived as entirely self-supporting, as is the one at Albrechtsburg in Meissen, Germany.

Benedikt Ried, the royal master builder to the Court of Prague, created one of the most incredible interior spaces of all time with the Vladislav Hall in Prague Castle. The hall is 203 ft long, 52 ft wide and 42 ft high (62 x 16 x 13 m), and is spanned by a stupendous lierne vault whose ribs twist in wide sweeps that appear to be weightless. Partially detached from the surface of the ceiling in places, they attain dazzling freedom.

For French businessman and finance minister Jacques Coeur, who was granted a peerage in 1441 by King Charles VII, the construction of his city palace in Bourges was primarily an outward expression of his new status. The richly and ornately decorated facade of this four-winged complex outdid every other late Medieval city palace in France.

The desire for extraordinary prestige even extended beyond this life: the monastic church of Brou was founded by the Dutch regent, Margaret of Austria, and was designated as the tomb of her husband, Philibert the Beautiful, who died young. The exquisite architecture and marvelous furnishings make this church a late Gothic masterpiece.

is a continuous entablature, which provides a transition to the upper story. Terracotta medallions are mounted in the spandrels of the arcades. The complex as a whole exudes classical balance, structural logic and self-assured elegance.

The importance of Brunelleschi's buildings as herald of the Renaissance is matched by the writings of Leone Battista Alberti, who was one of the first to take an interest in Vitruvius. Alberti studied and measured the

Renaissance Architecture

The Renaissance—the revival of the classical world of Greece and Rome—began in Florence, Italy, with architecture playing a key role. The ten volumes of Vitruvius' *De Architectura*, a treatise that describes the architecture of classical antiquity, albeit without illustrations, had been discovered in 1414. Vitruvius' writings triggered an architectural revolution. From this point onward, models drawn from classical antiquity determined architectural

design: the Middle Ages had finally been overcome. Balanced, harmonious proportions that mirrored the human body became the new ideal. Leonardo da Vinci visualized this principle in his Vitruvian Man (see p. 170).

If there is indeed a "seminal building" behind the Italian Renaissance, that honor would have to go to Filippo Brunelleschi's loggia for the Ospedale degli Innocenti in Florence. The arched loggia, which stands before the orphanage, overlooks the Piazza della Santissima Annunziata. Slender columns with Corinthian capitals support the arcade of round arches. Resting on the arcade

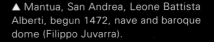

▲ Mantua, San Andrea, Leone Battista Alberti, begun 1472, nave and baroque dome (Filippo Juvarra).

◄ Rimini, San Francesco, also known as the Tempio Malatestiano, Leone Battista Alberti, begun 1446.

ancient buildings of Rome and ultimately composed his own work containing his philosophical and practical insights into architecture. His treatise, *De Re Aedificatoria*, (1451) was the first in a long series of theoretical writings that attempted to clarify the forms and functions of architecture.

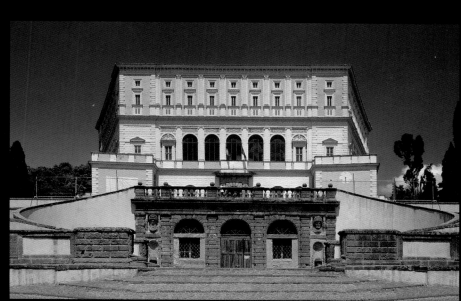

▲ Château de Blois, Domenico da Cortona, known as Boccador, 1515–1524, spiral staircase in the wing built by Francis I.

▲ Caprarola, Villa Farnese, Giacomo Barozzi da Vignola, 1559–1573.

Urban building enjoyed a brilliant revival. The notion of a social utopia inspired a plethora of ideal city plans, and secular architecture underwent a boom whose like had not been seen before. In the towns and courts, patrician and local palace owners rushed to join in: the enhancment of their palace facades with ascending orders of classical columns and rustication became an increasingly common hallmark of high status architecture.

Meanwhile, the traditional antique villa, located in the garden or park of great estates, also took on new life.

At the turn of the sixteenth century, Rome superseded Florence as the "capital city" of innovation. The Eternal City offered artists—including the likes of Michelangelo, Bramante and Raphael—ideal conditions in which to refine their knowledge and apply their skills. In Rome, in contrast to Florence, ancient classical models could be studied *in situ*. Furthermore, the ascent of Julius II to the papal throne endowed the world with a pope determined to return the city to its role and function as *caput mundi*.

The Sack of Rome—the plundering of the city by the troops of Charles of Bourbon in 1527—destroyed these burgeoning hopes. Many artists emigrated to the court of Francis I, where they achieved great success in the development of the great French châteaux. The Veneto also developed into a further center of creativity; here Palladio created villas that resembled the classical models more closely than any to date. Architects north of the Alps, in contrast, copied the classical details only superficially, glossing a Renaissance veneer onto late Gothic structures without concerning themselves even tangentially with the complex theoretical "philosophy" of Italian theoreticians. Not until the construction of the Italianate Residence in Landshut, Germany, and the antiquarium of the Residence in Munich did buildings in the pure Renaissance style make their way over the Alps.

◄ Munich, Residence, Jacopo Strada and Wilhelm Egkl, begun 1569–1571, antiquarium.

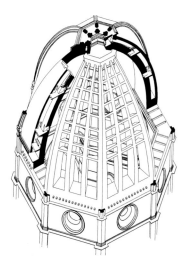

◀ Florence Cathedral, view showing dome by Filippo Brunelleschi, begun 1418.

▼ Axonometric projection of the dome of the cathedral.

Brunelleschi and the Early Renaissance

Fifteenth-century Florence achieved a veritable revolution in the arts. The break with tradition was at once extreme and deeply rooted in the past. The models for the new, clearly structured architecture with its characteristic colored marble inlays and classical details are already evident in the facades of such Romanesque buildings as the baptistery and church of San Miniato al Monte. For this reason, the style is now known as the "Tuscan protorenaissance." Historically, however, these buildings were once understood as testaments to classical antiquity.

Whether inspired by "true" or apparent antiquity, Filippo Brunelleschi succeeded in developing a new style of architecture. The geometrical organization and logically structured ornamentation of the Pazzi Chapel near Santa

The Importance of Perspective

For Renaissance artists, a command of the principles of perspective was *sine qua non*. It was an essential skill for convincing representations of the visible world. Again it was Brunelleschi who introduced the method: a system for rendering images with perspective is seen in his "peep-hole" view of the Florentine baptistery. By using a grid and two vanishing points, he transposed the three-dimensional image onto a flat surface. Brunelleschi's technique reached a broad audience through the treatise of Leone

▶ Reconstruction of Alberti's perspective diagram with two vanishing points.

▶ Albrecht Dürer, wood cut for *Unterweysung der Messung*, 1525.

Battista Alberti, *Della Pittura* (1435/1436). Albrecht Dürer took Alberti's methods even further. He developed numerous aids, which he presented in his artist's manual *Unterweysung der Messung* ("Instruction in Measurement," published in English as *The Painter's Manual*) of 1525.

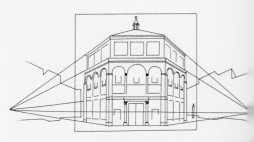

Croce displays this new approach with extreme economy. This mausoleum of the influential Pazzi family is an austere cube, crowned by a twelve-sided melon-shaped dome and brightly illuminated by round windows. The definitive motif is the triumphal arch, which lends the chapel its noble appearance. Aesthetically, Brunelleschi's work established both the vocabulary and syntax of a new formal language; technically, the construction of the cathedral dome amounted to a heroic feat.

Creating a dome that would span such a great distance—in this case, nearly 140 ft (45.52 m)—had long been considered an almost impossible challenge. Yet the stipulations of the project remained: the dimensions for the reconstructed choir of the church had been established in the middle of the fourteenth century and the master builders of the project even had to swear an oath to carry out their work. When a new competition for the design was announced in 1418, Brunelleschi came up with a brilliant solution for the construction of the dome. He proposed a self-supporting double shell strengthened with internal ribs. Requiring no substructure, the dome could be raised section by section. The gigantic work took sixteen years to complete, and it would be another twenty-five years before the lantern turret of the unique construction could be completed.

▼ Florence, Pazzi Chapel at Santa Croce, Filippo Brunelleschi, after 1442–ca. 1470, view of the interior.

▲ Florence, Baptistery, ca. 1060–1150, facade, an example of the Tuscan proto-renaissance.

Florentine Sacred Architecture

Brunelleschi's ecclesiastical architecture in Florence elevated the forms he had experimented with in the construction of the Innocenti to a monumental level. San Lorenzo (begun 1420) and Santo Spirito (begun 1436) take up the model of the flat-roofed early Christian basilica and translate it into the language of the Renaissance. The three-aisled nave is divided by rows of Corinthian columns whose impost blocks support arches, a continuous architrave and the clerestory. Both plan and elevation are based on a logical module arising from the crossing and the choir. The ultimate principle of design includes clear organization, harmonious proportions based on the human body, and simple classicizing ornament.

Commissioned by the Medici family, San Lorenzo must be seen as a pioneer in the principle of modular design. Santo Spirito, in contrast, is the most mature of Brunelleschi's works, even though the artist did not live to see its completion. As at San Lorenzo, the church is built on a Latin cross plan and features a projecting transept. In comparison to the older San Lorenzo, the interior of Santo Spirito was logically designed down to the last detail. Arches line the whole interior, including the transept arms and choir.

The style developed for the Florentine basilicas influenced church architecture for decades to come in Tuscany, where the basic ideas were also applied to centrally planned buildings (see pp. 154–155).

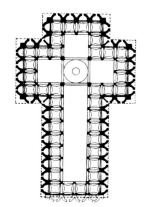

▲ Florence, Santo Spirito, Filippo Brunelleschi, begun 1436, interior view and floor plan.

◄ Florence, San Lorenzo, Brunelleschi, begun 1420, interior view and floor plan.

The Problem of the Facade

A striking number of Early Renaissance churches lack a facade—or at least a contemporary one. Even the fronts of

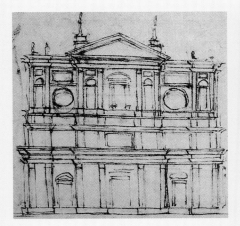

▲ Florence, San Lorenzo, Michelangelo, facade design, 1516/17–1519, Casa Buonarotti.

▲▲▶ Florence, Santa Maria Novella, begun 1246; gable and facade redesigned by Leone Battista Alberti after 1458.

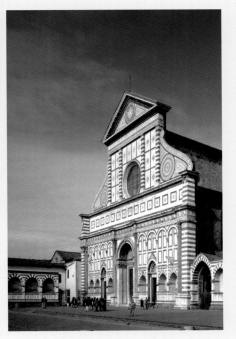

well-known churches, such as the cathedral in Florence or the Franciscan Church of Santa Croce, were chiefly constructed in the nineteenth century in a historicizing style. Brunelleschi's

trailblazing churches, San Lorenzo and Santo Spirito, as well as Santa Maria del Carmine (known for Masaccio's frescoes), remain unclad today. The reasons for this probably lie in the difficulty of transferring the temple facades prescribed by the Renaissance style onto the basilica with its ascending staggered profile.

It was Leone Battista Alberti, supported by his visionary patron Giovanni Rucellai, who accomplished an extraordinary solution on the facade of Santa Maria Novella. The church represents an ideal synthesis of the structures of the thirteenth and fourteenth centuries with those of the Early Renaissance. Alberti solved the problem of the transition between the high central nave and the lower side aisles by means of huge volutes that pull together the massive triangular gable and the broad attic story. These elements would become a staple of the baroque.

The Christian Temple

During the Renaissance, churches were intended to embody absolute perfection. For Alberti and his contemporaries, this meant turning away from traditional floor plans based on the Latin cross and from the typical staggered basilica profile. Instead, Alberti recommended centralizing floor plans such as the circle, square, hexagon or octagon. Nature, the "divine teacher of all things," was thought to prefer circles and polygons, along with their derivatives. In drafting their architectural theories, humanists primarily looked to classical and Early Christian structures as models for contemporary churches; Alberti himself referred to churches as "temples." For him, it was apparently of no consequence that his chosen models were chiefly derived from pagan architectural forms. The non-Christian origin of these designs was, in fact, an issue of no small consequence. In spite of the controversy, however, none of the greatest Renaissance architects felt hindered from following Alberti's theories. Thus, until Charles Borromeo damned the circular form as heathen during the Counter Reformation, a series of important centrally planned sacred buildings was erected.

Among the clearest, and probably also the most beautiful, examples of this style are the martyrium Santa Maria delle Carceri in Prato, which was begun by Giuliano da Sangallo sometime after 1484 on a Greek cross plan, and Santa Maria della Consolazione in Todi, begun in 1508, where four apses were added to the basic cruciform core. Here, as also in San Biagio near

◀ Todi, Santa Maria della Consolazione, Cola da Caprarola (probably based on designs by Bramante or Leonardo da Vinci), begun 1508.

Montepulciano, begun in 1518 as the most "intellectual" of the churches in this group, yet another of Alberti's required elements came into play: San Biagio was built on an elevated location that removes the "temple" from the vicissitudes of daily life.

The variety of ideal designs can best be followed in the numerous drawings and illustrations in the treatises of the time. In what is called Manuscript B, at the Institut de France, Leonardo da Vinci left a veritable catalogue of extremely varied architectural solutions based on geometric figures. The extraordinary importance intrinsic to the design process is made clear in Leonardo's Vitruvian Man. This diagram superimposes a circle and square on the human body, thereby deriving the proportions of a building from the limbs of a man with outstretched arms and spread legs. The well-formed man is the image of the cosmos; the geometry and perfect proportions of the human form are equivalent to the essence of divine harmony (see p. 170).

▲ Mantua, San Andrea, Leone Battista Alberti, begun 1472. The facade combines the structure of a classical triumphal arch with the motif of the temple front.

▼ ▼ Pilgrimage church Madonna di San Biagio near Montepulciano, probably based on plans by Antonio da Sangallo the Elder, ca. 1518–1540, view and detail of facade.

City Palaces

If the Italian cityscape of the trecento was dominated by religious, sacred and civic architecture, the monumental and usually freestanding palazzi of the patricians confidently took its place alongside these older buildings during the quattrocento. Private patrons adapted and reinterpreted the formal architectural characteristics that were typical of medieval municipal palaces: the block form, the arrangement of their stories and, above all, the rusticated masonry of the facades, which was symbolic of power and dignity.

The organization of the various elements, their proportions, harmony and symmetry, became a field of decisive innovations. Inner courtyards underwent a fundamental revision, becoming regular square areas surrounded by arcades. The hitherto freestanding stairs rising from the courtyards migrated inside one of the wings, thus gaining protection from the elements. The *cortile*, the courtyard with its classically arranged columns, became an essential component of every Renaissance palace.

Construction on two pioneering architectural works began within a few years of each other: the Palazzo Medici, begun by Michelozzo di Bartolomeo around 1440/44, and the Palazzo Rucellai, begun in approximately 1446 according to the plans of Leone Battista Alberti. The former building, designed for Cosimo de' Medici and his family, includes a square interior

▲ Florence, Palazzo Rucellai, Leone Battista Alberti and Bernardo Rosselino, begun 1446.

◄ Florence, Palazzo Strozzi, Giuliano da Sangallo and Benedetto da Maiano, begun ca. 1490.

courtyard whose three stories are differentiated through columned arcades, window fronts and loggia. The exterior is dominated by a horizontal organization and rustication, which becomes increasingly shallow as the building gains in height. A massive cornice crowns the entire structure.

In the palace designed for Giovanni Rucellai, Alberti formulated other important principles of design. In accordance with the theories he had formulated in his treatise *De re aedificatoria*, Alberti lent the facade an additional vertical organization by means of pilasters set before the wall. True to Vitruvian principles, the order of the pilasters ascended from Doric at street level to Ionian in the second story and Corinthian on the third. Initially, however, the model of the Palazzo Medici found more resonance: the Palazzo Strozzi, begun in 1490,

▲ ▼ Urbino, Palazzo Ducale, Luciano Laurana and Francesco di Giorgio, 1460–1482, exterior view and interior courtyard.

clearly takes up its organizational elements and raises them to an even more sublime form.

In the small residential city of Urbino located in the Marche, the prince-general Federico da Montefeltro erected an extraordinary palace complex. Designed by Luciano Laurana and Francesco di Giorgio, the complex emblematically combines ancient imperial elements with medieval. The humanistic philosophy of the owner reveals itself in the interior courtyard: above the elegant composite arcade is a Latin inscription in praise of the prince. On the west facade of the complex, other classical motifs emerge in the grandiose three-storied loggia, which offers a sweeping view of the extensive Renaissance garden.

▼ Urbino, Palazzo Ducale, detail of the facade.

The Medici Villas

The creation of a villa—a freestanding estate house incorporated into a garden or park—had been a highly respected architectural project since the days of the Roman emperors. With the rediscovery of classical antiquity and the writings of Vitruvius, the concept of the villa was reborn. Again, it was Leone Battista Alberti, with his *Ten Books of Architecture*, who reintroduced this architectural model. He supported it with many examples and offered proposals for the ornamental details of the building. In the sixteenth century, Palladio and Vincenzo Scamozzi would perfect the villa. In the process, the center of activity for villa construction migrated from Florence, across Rome and Latium, and ultimately to the Veneto.

It is no accident that the necessary conditions for the triumph of villa architecture existed precisely in Florence, for it was the Florentine patriarchate, in particular the banking family of the Medici, that propagated a new, more intimate lifestyle, and that at least occasionally sought to withdraw from the city into "free" nature. The villas constructed at the Medici's behest in the second half of the fifteenth century in the hills of Tuscany did indeed unite the pleasures of country life with seigniorial splendor. The Villa Medici di Careggi and Villa Cafaggiolo, both designed by Michelozzo di Bartolomeo, retain the defiant character of medieval palaces. The Villa Medici in Poggio a Caiano, in contrast, by Giuliano da Sangallo, greets visitors with an elegant Ionic portico and curved stairways. The unity of house and garden, the symmetrical layout of the surrounding park (laid out in the form of an H), as well as the temple front on the facade, remained hallmarks of the villa even into the eighteenth century—although, after the early sixteenth century, the centralizing plan was often discarded in favor of parallel series of rooms.

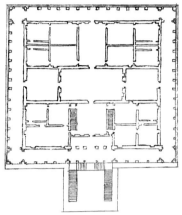

▲ ▲ Poggio a Caiano, Villa Medici, Giuliano da Sangallo, ca. 1485, Hall of Leo X with frescoes from the 16th century; proposed floor plan.

The Art of the Renaissance Garden

Gardens also came under the purview of Renaissance design principles based on the classical view of harmony and perfection. The balanced proportions of nature's laws were mirrored in the geometric design of garden beds and pools, in the axes of paths, and in the rhythmic inclusion of terraces and stairs. This order also reflected the Arcadian dream of paradise on earth. Not only is the garden the realm of the ancient deities, whose statues grace fountains, grottos and ruins; it is also the world of ideal architectural structures that melt into their natural environs. A further principle emerges in the topiary, whose precise form displays human ability to intervene creatively in nature.

◀ Villa Cafaggiolo near Florence, with gardens, expansion by Michelozzo di Bartolomeo begun 1451, detail from painting by Giusto Utens, ca. 1600.

The interior of most villas was arranged around a central hall, a design derived from the open colonnaded atrium of classical houses, but now enclosed. Public rooms were annexed at opposite sides of the hall. The summer dining room opened toward the garden, while the winter dining room could be heated. Comfort and ease became increasingly important. Frescoes on the walls and ceilings praised the lord of the manor and schematized the cheerful, informal atmosphere of these private "earthly paradises."

◀ Poggio a Caiano, Villa Medici, Giuliano da Sangallo, ca. 1485.

▶ Careggi near Florence, Villa Medici, Michelozzo di Bartolomeo, begun 1457, garden facade.

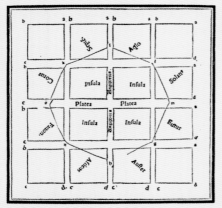

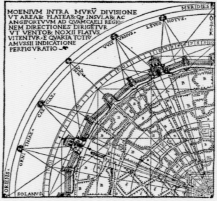

▲ ▲ Vitruvian city plans, Marcus Vitruvius Pollio, *De Architectura Libri*

Decem, Venice edition 1511 (left), Como edition 1521 (right).

The Ideal City

The desire to create a perfect world order based on reason and functionality can also be seen in urban planning. The supposedly chaotic organization of the medieval city was to be replaced with clear and geometric structures—an ideal embodied in Urbino in a series of painted wood panels that were probably inspired by Vitruvius. In practice, it was again the writings of Alberti that indicated the direction that the new

▲ A view of an ideal city, painted wood panel, ca. 1470, Urbino, Palazzo Ducale.

▼ Pienza, city center, Bernardo Rosselino, 1460–1464, trapezoidal plaza with cathedral and papal palace.

urban reality would follow. The aesthetic and social utopias Alberti formulated led to a multitude of ideal city plans. Among them was the design of the urban utopia Sforzinda proposed by Antonio Averlino, also known as Filarete, for the Milanese duke Francesco Sforza (see p. 170). Conceived as an octagon with a radial system of streets, the center was to be dominated by a palace and the cathedral. Almost simultaneously, Pope Pius II ordered his home town, Corsignano, which was south of Siena, redesigned as a signature model community called Pienza. The trapezoidal plaza, monumentalized by means of optical tricks, was flanked by a hierarchical arrangement of cathedral, papal palace, episcopal palace and Palazzo Comunale.

Reaching its peak in the sixteenth century in the fortified city of Palmanova (Veneto), this development formed the prelude to the construction of the complex star-shaped fortresses of the baroque period. According to Alberti's plans, even Rome would have become an enormous religious planned city; however, this utopian design was doomed to failure. Not until the sixteenth century did a rather pragmatic solution emerge, namely to extend the existing axes of the city and to connect the city and its main churches by means of two fan-shaped networks of streets.

Among the largest urban projects undertaken during the Renaissance is the redesign of the Capitol, the administrative center of Rome. The classical equestrian statue of Emperor Marcus Aurelius—long believed to be that of Constantine—had already been erected on the Capitoline Hill in 1538. Placed on a new pedestal designed by Michelangelo, the statue became the pivot of the new city plan, the role of the monument being clearly accentuated by the star pattern created by the paving stones radiating from it. The massive platform stairs that lead visitors to the trapezoidal plaza were constructed between 1546 and 1554. Opposite these stairs was the Senator's Palace (still in its medieval form at that time), before which Michelangelo placed a double stairway and a new portal. Between 1582 and 1605, Giacomo della Porta and Girolamo Rainaldi raised the present building, incorporating into it the earlier structure and reorienting it toward the interior of the plaza. The Palazzo dei Conservatori (on the right of the area) was also completed by della Porta according to Michelangelo's plans. The enormous Corinthian pilasters that unite both stories of the building dominate its facade. This motif, atypical of the classical age, was to become increasingly popular during the baroque period. Construction on the Capitoline Museum opposite the Conservatori did not begin until

approximately 1650 and followed the pattern established by the Palazzo dei Conservatori. The scenic quality of the composition, the intelligent disposition of the buildings, as well as the virtuoso play with open areas around them made the Capitol into an ideal center for Rome.

▲▲ Michelangelo's design for the Capitoline Hill, Rome (1538), engraving by Ètienne Dupérac, 1569.

▲ Rome, Palazzo dei Conservatori, on the Capitoline Hill, Giacomo della Porta, after a design by Michelangelo, 1564–1575, colossal-order facade.

Rome and the Beginning of the High Renaissance

In 1496, the young Michelangelo took up residence in Rome for the first time. Three years later, Bramante fled from French-occupied Milan and also found his way to the city, and Raphael arrived in 1508. There all three found fertile ground for the development of their careers. On one hand, the Eternal City allowed them to study classical antiquity at the site of its origin. In addition, when Julius II became pope in 1503, Rome gained a pope who expressly fostered both artists and the arts. It was no accident that these factors triggered a flood of innovations that mark the transition from the Early to the High Renaissance.

The incunabulum of the "classical" Renaissance period is Bramante's first work in Rome, the Tempietto in the court of San Pietro in Montorio. It was a gift of King Ferdinand and Queen Isabella of Spain, who wanted to erect a memorial at the site of the crucifixion of St Peter. Begun in 1502, the circular temple designed by the 60-year-old Bramante (who had once been a pupil

▲ Rome, Belvedere Court in the Vatican, Bramante, pen drawing by Giovanni Antonio Dosi.

of Luciano Laurana) more closely approximated the classical ideal than any structure before it. In spite of the temple's small size, Bramati achieved a wholly new monumentality and plasticity of form. The balanced proportions fit harmoniously into the narrow space of the cloister courtyard. The controlling order of Doric columns around the base reveals a sound knowledge of archaeology. Bramante's Tempietto carried the quattrocento principle of the central plan to its consummation.

Moreover, as a combination of a classical temple and martyrium, the building serves as a significant symbol for the historical continuity of Roman churches.

Immediately upon the elevation of Julius II to the papal seat, work began on the Cortile del Belvedere—over 1,000 ft (300 m) long—in the Vatican Palace. Later divided to produce a separate upper and lower court, the plan was unique in its time as a combination garden and fortified court. Three years later, in 1506, Bramante developed the first concrete plans for the rebuilding of St Peter's. Between 1513 and 1518 Raphael decorated the Logge (also designed by Bramante) overlooking the lower Belvedere court with scenes from the Old and New Testaments; the grotesque figures framing the frescoes were among the favorite decorative motifs of the sixteenth century.

The classical style, with a new monumentality, also triumphed in the design of Roman palazzo. A new era in secular architecture began with construction of the Cancelleria and the design of the rhythmically structured facade of the Palazzo Farnese, which was begun by Antonio da Sangallo the Younger.

◀ Rome, Palazzo della Cancelleria, begun 1483, two-story arcaded passages in the courtyard.

▶ Rome, Tempietto, San Pietro in Montorio, Bramante, begun 1502.

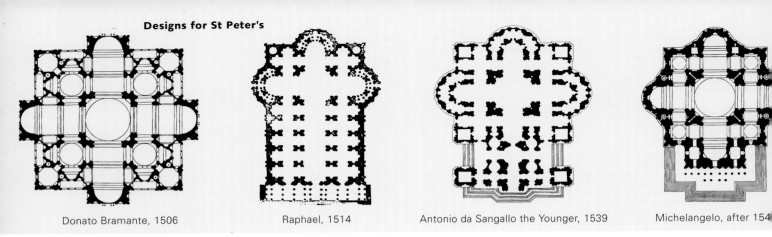

Donato Bramante, 1506   Raphael, 1514   Antonio da Sangallo the Younger, 1539   Michelangelo, after 154

The Rebuilding of St Peter's

In 1506 Julius II gave his official approval for the rebuilding of St Peter's, thus contradicting his predecessor's plans for a thorough restoration of the old church. The della Rovere pope wanted to create a whole new work, a building fit to carry the glory of the Catholic Church and its founder out into the world. Immediately following this decision, Bramante and his colleague Giuliano da Sangallo submitted the well-known "parchment plan," which is now preserved in the Uffizi Museum. The design called for a centrally organized structure rising above a Greek cross. According to Bramante, the building would "pile the Pantheon onto the Constantinian basilica."

Although the project was not carried out in this form, the design was nonetheless clearly formative for subsequent plans, all the way through to the construction of the dome by Michelangelo. When Bramante died in 1514, the crossing piers and arches—which were about 150 ft (45 m) high—were already completed. Raphael, Bramante's successor as master builder of the cathedral, had to accept the arches as a given, but altered Bramante's plans by adding a three-aisled nave with side chapels to the central structure. However, Raphael's sudden death in 1520 brought an end to this project. His immediate successor, Baldassare Peruzzi, revived Bramante's concept, whereas Antonio da Sangallo the Younger, who replaced Peruzzi, preferred Raphael's added nave. The project stagnated. Nonetheless, by the time Sangallo died in 1546, he had completed vaulting the southern and eastern arms of the church and had built the grottos for the papal tombs. (The grottos were intended to compensate for the differences in levels on the Vatican Hill and to serve as back-up containers for groundwater.)

Toward the end of 1546, the 71-year-old Michelangelo took over the work on St Peter's. Holding fast to the idea of a centrally planned building, he tightened and advanced the designs of his predecessors while increasing the monumentality and dynamism of the structure. It was then time to address the dome, whose construction followed the example set by Brunelleschi in the Florentine cathedral. There are no precise construction details concerning the project, however. At Michelangelo's death in 1564, only—or perhaps already—the drum and sidewalls of the dome were complete. Michelangelo's plans were finally implemented by his successor around 1590, but work dragged on and Christianity's most distinguished church was not completed until the seventeenth century.

▼ ▼ Rome, St Peter's, Michelangelo, western apse, exterior wall with colossal order pilasters.

▶ Rome, St Peter's, begun 1506, view of Michelangelo's dome from the Vatican Garden.

Michelangelo in Florence

Leo X, the first Medici to ascend the papal throne, shifted Michelangelo's sphere of work to Florence. Between 1515 and 1518 the artist produced designs (see p. 153) and a wooden model for the facade of San Lorenzo, but had to accept the fact that the pope prevented their implementation. To mollify the artist's resentment, Leo X granted Michelangelo the commission for construction of the Medicis' burial chapel in the New Sacristy at San Lorenzo. Formally conceived as a companion piece to Brunelleschi's Old Sacristy, Michelangelo's chapel broke the "bands and chains" (Vasari) inherited from Vitruvius that constricted the possibilities of architecture. Five tomb monuments were erected in the square room topped by a dome; the most splendid are the wall tombs of Lorenzo the Magnificent and Giuliano, Duke of Nemours.

Michelangelo's architectural innovations are evident in the vestibule of the Biblioteca Laurenziana, the Medici's library. As so often, fulfilling the patrons' requirements was not easy, and construction proceeded slowly. Nonetheless, the vestibule with its idiosyncratically curved stairway became a highlight of European architecture. The charm of this high, narrow room arises from its playful use of perception and its inversion of classical expectations. Michelangelo transported a facade organization to the interior of the building: the walls open into blind niches, and the volutes serve no purpose but to exist. Initially, contemporaries deplored the famed motif of the "trapped" columns as an "incomprehensible error"; and indeed

the notorious pairs of columns, instead of standing in front of the wall, are located within, or almost behind, the wall's surface.

▲ ▼ Florence, San Lorenzo, Michelangelo, Biblioteca Laurenziana, *ricetto* (vestibule), begun 1524, stairs and detail of the wall articulation.

◀ Florence, the Medici Chapel at San Lorenzo, Michelangelo, 1520/21, tomb of Giuliano de' Medici.

Palladio and the Architecture of the Veneto

After the Sack of Rome in 1527, many artists abandoned the Eternal City. Venice, which sought to rid itself of its medieval appearance, offered a rich field of activity for the exiles. However, the Renaissance was unable to assert itself easily in Venice. Not until the work of Sansovino around 1540 did classical architecture finally triumph in the City of Water. At the same time, Michele Sanmicheli erected the Palazzo Grimani, which translated the traditional Venetian palace facade into the language of the Renaissance.

Andrea di Pietro, better known as Palladio, was born in 1508 Padua, where he was also trained as a stone mason. In 1524, he arrived in Vicenza and discovered a friend and patron in the poet Gian Giorgio Trissino, with whom Palladio shared a humanistic attitude. Palladio began his successful career as an architect in 1540, and in 1570 he published *I Quattro Libri dell'*

Architettura (The Four Books of Architecture), a work that was considered fundamental to architects for centuries. As early as the renovation of the Basilica Palladiana in Vicenza, Palladio had made architectural history by elevating the Serlian window (a large arch flanked by trabeated narrow openings) to the main theme of the facade. Known thereafter as the Palladian motif (see illus. p.171), this theme would be copied thousands of times. In addition to various urban palazzi, the architect also erected the Teatro Olimpico in 1580, shortly before his death. That project was both the first freestanding theater architecture built since classical antiquity, and at the same time, a comprehensive reconstruction of the ancient Roman theater as described by Vitruvius.

The main field for Palladio's creativity, however, was the villa, whose classic ideal he revived in numerous variations. Palladian villas are characterized by symmetry, harmonious proportions, and their integration into the surrounding landscape. The Villa Capra, known as the Rotonda, is the most famous

▲ Venice, Il Redentore, Andrea Palladio, begun 1576.

◄ Vicenza, Teatro Olimpico, Andrea Palladio, 1580, interior.

of these, although Palladio himself saw the structure more as a palace, or at least a *villa suburbana*, since the building lacked an agricultural setting. The Rotonda is domed and set on a square core with a temple facade on all four sides—the statement could hardly be more impressive.

Palladio's other leitmotiv is the adaptation of the classical temple facade for religious buildings. As we have seen, Renaissance architects faced a number of problems in designing church facades. The Counter Reformation deemed the central plan, which had long been favored by theoreticians, to be a heathen structure. Proponents of the Counter Reforma-

tion demanded the Latin cross floor plan, the antithesis of Palladio's understanding of a "Christian temple." Nonetheless, in the Venetian churches Il Redentore (begun 1576) and San Georgio Maggiore (begun 1566, see pp. 146–147) Palladio succeeded in squaring the circle by setting various kinds of spaces in sequence and uniting them through a continuous wall articulation. The crossing is delineated by centralizing elements, and the basilical structure is concealed by the temple facades. The face of Il Redentore, for example, which rises above the Canale della Guidecca, is a stroke of genius: here, multiple temple fronts are superimposed to produce a theatrical facade crowned by a spacious, towering dome.

◀ Venice, Palazzo Grimani, Michele Sanmicheli et al., 1541–1575.

▼ Vicenza, Villa Capra (La Rotonda), Andrea Palladio, 1566–1580.

Architectural Theory

At no point in time has architectural theory played a greater role than in the early modern age. The plentiful comprehensive writings composed by scholars, connoisseurs, artists and engineers had a decisive influence on what was actually built. Architecture developed from an *ars mechanica*, a craft carried out by artisans, to emerge as a science. Of course, there had been theoretical discussions about architecture in the post-classical period. One might mention ideal plans for monasteries, pattern books for the master builders of cathedrals (by Villard de Honnecourt, for example) and the liturgical requirements of Abbot Suger. But there had been no complex, comprehensive organization of ideas.

It is no accident that this systematic treatment of architecture began in the Early Renaissance—this is yet another manifestation of the striving for autonomy experienced in all the arts in the fifteenth century. No longer the arcane lore of experienced master builders, architecture now became a proper object of study for humanists. Whereas theoretical writings at first circulated only within elite circles, the invention of the printing press hastened the spread of the tracts throughout Europe and provided the "modern" architect with the intellectual equipment needed for innovation.

Unquestionably, the "rediscovery" of Vitruvius' *Ten Books of Architecture* in the first half of the fifteenth century marks the beginning of early modern architectural theory. But this was not a true rediscovery, for various copies and translations had kept the ideas of Vitruvius alive throughout the Middle

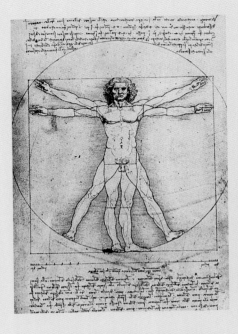

◀ Leonardo da Vinci, *The Vitruvian Man*, late 15th century.

▼ Filarete (Antonio Averlino), plan for the ideal city "Sforzinda," 1460.

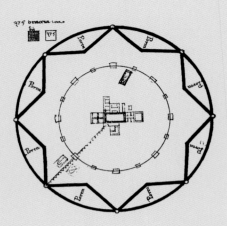

▶ Cosimo Bartoli, diagram of a pulley system in the first illustrated edition of Leone Battista Alberti's *Dell'Architettura*, Florence, 1550.

Ages—albeit without illustrations. Leone Battista Alberti was the first to deal with the classical sources systematically and to develop a comprehensive theory of the arts in his *De re aedificatoria libri decem*, published between 1442 and 1452. In this work Alberti laid the foundations for modern architectural criticism.

Following Vitruvius, Alberti's discussions considered issues such as the stability, utility and beauty of a building; material and construction; typology, i.e., the canon of the various classifications of buildings; and finally "ornament," according to which the column is "the most beautiful ornament of a building." The central issue in the debate was the question of a building's form and its integration with an order. As addressed by Vitruvius and Alberti, all these categories contain social and aesthetic components; furthermore, the categories define both the expression and duty of a society that wishes to adapt architecture to serve its needs.

Alberti's architectural treatise had no illustrations. It remained for subsequent generations to illustrate his ideas and formulate them more precisely. The ongoing research on Rome's ancient architectural heritage inspired painters and graphic artists to make detailed studies, which in turn were incorporated into architectural theory. The first illustrated treatment composed after the publication of the *Ten Books*, however, was a work of fiction, and was written in the vernacular: Antonio Averlino, known as Filarete, designed an ideal city, Sforzinda, for the Duke of Milan, Francesco Sforza.

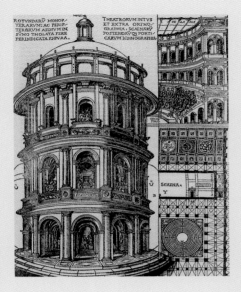

▲ Cesare Cesariano, woodcut from his *Di Lucio Vitruvio Pollione de Architectura*; elevation, section and floor plan of a Roman theater, Como, 1521.

The allegorical *Hypnerotomachia Poliphili* printed in 1499 presented an almost romantic vision of the classical age. The hero named in the title wanders through a classical dream kingdom. In writings that appeared between 1470 and 1492, the military architect Francesco di Giorgio Martini took up Alberti's antiquarian principles with the aim of making the knowledge won from antiquity available to modern times. Martini's anthropomorphic designs, in which he applied the proportions of the human body to architectural components, became famous. Leonardo apotheosized this principle by making man the measure of all things.

The commentary on Vitruvius written by Cesare Cesariano (1521) is unique. Cesariano unites classical theory and contemporary architectural practice, as when he discusses Vitruvian categories with reference to a cross-section of the (unexpectedly) Gothic cathedral in Milan. Over the course of the sixteenth century, the discussions about the number and form of the orders of columns took precedence over all other themes. The first to develop a canon of column orders was Sebastiano Serlio, who began in 1537 to establish five orders (Tuscan, Doric, Ionic, Corinthian, composite). Subsequently, in 1562, the *Regola delli cinque ordini d'architettura* by Iacomo Barozzi da Vignola was published and became one of the most successful text books on architecture that has ever been written.

Palladio's *Four Books*, with their high-quality woodcuts, numerous ground plans, and vertical sections of classical and contemporary buildings, provided a catalog of sorts that served as a reference for every classically inspired project into the eighteenth century in England. In 1615, the widely traveled architect and scholar Vincenzo Scamozzi made an attempt to gather the sum of architectural theory and practice at the end of the Renaissance in his fragmentary treatise *L'idea della architettura universale*.

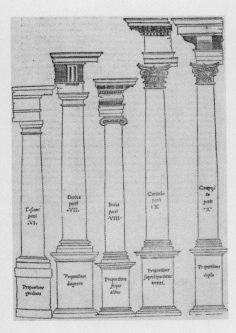

◄ Sebastiano Serlio, order of columns from *Tutte l'Opere d'Architettura et Prospettiva*, left to right: Tuscan, Doric, Ionic, Corinthian and composite; Venice, 1619.

▲ Andrea Palladio, frontispiece of the original edition of *I Quattro Libri dell'Architettura*, Venice, 1570.

▲ Andrea Palladio, front elevation of the basilica in Vicenza. This woodcut, from Book III, shows the Palladian motif (also known as the Serlian window or Serliana).

The Construction of French Châteaux

Renaissance impulses began to make their presence felt in France around 1500, an understandable consequence of the campaigns of Charles VII in Italy. From Urbino and Naples came convincing inspirations for the modernization of castles, and artists in Florence, Rome and Milan responded to the invitations extended by the French court. Among these artists was Leonardo da Vinci, who spent his final years in Amboise.

The château, attractively ensconced above the Loire, became the nucleus of Renaissance culture in France. From Amboise, the new style conquered the entire Loire region. The ascent of Francis I to the throne in 1515 initiated a feverish building boom that included new construction as well as extensive renovation of existing older structures. At Blois, the king ordered a radical modernization of the medieval fort. He commissioned Domenico da Cortona, known as Boccador, to build a new wing with a grandiose loggia facade that opened toward the city and the countryside. The courtyard was

dominated by the winding, open-well staircase (see p. 149), an elegant external stairway that became the setting for magnificent formal receptions. Immediately after 1515 work also commenced at Chenonceau; however, its distinctive long wing (200 ft, or 60 m) above the Cher River was not built until 1547, when Henry II presented the estate to his mistress, Diane de Poitiers.

In 1519, Francis I ordered the demolition of his royal hunting lodge at Chambord to make way for con-

struction of a far more splendid castle. This project, which was presumably also directed by Domenico da Cortona, resulted in one of the most magnificent palaces of the Renaissance. The core of the château is a square building with corner bastion towers reminiscent of a medieval keep. The center of the building, however, is dominated by a majestic double-helix staircase around which interior and exterior quadrangles containing symmetrical suites of rooms are arranged. This unique configuration is outrivaled only by the Château de

◀ Château de Blois, Domenico da Cortona, known as Boccador, 1515–1524, wing of Francis I.

▶ Château Chenonceau, begun 1515, Grande Galerie above the Cher River, completed ca. 1580.

Fontainebleau. The influence of the latter on French architecture, however, is due to the splendor of its individual rooms, rather than to a clear arrangement of the ground plan.

In 1541, Sebastiano Serlio arrived at Fontainebleau and assumed the office of *Architecte générale des bâtiments de France*. Although his designs remained confined to paper, with a few exceptions, Serlio's ideas provided the basis for the extension of the Louvre, which Francis I had been planning since 1528. The renovations were not actually carried out until the reign of Henry II, under the royally appointed direction of Pierre Lescot. The southwest portions of the Cour Carrée—i. e., the oldest structures—are the combined effort of Lescot and the sculptor Jean Goujon. The show-piece of the interior is the Salle des Caryatides, which occupies almost the entire ground floor of the west wing. This grandiose room, which functioned both as a banquet room and as the hall of justice, owes its name to the four antique classical female figures that support the musicians' balcony.

French religious buildings, meanwhile, remained true to late Gothic traditions, though classical motifs can occasionally be found in the decorations of the entrances.

▶ Paris, Louvre, Pierre Lescot, Salle des Caryatides in the Lescot Wing of the Cour Carrée, begun 1546.

◀ ▶ Château Chambord, begun 1519, exterior view (l) and grand stairway (r).

Villa, Palace and Garden

In the fifteenth century, the girdle of villas constructed by the Medici around Florence featured a more intimate and nature-oriented lifestyle. In the sixteenth century, the spark of this idea jumped to Rome. Between 1508 and 1511, the banker and art enthusiast Agostino Chigi engaged Baldassare Peruzzi to erect the Farnesina. An early example of the *villa suburbana*, or villa on the outskirts of a city, Peruzzi's campus, which drew its inspiration from classical writers, is completely devoted to *otium*, or leisure. The building layout opens to the surrounding terraces and gardens. At the heart of the villa is a broad garden loggia designed and decorated by Raphael and his coworkers. The Villa Madama attempts to approximate the classical villa even more closely. Raphael designed it in 1516/1517 around a circular courtyard surrounded by a wall interrupted by apses and niches. The grotesque figures ornamenting the villa were inspired by the paintings of Emperor Nero's Domus Aurea, which had been rediscovered a short time earlier.

As the Roman impulses for the design of palaces and villas spread beyond the city in the sixteenth century, they underwent further development. The Villa Imperiale near Pesaro, for example, took up the model of the Palatine Villa Farnese (destroyed, only the historic gardens remain). The picturesque Imperiale complex nestles on a hillside and offers an expansive view of the Adriatic from its terrace gardens. A glorious example of the extent to which architects freed themselves from the rules of classical architecture is the Palazzo del Te in Mantua, which represents the epitome of intellectual mannerist architecture (see p. 177). The sculptor and architect

▲ Florence, Palazzo Pitti, garden facade, ca. 1560.

▼ Bagnaia, near Viterbo, Villa Lante, begun after 1566.

Bartolomeo Ammanati carried these mannerist elements to Florence. The courtyard facade of the Palazzo Pitti, whose three stories (including their three orders of columns) are strongly rusticated, must have seemed like an assault against the classical understanding of facade design.

Remodeling the Villa Farnese in Caprarola (see p. 149) represented a particular architectural challenge. The massive pentagonal fortress was supposed to be transformed into a charming summer residence for a humanistic prince. Antonio da Sangallo the Younger, Peruzzi and Vignola worked together on the project for many years.

Vignola was also responsible for the expansion of the neighboring Villa Lante, a country estate that had served as a summer resort for many Roman cardinals since the fifteenth century. In accordance with the villa concept, the cultivated area is clearly distinguished from the wooded landscape area. The central axis is marked by a series of stairways that follow the water to the four ponds grouped around a magnificent fountain.

In France only a few palace-and-garden ensembles retained their sixteenth-century character; most were redesigned during the baroque period. The Renaissance style is best preserved in the châteaux of Chenonceau and Azay-le-Rideau. Taking advantage of the river terrain of the Loire region, these estates also incorporated water as a unifying motif: the Grande Galerie of Chenonceau juts boldly above the Cher River, while Azay-le-Rideau lies on an island in the Indre River. The palace is picturesquely framed by corner bastion towers, which clearly reveal the former defensive character of the site. Château de Villandry was completed in 1536, but its wonderful gardens, which were created at the beginning of the twentieth century, play freely with historical models.

▲ Château de Villandry, completed 1536, view from the ornamental garden toward the Renaissance building and older keep.

▼ Château d'Azay-le-Rideau, 1518–1527, located on an island in the Indre River.

Mannerist Architecture

If one were to judge Renaissance architecture by the standards of the Florentine humanists themselves, it is likely that only a few buildings would pass muster: Brunelleschi's works, for example, Alberti's facades and Bramante's Tempietto. Even the work of Michelangelo, in particular the *ricetto* (vestibule with staircase) of the Biblioteca Laurenziana, almost glories in architectural "violations" willfully employed by the artist to increase the dramatic effect of the wall. The Palazzo del Te, mentioned earlier, also represents a milestone in this development. Giulio Romano's facades play expertly with the elements of classical architecture (such as rustication, columns, entablatures) but set them into new, non-classical relationships, contrary to Renaissance "rules." Under mannerism, what assumes preeminence is neither the perfect balance of the proportions nor the clear logic of weights and

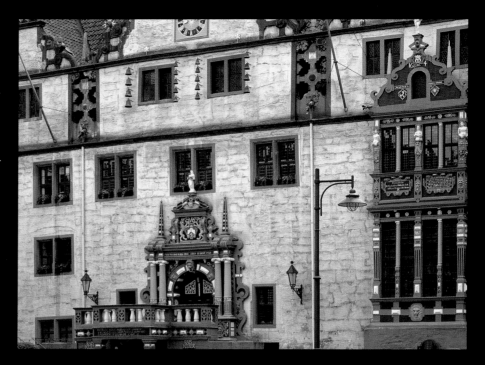

supports, but rather individualistic scene-setting and a dramatic effect.

The architecture of the Uffizi, the elongated office building between the Palazzo Vecchio and the Arno River, borrowed motifs by Michelangelo. The endless extension of the axes may be

seen as an effective modern element in terms of urban architecture. The elegant conclusion of the "corridor" (the street-like courtyard) forms a loggia with archways reminiscent of a triumphal arch; in fact, they form a *serliana* that opens toward the river.

Beyond Italy's borders the mannerist style became the norm. In regions untouched by classical culture, the new freedom in the interpretation of the Vitruvian heritage opened manifold innovative design possibilities, completely independent of any form of "classical considerations," according to the architectural historian Erik Forssman.

The assimilation of late Gothic, Renaissance and mannerist elements gave rise to a new style, which inspired extraordinarily charming buildings. The tracts and treatises that circulated throughout Europe in the second half

◄ Florence, Uffizi Corridor, also called the Vasari Corridor, Giorgio Vasari, begun 1560.

of the sixteenth century played an important role in the success of mannerism. An example of the open-minded stance typical of the tract literature can be seen in the writings of Hans Vredeman de Vries, who offered a veritable firework display of decorative motifs that would enrich architecture north of the Alps well into the seventeenth century. The facade of St-Ètienne-du-Mont in Paris might well have stemmed from a manual of mannerist patterns, even though the building wasn't begun until 1610. The church's three dissimilar gables, which tower one above another, lend the building a striking vertical thrust. Whereas the lower story is designed as a temple facade with rusticated columns, a Gothic rose window stands in splendid defiance under a broken segmented (arched) gable in the story above, and the whole ensemble is crowned by an extremely steep triangular gable. Last but not least, a tall asymmetrical bell tower contributes yet another individualistic note to this dynamic facade.

The term mannerism was coined by art historian and critic Giorgio Vasari, who used it to describe an individual style. Long a subject of debate, it has asserted itself as a designation for the transitional phase between the Renaissance and baroque periods.

▲ Mantua, Palazzo del Te, Giulio Romano, begun 1526.

◄ Paris, St-Étienne-du-Mont, facade, begun 1610.

▶ Château Anet, Philibert de l'Orme, 1547–1552, view into the dome of the palace chapel.

Belgium and the Netherlands

The city of Antwerp, Belgium's most important port, made an immense contribution to sixteenth-century architecture—although less through the buildings erected there than in its role as the center of book printing. Antwerp was the locus of the first translation of Serlio, and the most influential architectural theoreticians of northern Europe, Cornelis Floris de Vriendt and Hans Vredeman, both lived within the city's walls.

Cornelis Floris, who lived in Rome between 1540 and 1547, published two series of ornament collections after his return. These works spurred on the spread of mannerism. His drawings of Roman grotesques and his invention of manifold decorative forms, such as masks, cartouches, scrollwork and festoons of fruit, were eagerly taken up throughout Europe and ap-

▲ Antwerp, City Hall, Cornelis Floris, 1561–1566.

▶ Antwerp, guild houses on the Grote Markt, 16th or 17th century.

pear thousands of times in facade decoration. His sole surviving architectural work, Antwerp City Hall, has a generally classical style, but the facade's projecting central bay with its forceful double columns and towering gable represent the quintessence of Flemish mannerism. Hans Vredeman de Vries even outdid his predecessors in the didactics of architecture. His textbooks—for example, his pattern books of columns—offered artists and craftsmen a comprehensive range of tools for putting classical orders and architectural types into practice.

After the separation of the Protestant north (now Netherlands) from the Catholic south (now Belgium) in 1579, the most significant building projects in the region were city palaces, citizens' houses and communal buildings such as town or city halls, guild halls, cloth halls or the *waaghuis* (weighing house) found in each city. Various treatments of Renaissance forms can be seen in

◀ Haarlem, Netherlands, Vleeshal, Lieven de Key, begun 1601.

the former fishmongers' guild house in Mechelen (now called The Salmon) and the Ancienne Greffe (the Old Chancellery) in Bruges, both in Belgium. In these buildings, late Gothic structures, Renaissance decoration and mannerist gables complement each other most charmingly.

Toward the end of the sixteenth century, classical architecture lost ground, mainly due to Haarlem architect Lieven de Key. He began leading construction of the Waaghuis (municipal weighing house) in that city in 1598, a project that demonstrates a conscious use of Italian ideas in spite of certain mannerist details. Moreover, the construction history of the Vleeshal (Butchers' Hall) in Haarlem demonstrates that the Italian style was just one of several options available at the time. When de Key received the commission for that project in 1601, he had submitted two proposals, one in the classical Roman style, and the other in the tradition of the Dutch Renaissance with its lively ornamentation and eccentric silhouette. The latter proposal was awarded the contract.

The Renaissance and Mannerism in Germany

In Germany, the stylistic repertoire of the Renaissance made inroads only slowly. In 1509, the Fuggers, a wealthy merchant family in Augsburg, were the first to import Italian ideas and forms in the design of their burial chapel. In the 1530s, the princely houses of central Europe began to take up the new style as well. In Torgau, the Saxon prince elector Johann Friedrich the Magnanimous had the medieval fortress of Hartenfels rebuilt as a palace. The heart of the building is the spiral staircase, which has no central supporting column and is decorated with grotesque figures. Also among the important palaces of the sixteenth century is Augustusburg near Chemnitz, whose austere, regular arrangement of buildings around a cruciform courtyard can be explained only with reference to French models. The two-story chapel is spanned by a broad barrel vault with mannerist strapwork. Northern Italian ideas come into play in the first "modern" city palace to be built on German soil in Landshut. The reconstruction of the Munich Residence with its "classical" antiquarium (see p. 149) is one of the earliest museum buildings north of the Alps.

In the middle of the sixteenth century, the Renaissance style was widely accepted in German secular architecture, although most of the designs bore traces of the mannerist pattern collections. The most beautiful example is the grandiose west facade of the Ottheinrich wing of the Heidelberg

◀ Torgau, Schloss Hartenfels, view of the Johann Friedrich wing with the grand spiral stairs (1533–1536) and Albrecht wing, built in the late 15th century.

◀ Heidelberg, castle, begun 1556, detail of the facade of the Ottheinrich wing.

▲ Augsburg, Fugger Chapel, 1509–1518.

▲ Schloss Augustusburg near Chemnitz, castle chapel, 1569.

Castle, which was transformed into a picturesque ruin by a fire in 1764. Rhythmically organized by orders of pilasters, the complex allegorical building design does honor to its patron.

Similar to the trend in the Netherlands, the facade of the German city hall developed into an impressive architectural enterprise. Guildhalls and civic buildings followed a similar direction.

Even in the seventeenth century, however, the traditional half-timbered construction was still preferred in many places; it was simply dressed up with a chic Renaissance "costume."

The Weser Renaissance

The area along the Weser River had an economic boom in the sixteenth and early seventeenth centuries. Nobility built imposing palaces, and wealthy families competed to create splendid facades. These "Weser Renaissance" buildings have a variety of styles. Regular rectangular layouts with four wings were accompanied by late-Gothic stair towers, gables, bays and portals. The mannerist display of playful ornamentation was likely drawn from pattern books. Around 1600, the architectural features became more balanced, with a prevalence of classical elements that emphasized the horizontal dimension. Principles of construction, both half-timber and stone, were still modeled on late medieval gabled dwellings, thus retaining their vertical momentum. Decorative elements such as pilasters, grotesques and volutes began to appear alongside mannerist scrollwork and baroque ribbon motifs. Obelisks re-placed late Gothic pinnacles. An example of this style is the market-square facade of the City Hall in Hannoversch-Münden with its cross gable and two-story bay (see p. 176).

◄ Hameln, Leisthaus, 1589.

▶ Osnabruck, Willmannsches Haus, 1586.

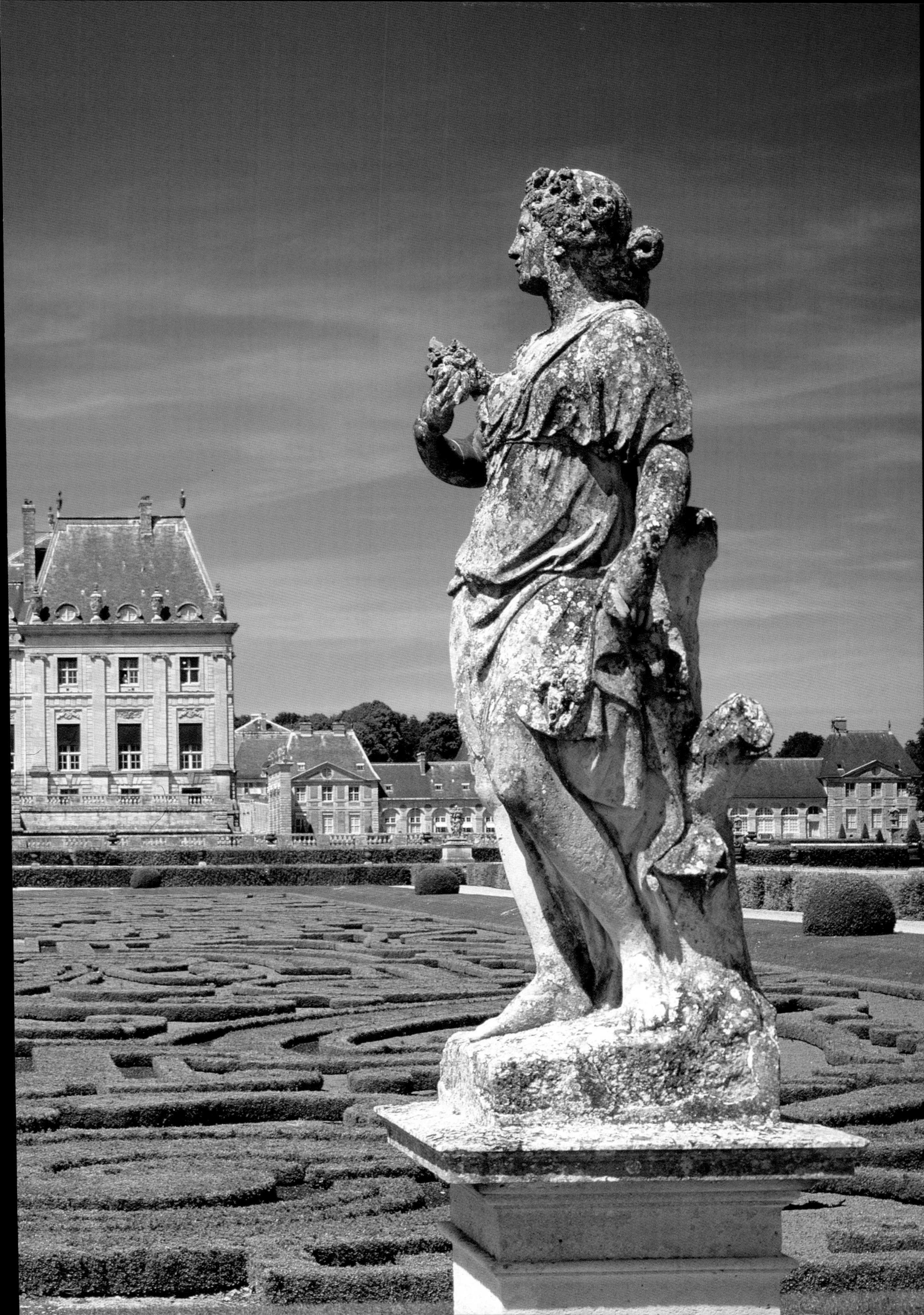

VIII. Baroque and Rococo

Baroque Architecture

Baroque architecture was at the service of spiritual and worldly powers alike. Both sensory and intellectual, it was intended to impress, to stir the emotions, and to convince humankind of the hidden order of things, and it did so in union with the other arts. Once again it was Rome where the transition took place—this time from mannerism to baroque—and it was Roman artists who introduced the new, sensualist architectural style to the world. Other regions did not emerge from the shadow of the city on the Tiber until the late seventeenth century. Rome owed its preeminence to the power of the Roman Catholic Church and the ambitions of the popes, who established the great urban axes and had them decorated with fountains and obelisks, and commissioned the renovation of countless churches, as well as lavish palaces for themselves.

The Jesuits played a decisive role in the dissemination of baroque architecture, at least in terms of sacred buildings. They had a tightly knit organization at their disposal

▼ Royal Seat of San Lorenzo del Escorial, Juan Bautista de Toledo and Juan de Herrera, 1563–1584.

▲ Salzburg, collegiate church, Johann Bernhard Fischer von Erlach, 1694–1707.

▲ Vienna, Upper Belvedere, Johann Lukas von Hildebrandt, 1721–1722, sala terrena.

that spread the architectural style of the Counter Reformation throughout the world.

So it was that the preferred baroque form of the cross-in-square church was based on the ideas of the Council of Trent (1545–1563), which called for a uniform preaching area with an unimpeded view of the high altar. These ideas took shape in the aisleless church of Il Gesù in Rome, where construction began in 1568. This groundbreaking Jesuit building was copied and varied hundredfold, and remained an archetype well into the eighteenth century. Built almost concurrently, the Royal Seat (both palace and monastery) of San Lorenzo

del Escorial embodied the perfect union of ecclesiastical and worldly power at the beginning of the absolutist era.

Votive churches represent a characteristic feature of baroque sacred architecture. They reveal the private devotion of the sovereign patron and express praise for having survived a personal or state crisis.

Palaces were conceived in an entirely new way in the baroque era. With their hierarchical sequences of rooms, prestigious stairways, theaters and royal chapels, they became the leading architectural enterprise of the time. Abandonment of the fortress type resulted in an openness toward nature. A new kind of palace came into being,

Versailles, near Paris, Louis Le Vau,
Jules Hardouin-Mansart and others, begun
1668, gardens by André le Nôtre.

generally with a horseshoe-shaped
entre cour et jardin (between courtyard
and garden) arrangement, which
reached out into the landscaped surroundings. Its most beautiful expression is the *sala terrena*, a ground-floor
room with access to the gardens that
united manmade architecture with the
utopian fantasy of rural Arcadia.

The art of garden design illustrates
the contradictions of the baroque like
no other medium. Its axial system

of allees embodies the strongly delineated order of absolutism, while at the
same time, sculptures, fountains and
architectural decoration transported
observers into a world of illusion. The
art of baroque gardening reached its
zenith at Versailles, and the French
garden became the embodiment of
modernity and culture. The axial
orientation of park allees also influenced city planning, which was based
on feudalistic requirements well into
the nineteenth century.

St Peter's Square constitutes the
peak of Roman baroque urban architecture. Despite restrictive guidelines,

▼ Bath, The Circus, John Wood, 1754.

Bernini created an urban space that
exceeded even the most audacious
expectations. The final draft of 1657 is
based on a dramatic double piazza, in
which the facade of St Peter's with
its benediction balcony looms large
behind it as if part of a theatrical set.
Its rationalistic counterpart is the
Circus in Bath, England, where impulses toward classicism are evident.

◄ Rome, St Peter's Square, Gianlorenzo
Bernini, 1656–1671.

BAROQUE   185

The Development of the Baroque in Rome

From 1568, when Giacomo della Porta designed the facade of the Church of Il Gesù, the mother church of the Jesuit order, the anti-classical tendencies that would lead to the development of baroque architecture were given free reign. But interior design was also undergoing decisive innovations. At Il Gesù, Giacomo Barozzi

▲ Rome, Il Gesù, Giacomo Barozzi da Vignola, interior view, 1568–1584.

▶ Rome, Il Gesù, Giacomo della Porta, facade, 1568–1584.

▲ Rome, Santi Luca e Martina, Pietro da Cortona, 1635–1650, facade.

▲ Rome, Santa Susanna, Carlo Maderno, 1597–1603, facade.

da Vignola successfully designed a church space that expressed the concepts of the Council of Trent to perfection. The church is compact. It has a single aisle with a barrel-vaulted nave, chapels, and barely projecting cross arms that permitted a large number of the faithful to see clearly what was happening at the altar. The room culminates in the spacious crossing, which is covered by a powerful dome resting on a drum. Il Gesù became the prototype for Roman Catholic church buildings both in Europe and the New World.

Special attention was paid to facades during the baroque era, not least because of their effect on urban development. Carlo Maderno's facade of Santa Susanna was a milestone: the sculptural and dynamic architectural language explored on Il Gesù was carried to perfection. Not surprisingly, Maderno was comissioned that same year to add a long nave and facade to St Peter's, which had begun as a centrally planned structure.

The works of Pietro da Cortona (born in 1597 as Pietro Berrettini) mark the transition to high baroque. This outstanding painter, draftsman and stage designer considered architecture merely a hobby. Although he completed very few buildings, they became the embodiment of baroque interior design. Thus, he drafted plans for the Church of the Accademia di San Luca, a centrally planned structure on a Greek-cross plan. Its interior is exceptionally and vividly three-dimensional. The walls melt away in the interplay of columns and pillars; white and gray reliefs articulate the remaining wall and vault surfaces. The convex curve of the facade, something never before seen, is held fast between the double pilasters that frame it. The facade of Santa Maria della Pace, also designed by da Cortona, is even more ingenious. Its entryway is a semicircular portico that extends into the small square in which it stands, framed by two concave wings. The flowing movement of the whole is highly theatrical.

The Completion of St Peter's in Rome

The bewildering architectural history of St Peter's continued in an equally confusing manner during the baroque period. Pope Paul V ordered an extension of the centrally planned building toward the east (St Peter's had been west-facing since its founding), even though that did not correspond to the liturgical ideas of the Counter Reformation. It fell to Carlo Maderno, who headed up the cathedral building site

from 1603, to carry out construction of the long nave, vestibule and powerfully articulated facade. The new St Peter's was consecrated in 1626. After his election as pope, Urban VIII commissioned Bernini to complete the interior. Work on the papal altar and the baldachin above the grave of St Peter began in 1624. Soon afterward, the sculptor-architect was commissioned to furnish the crossing columns with niche figures and to give a new interpretation to the monumental relics. Both assignments were subject to a compelling theological idea: the balda-

chin, with its imposing twisted bronze columns, memorialized the Constantinian St Peter's as well as the Temple of Solomon in Jerusalem. The 13-foot (4-m) high niche figures dramatically present the main relics of St Peter's.

Bernini began construction of the clock towers in 1626. After the first one collapsed due to structural defects, that project was abandoned. But Bernini's remodeling of the apse with the *Cathedra Petri* (altar with the throne of St Peter), carried out between 1657 and 1666, resulted in a triumphal *gesamtkunstwerk*, or total work of art.

▲▲ Rome, St Peter's, view into the cupola, designed by Michelangelo, ca. 1546.

▲ Rome, St Peter's, facade, Carlo Maderno; St Peter's Square, lateral view, 1607–1612.

▲▲ Rome, St Peter's, facade, Carlo Maderno.

▶ Rome, St Peter's, baldachin, Gianlorenzo Bernini, 1624–1633, with the *Cathedra Petri* in the background, 1657–1666.

Bernini and Borromini

Bernini spent almost all his life in the Eternal City and bequeathed it a range of his sculptural and architectural masterpieces. His works are three-dimensional paintings, illusionistic spaces, which opened up new artistic perspectives. Bernini's career as an architect began when Pope Urban VIII commissioned the inexperienced artist with the renovation of Santa Bibiana. In 1629, following Maderno's death, he took over as *capomaestro* at St Peter's while continuing to work on the Palazzo Barberini. Around 1660, Bernini was commissioned to build three additional churches, the most important of which was Sant'Andrea al Quirinale.

In this small elliptical church, the altar is crafted like a theatrical stage on the short axis. The facade of the church was magnificently set in relation to the street: a canopy atop two Ionic columns juts far out from the front of the church, while concave flanking walls create a conceptual forecourt. Bernini's most important secular building, the Palazzo Chigi-Odescalchi, dates back to 1664–1665. The remodeling of the Pons Aelius into the baroque Sant'Angelo Bridge, which was reinterpreted as a crossroad (Via Crucis, or way of the cross) leading to St Peter's, coincided with the pontificate of Clement IX.

Francesco Borromini was in his twenties when he arrived in Rome, where he worked as a stonemason at the St Peter's construction site. When Bernini took over as head of papal projects, this sparked off a lifelong rivalry between the two artists. Borromini went off in search of new patrons. He created his first masterpiece, the church of San Carlo alle Quattro Fontane, for the Discalced Trinitarians. The interior space, both brilliant and bewildering, and the billowing, concave-convex-concave facade "moved" the architecture in every sense of the word. In the collegiate church of Sant'Ivo alla Sapienza, Borromini increased the plasticity of his architecture further still. Its facade, recessed into Giacomo della Porta's narrow courtyard, is shaped like an exedra, while the domed church itself rises up in a contrary motion behind it. The walls of the central

◄ Rome, San Carlo alle Quattro Fontane (San Carlino), Francesco Borromini, facade, 1665–1667.

▲ Rome, San Andrea al Quirinale, Gianlorenzo Bernini, facade, 1658–1661.

interior dissolve into niches, balconies and apses.

Innocent X preferred Borromini over Bernini and assigned him the renovation of the Constantinian basilica of St John Lateran. After 1653, Borromini led the work on Sant'Agnese in Piazza Navona, a church that belonged to the pope's family palace. There were fierce arguments over the layout of the ensemble, and Borromini was again forced to vacate his post. However, he did complete the interior to a large extent, along with other aspects such as the generously curved, twin-towered facade.

▼ ▶ Rome, San Ivo alla Sapienza, Francesco Borromini, begun 1643, view into the dome; courtyard with facade of the University Church.

The Rivalry Between Bernini and Borromini

The rivalry between the urbane sculptor and architect Gianlorenzo Bernini (1598–1680) and the taciturn Francesco Castelli (1599–1667), called Borromini, who was originally trained as a stonemason, gave rise to numerous legends and much speculation. During construction of the baldachin and clock towers of St Peter's, a breach must have occurred between Borromini and Bernini, who headed up papal projects from 1629 onward. What followed was a volatile, lifelong battle for Curial commissions and papal favor that only ended with Borromini's suicide in 1667. Over and above personal motives and differences in the men's temperaments, their conflict is also an expression of the divergent artistic currents in baroque Rome: academic classical invention (Bernini) as opposed to technical perfection and visionary creativity.

The City as a Stage

In the baroque period, even city planning was subject to the principles of theatrical staging. Sixtus V used them in the service of religion by connecting Rome's seven Early Christian basilicas to one another via wide processional routes, which he had scenically embellished with obelisks and fountains. Bernini's St Peter's Square also owes its sublime effect to scenic staging. The oval of the Piazza Obliqua with its Doric colonnades welcomes streams of pilgrims, just as the Church opens her arms to the faithful. The setting narrows in the direction of St Peter's toward the trapezoidal Piazza Retta, on higher terrain, making it an appropriate "pedestal" for Maderno's facade. The Piazza Navona, too, once the site of Domitian's stadium (Circus Domitianus), became a dynastic festival ground.

Late baroque and *barochetto*, the Roman version of rococo, preferred intimate scenarios. The Spanish Steps, a graceful design of Francesco de Sanctis, are an example of this. Setting off in three sections, they wind their way upward to the scenic facade of the church of Trinità dei Monti. At the Fontana di Trevi (Trevi Fountain), the display wall is constructed like a triumphal arch, displaying the new rationality and clarity. Nicola Salvi's work combines the backdrop of the fountain with the palace facade.

◀ (top) Rome, Piazza del Popolo; view toward Via Babuino, Via del Corso and Via Ripetta with twin churches of Santa Maria in Monsanto and Santa Maria dei Miracoli.

◀ Rome, Fontana di Trevi, Nicola Salvi, with facade of Palazzo Poli, 1732–1762.

◀ (left) Rome, Piazza Navona with Santa Agnese.

▶ Rome, Spanish Steps, Alessandro Specchi and Francesco de Sanctis, 1723–1726.

Sacred Architecture North of the Alps

Seventeenth-century church architecture north of the Alps is highly diversified. The Reformation, initiated in 1517, and the religious wars that ensued divided Europe not only along religious and political lines, but along cultural and stylistic ones, as well.

The Jesuit church of St Michael in Munich, a powerful expression of Counter Reformational trends on German soil, may be viewed as the earliest example of the baroque in the Holy Roman Empire. In this work by an unknown architect, commissioned by William V, Duke of Bavaria, the unifying spatial structure of Rome's Il Gesù is combined with indigenous pier church architecture. The pier church would reach its culmination during the late baroque period.

The construction of the new Salzburg Cathedral, on the other hand, which was begun by Santino Solari in 1614, demonstrated other impulses. This design combines a domed church with a triconch arrangement. But the main focus here was the interior, which was decorated with opulent stucco work that underscored the architecture. This is another characteristic that would be developed to the highest level of artistic maturity in the eighteenth century.

The Netherlands experienced an economic and cultural blossoming in the first half of the seventeenth century that encompassed both the Calvinistic north of the country and

▲ Munich, St Michael's Church, 1583–1597, view toward the nave.

▲ Salzburg Cathedral, Santino Solari, begun in 1614, view toward the nave.

the Catholic south. While Flemish architecture remained true to the Counter Reformation type, the architecture of the northern provinces developed in a different direction, one that resulted in a radical rethinking of sacred architecture. Thus, Amsterdam's Noorderkerk (North Church), for example, begun in 1620, embodies the ideal of the Calvinistic preacher's church that would become obligatory for the entire Protestant world. The dominant motif is the central space, whose geometric elements—square, octagon, circle or Greek cross—emphasized sobriety and systematic clarity. The pulpit and baptistery stand at the center, with the seating arranged around them as in a theater.

In England, the Anglican Church (a Protestant state religion) sought its own, unique solutions to ecclesiastical architecture. This makes it all the more surprising that after the Great Fire of London destroyed Old St Paul's Cathedral in 1666, Christopher Wren presented a blueprint for the new St Paul's that clearly demonstrates

▲ London, St Paul's Cathedral, Sir Christopher Wren, 1675–1711.

◀ Amsterdam, Noorderkerk, Hendrick de Keyser, 1620–1623.

a relationship to St Peter's in Rome. His Great Model of 1673 bears comparison with Michelangelo's centrally planned domed building. After many compromises and changes to the plans, what was actually built is a traditional long plan, crowned with a gigantic double-shell dome (364 ft/ 111 m high) above the crossing. The main facade, facing west, combines a two-story portico with paired Corinthian columns and flanking towers, based on the new facade of the Louvre in Paris.

Architectural Theory and Drafting

Naturally, critical engagement with the ideas of Vitruvius had an impact on architectural theory of the baroque period, but a more thorough scientific understanding and practicality were also called for. The learned Theatine priest Guarino Guarini provided both. Admired equally as a philosopher and an architect, he published a wide range of treatises, the most important of

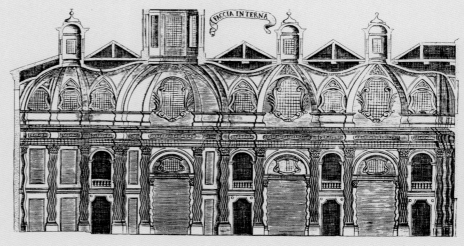

▲ Guarino Guarini, *Disegni di architettura civile*, Turin, 1686, Church of Divine Providence, Lisbon, cross section.

▲ François Blondel, *Cours d'architecture*, 1675–1683, frontispiece: Porte-St-Denis, Paris.

▶ Johann Bernhard Fischer von Erlach, *Entwurff einer Historischen Architektur*, 1721, Mount Athos.

which was *Architettura Civile*. Engravings from this work were circulated throughout Europe even prior to its publication. In contrast to earlier theoreticians, Guarini granted that architecture, and thus column order, possess a certain mutability. Classical antiquity was no longer the sole, standard-setting authority. The mathematician François Blondel, who would ascend to become the leading architectural theorist of absolutist France, also demanded a change in the Vitruvian canon of the column. The laws of nature, as well as *bon goût* (good taste) that all intelligent men possess, were the leitmotifs of his designs. Between 1675 and 1683, Blondel published the five-part *Cours d'architecture*, which he dedicated to Louis XIV.

Among the German literature on architecture, Paulus Decker's *Fürstlicher Baumeister* (The Princely Architect, 1721) may have garnered the most attention. Also highly successful was Johann Fischer von Erlach's *Entwurff einer Historischen Architektur* (An Outline of Historic Architecture, also published in 1721). This work is not a treatise, but rather the first comparative worldwide history of architecture. In England, Colin Campbell's *Vitruvius Britannicus* was the most influential work of its time. Appearing in three volumes between 1715 and 1725, it praised the work of Palladio and recognized it as the apogee of architectural achievement. At the same time, Campbell sought to improve Palladio's specifications

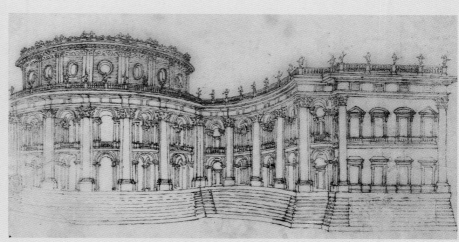

▲ Giuseppe Galli Bibiena, *Architetture e Prospettive*, 1740, *scena per angolo* (oblique view).

▲ Gianlorenzo Bernini, the first project for the Paris Louvre, 1664.

▼ Filippo Juvarra, competition drawing for the Accademia di San Luca, 1705, *Palace for Three Personages*.

selectively, and to adapt his work to British requirements.

During this period, architectural drawing gained increasing importance and independence. Drawings could serve as a means of presenting designs, as in the case of Bernini's Louvre sketches or Filippo Juvarra's competition entries for the Roman Accademia di San Luca. They were also a practical way of documenting the current state of a building or of its reconstruction. The character of architectural drawings could vary depending on whether they concerned reality or fantasy: the set designs of the Galli-Bibiena family or Giovanni Battista Piranesi's *capricci* are especially good testaments to the latter, demonstrating the immense power of imagination and the artistic freedom of their creators.

The quality of a drawing was determined by its purpose. While a sketch might be sufficient to record the creators' main ideas, blueprints had to be made with the utmost precision so that they could be used at construction sites.

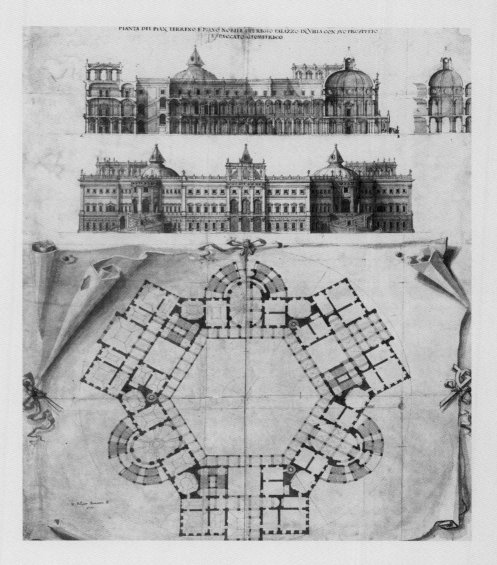

Paris

The urban complexes of King Henry IV formed the prelude to Parisian baroque architecture. Great care was taken to create a "new" city, one that would serve as a reflection of absolutist power. An intensive search for new solutions to traditional architectural enterprises began during the reign of Louis XIII and is evident in the clearly arranged blocks of Luxembourg Palace.

The Church of the Sorbonne with its courtyard facade is a milestone in the development of French baroque classicism. The picturesque and theatrical progression from the temple facade through the triumphal arch and hipped roof to the dome resting on its drum is an utterly willful fusion of classical and baroque elements.

Dominant cupolas became characteristic of nearly all Parisian churches. Val-de-Grâce thus acquired a tower-like dome on drum. A similarly majestic dome rises above the church of the Collège des Quatre Nations. The most fully developed French baroque building was produced by Jules Hardouin-Mansart, who designed Les Invalides. Consecrated in 1706, this church displays a stunning

▲ Paris, Church of the Sorbonne, Jacques Lemercier, begun 1626, courtyard facade.

▶ Paris, Les Invalides, Libéral Bruant and Jules Hardouin-Mansart, 1677–1706.

synthesis of two architectural elements: the block-like lower structure with its portal frontispiece, and the colossal dome on its drum, which is reminiscent of St Peter's.

Art was drafted into the service of the state when Louis XIV took the reins of power in 1661. All artistic production was controlled by the head of the *Académie* and *Surintendant des Batiments* (Superintendent of Buildings), Jean Baptist Colbert. His overriding concern was the expansion of the Louvre, which still lacked a prestigious facade overlooking the city. Although the most renowned architects, Bernini among them, delivered proposals, the eastern facade was finally completed according to a design by Claude Perrault, a doctor and mathematician. The facade is characterized by a sequence of widely spaced, paired Corinthian columns that lend it a solemn gravity.

◀ Paris, Louvre, east facade, Claude Perrault, 1667–1668.

Versailles

The Chateau de Versailles is the culmination of European palace architecture and a powerful symbol of absolute power. The expansion of this former hunting lodge began in 1668. Louis XIV called on the likes of Le Vau, Le Brun and Le Nôtre, the same team that had recently developed new ideas at Vaux-le-Vicomte. The highest priority was accorded the elevations of the main building, whose wide terrace opened out onto the gardens. The next step was to establish the axis system, and finally, the sprawling park surrounding the palace was designed. The king decided to move the imperial residence to Versailles in 1677–1678, an act that involved enormous planning, since the entire court was also compelled to relocate.

Jules Hardouin-Mansart, who would lead the construction for thirty years, completed the garden elevation first, where he set up a grandiose mirror gallery (the Hall of Mirrors) in lieu of a terrace. Salons glorifying the military victories of the king lie at either end of it. The king's apartments were located in the old core building. His bedroom was placed at the center,

▲ Palace of Versailles, marble courtyard, Philibert Le Roy, Louis Le Vau and Jules Hardouin-Mansart, 1631–1668.

▼ Palace of Versailles, garden facade, Louis Le Vau and Jules Hardouin-Mansart, begun in 1668.

precisely on the east-west axis, because the course of the king's day was meant to follow that of the sun. Hardouin-Mansart provided the three-winged central building (which enclosed the marble courtyard dating back to the time of Louis XIII) with

additional north and south wings that surrounded a second courtyard, the Cour Royale. The palace chapel, begun by Hardouin-Mansart in 1689 and completed by Robert de Cotte in 1710, synthesized elements of classical, medieval and baroque styles.

▲ Palace of Versailles, Hall of Mirrors, Jules Hardouin-Mansart and Charles Le Brun, begun 1679.

▲ Palace of Versailles, palace chapel, François Mansart and Robert de Cotte, 1689–1710.

The Court of the Sun King

The court of Louis XIV was understood as a mirror image of the cosmos. The king reigned as both Jupiter and Apollo (i.e., the sun shining over all that is), and was also patron of the arts and guardian of the peace. Complex iconography was used to express metaphorical content. However, the king himself was the most important symbol. His entire day paralleled the course and effects of the sun.

Every activity, even a walk in the gardens, became a symbolic act, a metaphor for his godly epiphany. Each room in Versailles correlated with a metaphorical interpretation; a private sphere simply did not exist. Louis XIV's bedroom, where the Exaltation (arising) took place, was located in the heart of the complex. It was both a cult site and the center of power. The iconography in the Grande Galerie presents the king's glorious history, while giant mirrors reflect sunlight. The sequence of rooms and concomitant degree of accessibility was part of the rite.

The ornate park, with its lyrical features, pleasure pavilions, fountains, arbors and sculptures offered the ideal setting for grandiose festivals and staged allegories.

◀ Palace of Versailles, Louis XIV's bedroom, after 1701.

Central European Imperial Residences

Versailles was the ideal upon which nearly all imperial residences (palaces) of the late seventeenth and eighteenth centuries were modeled. Balthasar Neumann, who began his career as a cannon and bell founder and rose to became a celebrated court architect, created the most magnificent palace in the Holy Roman Empire. His influence on eighteenth-century German architecture was second to none. The Würzburg Residenz was the seat of the Franconian prince-bishops and, like Versailles, it rested within a *cour d'honneur* (reception court). The vestibule with a double staircase lies on the central axis and, behind it, the oval sala terrena (see p. 184) transitions to the garden. Unique and formidable, the stairway occupies the entire height of the palace and contains a vault measuring about 105 x 59 ft (32 x 18 m). Decorated with frescoes by Tiepolo, the vault spans the impressive ascent to the Kaisersaal (Imperial Hall).

Between 1711 and 1718, Schloss Weißenstein near Pommersfelden came into being as a friendly collaboration between Johann Dientzenhofer, Maximilian von Welsch and Johann Lukas von Hildebrandt. The architecture, the furnishing of the *corps de logis*, or main block, with a magnificent three-tier staircase, the grotto design of the sala terrena, the vestibule, and the gorgeous marble hall all set new standards.

At Schloss Augustusburg in Brühl, architects Johann Conrad Schlaun

◄ Würzburg Residence, Maximilian von Welsch, Johann Lukas von Hildebrandt, Balthasar Neumann and others, 1720–1754, staircase with ceiling frescoes by Giovanni Battista Tiepolo, 1735 and 1751–1753.

and François Cuvilliés were confronted with the difficult task of converting a moated castle into a prestigious palace. Balthasar Neumann designed the triumphal staircase with opulent, colorful marble stucco.

▲ Brühl, Schloss Augustusburg, Balthasar Neumann, 1741–1744, staircase.

▼ Schloss Weißenstein near Pommersfelden, Johann Dientzenhofer, Maximilian von Welsch, Johann Lukas von Hildebrandt, 1711–1718, view from the courtyard.

▲ Vienna, Upper Belvedere, Johann Lukas von Hildebrandt, 1721–1722.

▼ Vienna, Karlskirche, Johann Bernhard Fischer von Erlach, 1716–1737.

Vienna

After a two-month siege of Vienna by Turkish troops of the Ottoman Empire was successfully ended in 1683, Vienna experienced a period of unique artistic flowering. And so it was that Johann Bernhard Fischer von Erlach and Johann Lukas von Hildebrandt were drawn to the imperial residence, where they created their greatest works in constant competition with one another.

While Hildebrandt was head of the imperial architectural office, beginning in 1711, Fischer von Erlach built the Karlskirche (St Charles Church), the architectural symbol of the Austrian Habsburgs. Fischer's concept combined the building's votive function (the church commemorated the plague of 1713) with stately prestige. A high dome on a drum spanning the longitudinal oval of the interior is the church's dominant feature. It rises up behind the classical portico, which is framed by two antique spiral columns and compact flanking towers.

Fischer and Hildebrandt also competed against each other in the design of buildings for the Viennese nobility, as in the construction of Prince Eugene's winter palace on Himmelpfortgasse, for example.

But Hildebrandt alone was responsible for the design of Schloss Belvedere, the summer palace. Terracing of the hilly terrain had begun by 1700, and work on the lower Belvedere followed between 1714 and 1716. The Upper Belvedere was originally intended to be simply the architectural crowning touch to the extensive parks. Instead, what Hildebrandt built in 1721–1722 became the culmination of European palace architecture. The enormous edifice rises from the ascending terrain like a stage set, its silhouette impressively graduated around the main wings, which curve toward the water. In its combination of independent building blocks, the French pavilion system found its way into German architecture.

The interior of the palace is no less grandiose. Visitors are greeted by a staircase decorated with trophies, a tribute to the prince's glorious "war-and-victory cabinets" (which are the theme of the entire structure). The stairs lead up to the great hall or down to the sala terrena (see p. 184), where the vaulting is supported by stalwart Atlas figures.

The Hofbibliothek (Imperial Library) in Vienna was a late work by Fischer von Erlach. Again, the architect based his design on a large oval hall. Two barrel-vaulted rooms, dedicated to war and peace respectively, flank

▲ Vienna, Schloss Schönbrunn, Johann Bernhard Fischer von Erlach, Joseph Emmanuel Fischer von Erlach and Nikolaus Pacassi, begun 1696, garden facade.

◄ Vienna, Hofbibliothek, Johann Bernhard Fischer von Erlach, 1723–1735.

the domed central area. Pairs of Corinthian columns separate these two wings. Complex allegorical iconography reflects each wing's theme of war or peace.

If Schönbrunn had been built according to Fischer von Erlach's ideas, it might even have surpassed Versailles. His design for a hillside pleasure palace, dated 1688, represented "the sum total of all sovereign architecture" and would have brought Emperor Leopold I worldwide fame. Certainly, this grandiose early project is increasingly understood in terms of ideal planning. It may well have been empty state coffers, however, that made it necessary to realize a more modest version of his design.

◀▼ Turin, Chapel of the Most Holy Shroud, Guarino Guarini, 1668–1694, view into the dome and drawing of the dome's exterior.

▼ Caserta, La Reggia, Luigi Vanvitelli, begun 751, view of the exterior and palace grounds.

Turin and Naples

Turin was the capital of the Duchy of Savoy and, from 1720, the imperial residence of the kings of Sardinia-Piedmont. Decisive contributions to the architecture of the baroque period were made there, thanks to the work of Guarino Guarini, Filippo Juvarra and Bernardo Vittone. Guarino Guarini, a native of Modena and a Theatine monk, was known as a philosopher and mathematician before dedicating himself to architecture and architectural theory. As court architect to the dukes of Savoy, he completed the Santissima Sindone (Chapel of the Holy Shroud) at Turin Cathedral between 1668 and 1694. The irrational quality of the reliquary chapel is not only due to the black marble sheathing on the walls; the completely anomalous cupola, comprised of thirty-six segmental arches arranged in layers, is also highly evocative.

Filippo Juvarra, an exceptionally gifted architect and draftsman, entered the service of Victor Amadeus II of Savoy in 1714. It was he who provided Turin with a new face, relegating Rome to the role of a spectator. One of his early works in Turin, the Basilica di Superga, was also to be his most important. It is picturesquely situated at the summit of Superga Hill, which stands almost 3,000 ft (700 m) above the city. Endowed in 1706, the towering, centrally planned building came to serve as a mausoleum for many members of the Savoy family. Low wings with bell towers flank its

cylindrical core, and a large classical portico stands before it. An elegant dome resting on a high drum rises high above the rest of the building. With the Superga, Juvarra had seized on Roman high baroque ideas and transferred them to a new setting, the countryside.

Juvarra also devised new concepts for the Venaria Reale and Palazzina di Stupinigi hunting lodges, as well as for the summertime Rivoli Residence. The ground plan for Stupinigi extends far into its surroundings The imperial apartments are housed in the wings, which are shaped like a splayed X and meet at an extremely ornate, oval-shaped Great Hall decorated with hunting scenes.

The united kingdoms of Naples and Sicily were under the control of the Spanish crown until 1713. After that, Austria, the Savoys and, finally, the Spanish Bourbons would control the fate of southern Italy. The cityscape of Naples has remained decidedly baroque and rococo to this day. From 1750, the classicizing architects

▲ Palazzina di Stupinigi, near Turin, Filippo Juvarra, 1729–1733, Great Hall.

◄ Turin, Basilica di Superga, Filippo Juvarra, 1717–1731.

Luigi Vanvitelli and Ferdinando Fuga dominated events there.

In 1751, Vanvitelli took over leadership of the construction of the Reggia in Caserta, the palace of the Bourbon kings of Naples. It was built on a vast scale. Vanvitelli devised a floor plan with a structure similar to that of the Escorial (see p. 184). Four intersecting wings are set inside a rectangle, which thus form four spacious courtyards, around which series of rooms are grouped. The octagonal vestibule at the center of the complex is superbly executed, and opens into a tri-partite staircase.

Libraries

The construction of magnificent libraries boomed during the baroque era. The entire written and printed knowledge of the day was collected, systematized and displayed in the most opulently furnished rooms. Library interiors not only resembled royal art galleries, they were also required to be pictorial encyclopedias of sorts.

Allegorical iconography was supposed to be instructal for visitors and researchers, revealing the philosophical, historical and religious roots of knowledge, and was rendered in both painting and sculpture. The library of the royal seat of El Escorial near Madrid, the Biblioteca Ambrosiana in Milan, and the Bibliothèque Mazarine (library of Cardinal Mazarin) in Paris were the first in a series of modern, highly prestigious libraries. As a result of the rapid dissemination of printed books, architectural library expansion had a visual aspect, too. The endless rows of leather-bound volumes created their own aesthetic.

At the beginning of the eighteenth century, Fischer von Erlach's Hofbibliothek (Imperial Library, see p. 205) in Vienna had set new standards. Thereafter, it was mainly monasteries that adorned themselves with magnificently conceptualized "halls of knowledge." Usually placed in elongated halls above the refectory, they appealed not only to observers' scholarly nature, but also to their aesthetic sense.

Many of these splendid buildings have been preserved, especially in the Alpine region, but the Strahov Monastery in Prague and the University of Coimbra in northern Portugal also have impressively designed libraries. Among the highpoints of Swabian rococo architecture is the Wiblingen Abbey library near Ulm. A gallery of varying widths, resting on thirty-two wooden columns, creates a sense of movement within the space. Blue-green, red, white and gold are the dominant colors. The Benedictine monastery library in St Gall was built around 1760. This, too, is a two-storied space dynamically articulated with massive piers and an encircling gallery. Over 2,000 manuscripts and 100,000 printed books are preserved there.

The circular construction of the Radcliffe Camera in Oxford is a special case, a genuine "temple of learning." The domed building rests on a rusticated base, while pairs of engaged Corinthian columns articulate the facade. This centrally planned building—which could possibly be a reference to the Wolfenbüttel Hofbibliothek—recalls works by Sir Christopher Wren.

▶ Wiblingen Abbey near Ulm, library, Christian and Johann Rudolf Wiedemann, 1737–1740.

◀ Oxford, Radcliffe Camera, James Gibbs, 1737–1749.

▶ St Gall Abbey, library, new construction from 1755, interior design by Gabriel Loser.

England

A fundamentally new, self-consciously mannerist style was introduced to late Renaissance architecture in England by stage designer Inigo Jones and the young Earl of Arundel, both of whom had studied in Italy. The Queen's House, the cornerstone of which was laid in 1616, serves as a clear example of this abrupt change. Located in Greenwich, it consists of two rectangular blocks joined by a bridge. The *piano nobile* (the main floor) soars above the rusticated ground floor and opens on the garden side with a wide, columned loggia. Apart from Inigo Jones, there were few important British architects. One of them was John Webb, who was related to Jones by marriage. Large parts of Winton House, including the elegant Cube and Double Cube state rooms, are credited to Webb in collaboration with Jones and the French landscape designer Isaac de Caus.

With Christopher Wren, classicism with a strong Roman flavor was finally established in England. After the Great Fire of London in 1666, Wren and his

colleagues were commissioned to suggest ideas for the extensive reconstruction that was needed. The new St Paul's Cathedral and fifty-one other sacred buildings are largely their work. Hampton Court, the summer palace of the English royal family, was commissioned by King William III and his wife, Mary, and was built between 1689 and 1692.

John Vanbrugh and Nicholas Hawksmoore augmented Wren's

▲▼ Greenwich, The Queen's House, Inigo Jones, 1616–1635, view into the inner courtyards; view of the exterior.

style in more monumental, yet also essentially picturesque ways. From 1699, they were commissioned to build Castle Howard. The *entre cour et jardin* layout (see p. 185) consists of a corridor-like apartment wing, the middle of which features a salon that opens onto the gardens, and a square great hall that faces the courtyard.

Vitruvius Britannicus came out in two volumes, in 1715 and 1717, and contained engravings of classic English buildings and a translation of Palladio's *Quattro Libri dell'Archittetura*. These volumes initiated another significant change in style, to neopalladianism, the goal of which was a return to the "right and noble rules" of antiquity, as interpreted by Palladio and rendered in the works of Inigo Jones. An important champion of this movement was the art connoisseur Lord Burlington, who came astoundingly close to the works of Palladio in his design for Chiswick House (see p. 232).

▲▲ Hampton Court Palace, Sir Christopher Wren, 1689–1692.

▲ Yorkshire, Castle Howard, Sir John Vanbrugh and Nicholas Hawksmoore, 1699–1712.

◄◄ Wiltshire, Wilton House, John Webb, Inigo Jones and Isaac de Caus (?), begun 1632, renovated after a fire in 1647, view of "The Double Cube."

◄ Oxfordshire, Blenheim Palace, Sir John Vanbrugh and Nicholas Hawksmoore, 1705–1724, detail of the facade.

◄ Jülich, Germany, citadel, Alessandro Pasqualini, 1549–1555.

Advances in defensive building also had an effect on civilian architecture. There was a tremendous boom in street and bridge construction from the sixteenth to the eighteenth centuries. Old wooden bridges were replaced with stone ones, and bridge building generally came to be regarded as an artistic enterprise. The design of the Castel Sant'Angelo Bridge in Rome, the marble Ponte Santa Trinità in Florence and the Pont Neuf in Paris are eloquent testaments to the art form.

Prior to its destruction, the Old Bridge in Mostar, Bosnia and Herzegovina (completed in 1566) was the longest single-span arched bridge in the world. It was the work of the Ottoman architect Mimar Hajrudin. All the most important architects of the late sixteenth century were involved in designing the Rialto Bridge in Venice, made of stone and lined with shops. The commission was finally given to architect-engineer Antonio da Ponte. Presumably, he alone was trusted to successfully build the bridge, which rested on unstable ground.

Fortresses and Architectural Engineering

The invention of firearms in the fifteenth and sixteenth centuries inevitably revolutionized the construction of fortresses and other defensive structures. Engineers and theoreticians, among them Albrecht Dürer, devised new "manners," systems that were intended to facilitate the defense of cities, castles and palaces. The bastion was an essential step in the direction of modern fortress complexes. Triangular projections in their walls allowed cannons to fire unimpeded by blind corners.

Both the town and the citadel of Jülich, Germany, are important examples of German defensive construction. These were developed during the second half of the sixteenth century, probably by Alessandro Pasqualini, a native of Bologna. The grid-like ideal city with its roughly hexagonal belt of

walls and bastions is certainly noteworthy, while the citadel and palace of Duke William V of Bavaria, Trausnitz Castle in Landshut, retained a Renaissance appearance. This square complex is also protected by bastions. In the seventeenth and eighteenth centuries, fortress architecture was perfected and adapted to regional needs. The most important theoretician and architect was Sébastien le Prestre de Vauban.

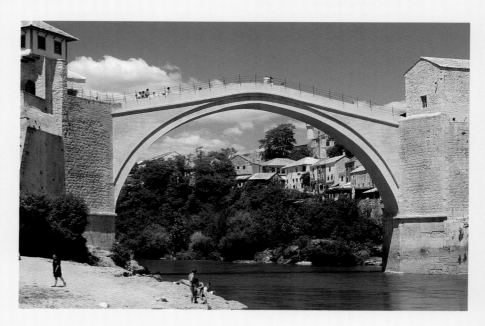

▶ Mostar, Old Bridge, Mimar Hajrudin, completed 1566, rebuilt 1996–2004 after its destruction in 1993.

Sébastien le Prestre de Vauban

Sébastien le Prestre de Vauban (1633–1707) was the most famous fortress designer of the baroque era. At the age of seventeen, he was already an engineer in the Spanish army. After being taken prisoner by the French in 1653, he found work as an engineering officer. Louis XIV appointed him architect and city planner, and he rose to become Marshal of France in 1703. Vauban is credited with over 400 projects and renovations, as well as thirty-three fortresses that he "personally" built. These were chiefly characterized by the further development of Renaissance methods and their adaptation to local conditions. Vauban's three systems of fortification were fundamental to military knowledge of the time. Several of his defensive compounds were still used in World War I. The Lille, Maubeuge and Neuf-Brisach fortresses are among Vauban's best-known works.

The latter was conceived as an octagonal grid city within a triple, star-shaped system of defense. Curtain walls and covered passages connect the bastions and ravelins (triangular outer fortifications). The Place d'Armes forms the center of the uniformly built city.

▲ Neuf-Brisach, Sébastien Le Prestre Marquis de Vauban, 1706, scale model, Paris, Musée des Plans Reliefs.

▼ Blaye, Gironde, Citadelle Vauban de Blaye, Sébastien Le Prestre Marquis de Vauban, 1685–1689, detail of the city fortification.

Rococo Architecture

Eighteenth-century art has many aspects, the loveliest of which is undoubtedly that of the *rococo*. Its essential buoyancy, playful charm, eroticism and exoticism enchanted all who dreamed of a return to a lost paradise. The term rococo first appeared in literature around the end of the eighteenth century. Initially, however, it was used derisively to describe excessive ornamentation.

Rococo architecture spanned the period between approximately 1710 and 1760. The artistic impulse for this new style originated around the beginning of the eighteenth century in France, where a new attitude toward life asserted itself as an antidote to the pathos and theatricality of the high baroque era. The rococo began

▼ Dresden, Zwinger Palace with Wall Pavilion, Matthäus Daniel Pöppelmann, 1709–1728.

▲ Birnau, Liebfrauenkirche, Peter Thumb (architect) and Johann Anton Feuchtmayer (stuccowork), 1745–1751.

as a decorative style that freed the high baroque from its structural stays (its "corset"). In the beginning, only interiors were ornamented—as in the Hôtel de Rohan-Soubise (see p. 216)—which was completely covered with a delicate web of stucco filigree. Outside of France, surface decoration was soon transferred to the exteriors

of buildings as well. The architect Matthäus Daniel Pöppelmann and sculptor Balthasar Permoser created the Zwinger Palace in Dresden, a grandiose rococo structure that was built between 1709 and 1728. Originally a jousting arena, its wooden architecture was carried over into the stone structure. Little by little, the impressively ornate "royal festival grounds" came into being. Unfortunately, due to lack of funds, only the nearly square courtyard with its pavilions and connecting galleries, as well as the exedras, were completed. At each end, Pöppelmann erected a delicate oval building: the Carillon and the Wall Pavilion. Today, these sumptuous facilities house the art collections of the Saxon princes.

Despite changes to the original concept, the Zwinger has retained

its theatrical character. It is an Arcadian building, an idyllic dream about communing with nature. Smiling herms, male pillar-like figures, carry the weight of the Wall Pavilion entablature. Satyrs, fauns and floral shapes enliven the cornices, while Hercules supports the globe. Nymphs bathe in an artificial grotto.

Frederick II, the philosopher-king responsible for creating Sanssouci, in Potsdam, outside Berlin, had his pleasure palace built in a vineyard instead (see p. 217). The Chinese Tea Pavilion, whose figures were created by Johann Peter Benckert and Matthias Gottlieb Heymüller, strikes a different note. This is where passionate admiration for Asian art and the longing for the exotic found their monumental analogues.

Churches could also afford beguiling furnishings. St Peter und Paul in Steinhausen, along with the Wieskirche (Meadow Church) and Vierzehnheiligen (Fourteen Saints), became the quintessence of exuberant, joyful decoration (see pp. 220–221). Swabian architecture and decorative arts reached their zenith in the Wallfahrtskirche (Pilgrimmage Church) in Birnau on Lake Constance, where Peter Thumb and sculptor-stucco work master Johann Anton Feuchtmayer created a lavishly resplendent sanctuary.

Cityscapes also reflected the new attitude toward life. Nancy, in the Lorraine region of France, for example transformed itself into a graceful rococo ducal seat under the direction of Emmanuel Héré de Corny.

City palace complexes wavered between refinement and utilitarian considerations. The Erbdrostenhof in Münster, built between 1753 and 1757 by Johann Conrad Schlaun for Baron Droste zu Vischering, is an outstanding German example.

◀ Potsdam, Sanssouci, Tea Pavilion in the palace gardens, Johann Peter Benckert and Matthias Gottlieb Heymüller, 1754.

▼ Nancy, Place Royale (today Place Stanislas), Emmanuel Héré de Corny, 1752, fountain and wrought iron gate by Jean Lamour.

▼▼ Münster, Erbdrostenhof, Johann Conrad Schlaun, 1753–1757, facade.

▲ Paris, Hôtel de Rohan-Soubise, Salon de la Princesse de Soubise, Germain Boffrand and Charles Joseph Natoire, 1735.

▼ Schloss Clemenswerth near Sögel, Johann Conrad Schlaun, 1736–1750.

Hôtels and Pleasure Palaces

Following the pathos and theatricality of the high baroque period, the nobility and bourgeoisie sought a more refined private lifestyle, individual freedom and intimacy. Nature offered suitable opportunities for retreat and, at least in a tamed form, began to quite literally "overgrow" the strict order of the baroque period. In terms of art and architecture, this is more apparent in the fittings of the Hôtel de Rohan-Soubise in Paris than anywhere else. The walls here are entirely covered in a delicate web of filigree stucco.

This foliate decoration disguises the transition between wall and ceiling, creating the illusion of a larger space. Shellwork takes on a framing role, among other things, and makes its triumphal march in the form of *rocaille* (artificial rockwork).

But the retreat into privacy and the natural world was not limited to interior decoration. New types of buildings came into being, namely *maisons de plaisance* (pleasure palaces), and older structures, such as the French *hôtels* (city palaces) and villas on the outskirts of town received a facelift.

The rococo attitude toward life was also embraced by crowned rulers. A wonderful example of this is Schloss Sanssouci near Potsdam, which King Frederick II (the Great) of Prussia had built as a vineyard palace. Plans for the light-hearted, comfortably situated structure were drawn up by the king himself. The idyllically elegant interior decoration, imitate foliage, vines and birds, are constantly reminding the visitor of the nearness of nature.

François de Cuvilliés, born in Belgium, became the greatest master of the rococo in Bavaria. He produced a truly enchanting work in the ballroom of the Amalienburg hunting lodge in Munich's Nymphenburg Park. An exquisite web of light blue and silver stucco covers the walls and ceilings, reflected many times over in the great crystal mirrors that infinitely expand the circular room.

Schloss Clemenswerth, a hunting lodge near Sögel, in northwestern Germany, has an entirely different character. Westphalian architect Johann Conrad Schlaun designed the complex as a series of pavilions, almost like a "stone encampment." But Schlaun's greatest work is the Erbdrostenhof in Münster, a city palace that has been cleverly adapted to accommodate an unusual triangular cour d'honneur (see p. 203).

▲ Munich, Amalienburg in Schloss Nymphenburg Park, François de Cuvilliés, 1734–1739, view of the interior.

▼ Potsdam, Schloss Sanssouci, Georg Wenzeslaus von Knobelsdorff, 1745–1747, detail of the facade.

◀ Neresheim Abbey
Church, Balthasar Neumann,
begun 1745, interior.

▶ Benedictine Abbey
of Melk, Austria, Jakob
Prandtauer and Joseph
Mungenast, begun 1701.

▼ Benedictine Abbey of
Einsiedeln, Switzerland,
Hans Georg Kuen, Kaspar
Moosbrugger and others,
new plans begun 1691,
construction from 1719,
view into the choir (begun
1674).

Abbeys and Monasteries

The splendor of imperial residences also had an effect on the architecture of abbeys and monasteries. Abbots and prelates cultivated patronage, just as worldly princes did.

Entirely rebuilt as a Benedictine monastery in 1702, Melk Abbey on the Danube is a unique ensemble in its integration with the countryside, its functionality and its symbolism. The picturesque, twin-towered facade of the domed church rises majestically above a steep rocky spur in the Danube valley. A balcony at the front provides a magnificent view of the countryside. Marvelous monasteries also sprang up in Bavaria and Swabia, including those in Weingarten, Zwiefalten and Ottobeuren.

The Vorarlberg school, founded in 1657 in Austria, was responsible for the enormous upswing in church construction in southern and southwestern Germany. In friendly collaboration with the Wessobrunn stucco artists, the Vorarlberg group determined the

course of architectural events in much of the German-speaking region. The Vorarlbergers preferred pier churches with chapel niches and galleries, and provided them with glistening, bright stucco decoration. The clear longitudinal alignment of the buildings gradually gave way to vibrant centralized spaces.

Neresheim abbey church glistens in cool white and is the legacy of Balthasar Neumann. Its slender, freestanding columns make it an architectural and aesthetic masterpiece.

With the Einsiedeln abbey church, Caspar Moosbrugger achieved a synthesis of centralized and longitudinal spaces. Behind the bowed, twin-towered facade, the interior forms an octagon containing the Chapel of Grace, followed by the transept-like pulpit area and the light-filled dome with frescoes by Cosmas Damian Asam. An illusionistic choir gate separates the public space from the choir.

◀ Wieskirche near Steingaden, Dominikus Zimmermann, 1745–1754, view into choir.

▶▶ Staffelstein near Bamberg, Vierzehnheiligen, Balthasar Neumann, 1743–1772, facade and interior view with the Gnadenaltar (altar shrine).

▼ Steinhausen, St Peter and Paul, Dominikus Zimmermann, begun 1727, view of the interior.

mistakes made by his building manager, Neumann superimposed a virtuoso floor plan of ovals and circles on the existing foundation walls. The heart of this plan forms the saints' sanctuary with the scenographic altar of the *nothelfer* (helpers in time of need)—the famed Gnadenaltar.

Pilgrimage Churches

From the late seventeenth century, there was renewed interest in pilgrimages. Miraculous holy images gave rise to splendid buildings and theatrically staged spaces.

The pilgrimage church of Steinhausen is garbed in solemn white. Dominikus Zimmermann gave it an elliptical ground plan with ten freestanding piers placed around it to support the groin vault. In 1738, a miracle happened in the home of a farmer's wife in Weis: an unpretentious statue of Christ began to weep. Responding to the stream of pilgrims, the neighboring abbey of Steingaden decided to build a pilgrimage church and commissioned Zimmermann with the design. Built to an approximately elliptical floor plan, the church reveals the sensuousness of the rococo as no other. The architecture, stucco work, sculptures and paintings are all part of a celestial ensemble.

Balthasar Neumann's pilgrimage church Vierzehnheiligen (Fourteen Saints) represents a clever solution to an emergency. In order to correct

◄ Prague, Villa Amerika, Kilian Ignaz Dientzenhofer, 1717–1720.

Architectural Dynasties

Architectural dynasties have shaped the development of the art of building since the Middle Ages. So it was that members of the Dientzenhofer family, originally from Upper Bavaria, created an unmistakable style that made the baroque architecture from Bamberg to Prague famous around the world.

Georg Dientzenhofer, the oldest of the clan, settled in Waldsassen around 1682, where he built the pilgrimage church of Kappel and subsequently worked in Bamberg. His brother Christoph remained in Bohemia for his entire life. His greatest works, St Nicholas Church in Prague's Mala Strana district and the church of St Margaret in Brevnov Monastery, display a knowledge of Guarino Guarini's œuvre in terms of their dynamic spatial organization, skilled vault construction and lively articulation of the facade. Christoph and his son, Kilian Ignaz, worked together on the Loreto Monastery in Prague.

Johann Dientzenhofer's path led from Prague by way of Fulda to Bamberg, where the powerful prince bishop Lothar Franz von Schönborn appointed him court architect in 1711. He built Fulda Cathedral, a magnificent church, in emulation of Il Gesù in Rome. But at the Benedictine abbey church of Banz, lying high on a bank above the Main River,

▼ Fulda Cathedral, Johann Dientzenhofer, 1704–1713.

▼ Prague, St Margaret's Church, Christoph Dientzenhofer, 1708–1721.

► Rohr (Lower Bavaria), monastery church, Assumption of the Virgin, Egid Quirin Asam, 1723.

the most obvious influence is Guarini's, as the elliptical bays of the nave alternate with those of the vault, and the space appears to be poised in the midst of soft undulations.

Kilian Ignaz Dientzenhofer also belonged to a new generation of artists. Trips to Vienna and study with Lukas von Hildebrandt gave him a broad knowledge of Austrian architecture, as is clearly seen in the Villa Amerika on the outskirts of Prague. The churches of St Mary Magdalene in Karlovy Vary and St Johann Nepomuk on the Rock in Prague are among the most beautiful rococo sacred buildings in Bohemia.

The Asam brothers, painter-architect Cosmas Damian and plasterer-sculptor Egid Quirin, were undoubtedly the most gifted and versatile artists of the German rococo, if not in all of Europe. Educated in Rome, they returned to Bavaria in 1714 to produce their scenographic and mystical masterpieces. Reality and illusion merge in their works. Through the harmonious use of all genres, the Asams created quintessential baroque *gesamtkunstwerke* (total artworks), for example in the church of Weltenburg Abbey with its dramatic altar staging of St George and its cupola frescoes. The altar of the monastic Church of the Assumption in Rohr is just as impressive, as is the one at the "Asam Church" (i.e., St Johann Nepomuk) in Munich, which served as a private chapel and burial place for Egid Quirin and was built alongside the Munich home of the Asam family of artists.

► ►► Munich, St Johann Nepomuk (also called Asamkirche),Egid Quirin Asam and Cosmas Damian Asam, 1733–1746, facade and interior.

The Baroque in Spain

Around the middle of the seventeenth century, other regions of Spain began to emerge from the shadow of the royal court. This architecture signaled a departure from the Herrerianism that characterized the Escorial (see p. 184).

Architectural developments in Galicia culminated in the building of a new cathedral facade in Santiago de Compostela, designed by Fernando de Casas y Novoa. The task demanded the highest aesthetic and engineering standards. The new facade was intended to cover and protect the twelfth-century, Romanesque Portico de la Gloria. Furthermore, it had to incorporate the baroque flight of steps on which work had already begun. Casas y Novoa responded to these challenging parameters by concealing the Romanesque portal behind the facade, which consisted of three bays flanked by two towers. In addition, he opened up the front by means of gigantic windows, a masterful technical achievement. The dynamic vertical articulation of columns placed on top of another, the staggered placement of the towers and central gable, and the filigreed dissolution of the wall reminded his contemporaries of goldsmithery, such that they called it *la fachada del obradoiro* (the workshop facade).

Central Spain was the province of the Churriguera family of artists, whose name would become a synonym for morbidly ornate decor in the nineteenth century. In fact, the retable of St Stephen in Salamanca was an architectural and sculptural gesamtkunstwerk that was formative of the architectural aesthetic of eighteenth-century Spain. Its theatrical design, profuse ornamentation and bold use of Salomonic (twisted) columns and *estípite* (a type of baluster) became the prototype for the exuberant decoration of Spanish facades. The Plaza Mayor in Salamanca, on the other hand, displays signs of the delicate balance and refinement associated with French *Places Royales*.

The most idiosyncratic and magnificent achievement of Spanish baroque architecture can be seen in the lavish interiors of two Carthusian monasteries. Their creator was Francisco de Hurtado Izquierdo. Derived from classical elements that were prismatically broken apart and replicated, his decorative forms continued to influence Andalusian and Spanish colonial architecture for decades.

Hurtado's first groundbreaking work was the sagrario for the Monasterio de la Cartuja, Granada's Carthusian monastery. He conceived the tabernacle as a colossal shrine whose "reliquary" was a square, dome-vaulted space. In 1718, Hurtado designed another sagrario for the Carthusians of

▲ Salamanca, Plaza Mayor, Alberto de Churriguera and Andrés García de Quiñones, 1728–1755.

▶ Santiago de Compostela, Fernando de Casas y Novoa, 1738, facade.

◀◀ Granada, La Cartuja Monastery, Francisco de Hurtado Izquierdo, 1702–1720, sagrario.

◀ Toledo Cathedral, *El Transparente*, Narciso Tomé, 1721–1732.

El Paular that was based on its predecessor in Granada. Finally, Narciso Tomé's *El Transparente* in the Toledo Cathedral also deserves mention. These are monumental tabernacles or monstrances, both enshrining and displaying the Host (communion wafer). Massive cousins of the heavily bejeweled reliquaries and monstrances found elsewhere in Europe, these distinctively Spanish architectural versions masterfully unite a great many artistic genres.

Neoclassicism and Romanticism

The buildings of ancient Rome and above all ancient Greece were the prototypes for neoclassical architecture. The name implies monumentality, strict proportions and severe, unadorned forms. Johann Joachim Winckelmann, a pioneering art historian, praised the classical ideal as embodying "noble simplicity and quiet grandeur." Neoclassical architecture was valued as a highly rational, conceptually perfect mirror of a new age governed by reason.

This interest in ancient architecture did not come out of nowhere. In England it took the form of neopalladianism, buildings with structural details reminiscent of the work Andrea Palladio (1508–1580), the Italian architect whose writings had kept classicism alive during the baroque era. Excavations of Herculaneum (1711) and Pompeii (1748) also renewed interest in all things classical, as did the travels of learned men, many British, who first presented to the

▲ Bordeaux, facade of the Grand Théâtre, Victor Louis, 1772–1780.

general public the largely unknown monuments of the ancient Greek world. In France, interest in new variations on the ancient architectural canon had a strong theoretical foundation. In his famous *Essay on Architecture*, the Jesuit Marc-Antoine Laugier called for a return to the original "pure" architecture. His work appeared around the same time as philosopher Jean Jacques Rousseau's theory of Natural Man, which emphasized mankind's

innate capacity for freedom of expression. The yearning for antiquity further expressed itself in a second movement that developed parallel to neoclassicism. Romanticism was often deeply rooted in the rediscovery of national identity. A veritable flood of archaeological and sociopolitical literature followed. Goethe's essay *On German Architecture* (1773) set off a wave of enthusiasm for Gothic-style buildings. The revival of Gothic architecture developed into a national movement in the post-revolutionary period.

Neogothic monuments include a good many cathedrals and castles that seem to be genuine Gothic, each one conjuring the illustriousness of the German Middle Ages. In 1814, Johann

▼ Donaustauf near Regensburg, Germany, interior of the Walhalla, Leo von Klenze, 1830–1842.

▼ Near Koblenz, Schloss Stolzenfels, Karl Friedrich Schinkel and Friedrich August Stüler, 1825–1845.

loseph von Görres called for the completion of Cologne Cathedral, where no
serious construction had taken place
since 1560. Crown Prince Ludwig I of
Bavaria, desiring a "German Pantheon"
first came up with the idea of the
Walhalla Temple in 1807. It was completed in neoclassical style in 1842
under the influence of architect and
scholar Leo von Klenze. He designed a
building to be set picturesquely atop a
hill, reachable by an outdoor flight of
stairs. The exterior of the building was
modeled after the Parthenon.

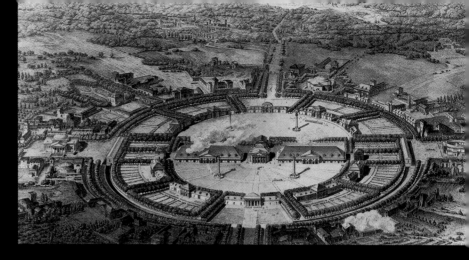

Utopian Architecture

The architecture of the period around
the French Revolution remained on
paper, to a large extent. It nevertheless
represents a decided effort to bring
architecture to a wider public. In the
spirit of the Enlightenment, French
architects of the eighteenth century,
among the first of them Claude Nicolas
Ledoux (1736–1806), sought to make
statements by means of style, form
and decoration. In reality, the ideal of
employing simple, basic forms often
evolved into exaggerated, megalomaniac arrangements of plane and solid
geometry. Spheres, squares and cubes
were repeated in numbers beyond all
reason, preferably in conjunction with
endless rows of columns and broad-
surfaced walls. The end result was
more exhausting than enlightening. In
the end, buildings and complexes were
incapable of teaching anything, despite
the idealism behind their design.

Many of these ideas were described
in Ledoux's 1804 book, *Architecture
Considered in Relation to Art, Morals
and Legislation*. One of the few buildings ever built from the designs published was the Royal Saltworks at Arc-
et-Senans (1774–1779), distinguished
by its semi-circular plan and decorative
motives of barrels and salt mines.

▲ ▼ Saline Royale (Royal Saltworks)
at Arc-et-Senans, France, Claude-
Nicolas Ledoux, 1775–1779, and its
intended plan (above), from an 1804
engraving showing the director's
pavilion in the center of the complex.

▼ Design for a cenotaph for Sir Isaac
Newton, Etienne-Louis Boulée, 1794,
Paris, Bibliothèque Nationale.

Architectural Follies

The full range of styles popular in the nineteenth century also appeared in the form of follies, the term used to describe the largely decorative constructions that often grace the picturesque "natural" landscapes of English country estates. These were commonly small-scale buildings representing the most current architectural trends, but executed with considerably more freedom. Romantic reconstructions of castle ruins and Gothic chapels belong in this category, along with classical temples, Palladian bridges and Chinese pagodas. Follies were

▲ Kassel, Germany, Löwenburg at Schloss Wilhelmshöhe, Heinrich Jussow, 1791–1799.

received in their time not as canonically perfect copies, but as aesthetic and emotional works of art.

This artistic license and widespread passion for antiquity did not preclude scholarly inquiry; in fact, it led to a notable increase of interest in researching ancient monuments. Information flowed directly from

▼ ▼ Aranjuez, Spain, exterior of the Casa del Labrador (l) and Round Temple in the castle gardens (r), Isidoro González Velázquez.

▲ London, Chinese Pagoda at Kew Gardens, William Chambers, 1761.

the archaeological excavations taking place at the time to the folly architects. Just as the mid-eighteenth-century passion for the subject of Greek art—barely known at that time—led to the development of the scholarly discipline of Classics, the rediscovery of the Middle Ages now aroused Christian, patriotic feelings that eventually led to the emergence of romanticism.

Both of these stylistic movements, the classical-archaeological and the medieval-romantic, could be experi-

The English Garden

The English garden was a response to the strictly regimented, symmetrically designed baroque garden as seen, for example, at Versailles. The open plan of English gardens, in contrast, respected the natural landscape, making a political—liberal—statement as well as an artistic one.

Typical English gardens avoid hierarchal structures and geometric paved areas. Instead, visitors follow a winding path through an Arcadian landscape dotted with architectural follies, encountering ever-changing, always surprising views. Seemingly untamed nature runs wild across the terrain. The relationship between English gardens and the writings of French philosopher Jean-Jacques Rousseau is evident, although the earliest English gardens (at Blenheim, Stowe and Stourhead) precede his work by several years. The style spread like wildfire, conquering most of Europe and the New World by the mid-eighteenth century.

Among the first designers of these vast works of art were William Kent and Lancelot "Capability" Brown. Sir William Chambers added an exotic element with his Chinese Pagoda in Kew Gardens, London.

▲ Wiltshire, England, Stourhead, bridge in the landscape garden, 1753–1754.

▼ Stowe, England, Palladian bridge in the gardens, James Gibbs, 1740.

enced—often side-by-side—in an English garden landscape. Germany played an important role in the development of gardens of this type, follies included. Contemporaries considered the Dessau-Wörlitz Garden Realm, also known as the English Gardens of Wörlitz, an important model. Planned and designed for Prince Franz von Anhalt-Dessau by his architect Friedrich Wilhelm von Erdmannsdorff and garden designer Johan Eyersbeck, the grounds include the Gothic House, a smaller version of Rome's Pantheon, a temple dedicated to Flora, another to Venus, and an Arcadian (wooded)

landscape. Bridges in various styles abound. There is also Rousseau's Island, named after the famous philosopher, and a fire-spewing volcano—Vesuvius (of course)—to startle onlookers. The gardens are a trip into both natural and architectural history.

The architecture of follies became less and less canonical over time. At Löwenburg, the castle of Count Wilhelm IX of Hessen-Kassel, the rooms of the medieval ruin are furnished to the highest degree of comfort. The estate park of the Casa del Labrador in Spain alternates romantic idylls with peaceful meadows. The Bourbon king

Charles IV kept his large collection of antiques in a three-winged building set atop what were supposed to be the foundations of a simple country house.

The fantasies of the patrons surpassed all stylistic, chronological and geographical boundaries. Prehistoric settlements, Egyptian monuments, Turkish baths and Chinese towers embellished all manner of gardens and castle grounds, beckoning visitors into a kingdom of dreams. The follies also provided a means for an architectural discussion to take place, one free from the dogmatic constraints of neoclassicism.

Neopalladian and Greek Revival Architecture

The beginning of the eighteenth century in England was marked by a significant shift in architectural tastes. A new generation of young architects turned against the pathos of seventeenth-century baroque architecture, which in England had been chiefly defined by the works of Christopher Wren. The younger generation called for architecture free of meaningless embellishment. It favored buildings that were "founded in truth and nature." The first two volumes of *Vitruvius Britannicus*, published by Colen Campbell in 1715 and 1717,

▲ ▼ Middlesex, Chiswick House, Richard Boyle, Third Earl of Burlington, 1725–1729, gallery (above) and facade (below).

consisted of a book of engravings of British buildings and a translation of Palladio's *Four Books of Architecture*. In 1727, architect William Kent published a series of plans and elevations of the works of the Renaissance architect Inigo Jones. Both Campbell and Kent belonged to the intellectual circle founded by Richard Boyle, Third Earl of Burlington. The "Architect Earl" was the acknowledged head of the neopalladian movement. His goal was a return to the "noble and just proportions" that originated in ancient Greece, which were interpreted by both Palladio and the English architect Inigo Jones.

A combination of classical forms and national traditions would define the architecture of England for several

decades. The art-loving members of the Society of Dilettanti gathered around the Earl of Burlington primarily influenced the design of secular architecture, rather than sacred. The earl himself designed one of the most thorough examples of neopalladian architecture. His own Chiswick House, in Middlesex, near London, is remarkably close to Palladio's Italian villas, despite its smaller scale. In plan, it resembles Palladio's famous Villa Rotunda, which was also based on a square with a central octagonal space. The interior decor follows the work of Inigo Jones for the most part. Jones was himself an early interpreter of Palladio's ideas.

By the late eighteenth century, the movement toward buildings that resembled ancient prototypes as closely as possible had moved to the forefront of neoclassicism. Bolstered by the publications of British scholars, the Italian-born architect Joseph Bonomi built a "Pompeiian Gallery" on the grounds of a Great Packington estate. His design was based on the most up-to-date archaeological information.

By the beginning of the nineteenth century, Greek architecture had moved even further to the forefront, leading to the style known as Greek Revival. Doric was the preferred order, held in highest esteem due to its sublime elegance. The ideals of the Greek Revival style were especially influential on the design of public buildings. Doric

▲ London, St Pancras Parish Church, sacristy with caryatid porch, William and Henry William Inwood, 1819–1822.

◄ Warwickshire, Packington Hall, Pompeian Gallery, Joseph Bonomi, ca. 1782.

temples were reconceived as museums, government buildings and monumental gateways. Eventually, other Greek styles made appearances. The sacristy of St Pancras parish church in London, for example, has a copy of the Caryatid Porch of the Erectheion on the Athenian Acropolis. Before long, neogothic architecture would also profit from archaeological investigation and architectonic reconstruction.

◀ Wörlitz, Germany, landscape garden and castle by Friedrich Wilhelm von Erdmannsdorff, 1769–1773.

▶ Arras, France, interior of St-Vaast, Pierre Contant d'Ivry, ca. 1755.

The Early Neoclassical Period in Central Europe

Neoclassicism became popular in Germany in the middle of the eighteenth century. The center of the neoclassical movement was Saxony, where a group of art-loving intellectuals assembled around art historian Johann Joachim Winckelmann and Adam Friedrich Oeser. A second group led by Georg Wenzalaus von Knobelsdorff and his patron, Friedrich II of Prussia, met in Rheinsberg and Berlin. Their goal was to give Berlin, the city of the Prussian royal residence, a more "enlightened" appearance.

The true cradle of Germanic neoclassicism, however, was Wörlitz. With his design for the summer royal residence of the Prince of Anhalt-Dessau, Friedrich Wilhelm von Erdmannsdorff took Winckelmann's concept of "noble simplicity and quiet grandeur" and translated it into architectural terms. The castle represented a rejection of every traditional rule regarding imposing and lordly edifices. Instead, Erdmannsdorff designed a rectilinear building with four symmetrical wings and an interior peristyle courtyard. Visible structural elements include a classical portico supported by monumental Corinthian columns. The only decorative elements are the window details, which resemble classical arches and pediments, and a sculpted dentil frieze running beneath crown molding.

The noble proportions and unmistakable strength of the symmetrical elevation bring the building to life. The design models are very obviously the Palladian villas in Italy that Erdmannsdorff had either visited or

studied from volumes of prints that were in circulation.

Another influence was the growing interest in the relationship between cultural and natural experiences. The prince had commissioned a landscape-style "English" garden, scattered throughout with grottos, ruins, small temples and statues. The strictly rule-bound gardens of the baroque period were no longer in favor. Instead, the neoclassical ideal promoted garden designs that were picturesque, intimate and superficially natural. In the summer residence at Wörlitz, these two opposing elements of neoclassicism were united. The clean, rational symmetry of the buildings is set against the melancholy, sentimental backdrop of a landscape developed according to the English garden type.

Other regions were also influenced by Western European trends. St-Vaast in Arras, France, is an early masterpiece of neoclassical ecclesiastical architecture. Two French architects, Pierre Michel d'Ixnard and Nicolas de Pigage, were responsible for St Blaise in the Black Forest (left and pp. 226–227), a key building in the movement of the new architectural style into southwest Germany. St Blaise is a massive structure supporting an enormous dome on a tall drum. Rounded corner towers and a Doric vestibule give the building weight and gravity. Windows in the rotunda, which was originally planned as a mausoleum, bathe the interior in bright light.

◀ St Blasien, Germany, St Blaise, interior of the former Benedictine abbey church, Pierre-Michel d'Ixnard and Nicolas de Pigage, 1768–1783.

▶ Versailles, main facade of Petit Trianon, Jacques-Ange Gabriel, 1762–1764.

▼ Paris, Pantheon, formerly St-Geneviève, Jacques Germain, Soufflot, begun 1756.

◀ Paris, Hôtel Beauharnais, Four Seasons Salon, after 1803.

▲ Versailles, Hameau de la Reine, mill, Richard Mique, 1783–1785.

Paris and Versailles

In France, the Académie founded by Jacques-François Blondel in the mid-eighteenth century ensured that classicism, never entirely absent from French architecture, enjoyed a new wave of popularity. A parallel development was the overwhelmingly positive reaction to the rationalist *Essai sur l'architecture* by the Jesuit Marc-Antoine Lauguier, which called for a return to ancient forms of building.

The Petit Trianon in the estate park surrounding Versailles Palace is an important early work in the new ancient style. Designed by Jacques-Ange Gabriel, this massive yet delicate building is fronted by a Corinthian peristyle opening onto the gardens. Its style is primarily based on British neopalladianism. St-Geneviève Church, designed by architect Jacques-Germain Soufflot, represents a stricter interpretation. Soufflot aspired to achieve the perfect synthesis of "Greek solemnity and Gothic weightlessness." His church is a Greek cross plan with the addition of a classical portico. The neoclassical interior, strictly adhering to the academic proportions, gives the impression of unrestrained lightness.

Claude-Nicolas Ledoux and Etienne-Louis Boulée are among the most important utopian architects. These men sought to design buildings that were expressions of artistic and moral qualities (see p. 229).

The French royal court, weary of its stiff baroque ceremonies, chose instead to live within a dream of earthly paradise. The classic expression of this sentiment is the fairytale farm village, complete with mill and dairy, that architect Richard Mique built for the French queen Marie-Antoinette in the estate park of Versailles Palace. Of course, the *Hameau de la reine* (Queen's little hamlet) also included a theater, library and Temple of Love. But the idyll was deceptive. Its construction was the final architectural effort at Versailles before the French Revolution. A few years later, both Mique and his patroness ended up on the guillotine.

By the beginning of the nineteenth century, French architects were going off in new directions. As enamored as the nation had been by republican ideals, the crowning of Napoleon as emperor brought the Roman Empire

▲ Paris, St-Madeleine, Alexander Vignon and Jacques-Marie Huvé, 1807–1842, interior view.

▼ Paris, Arc de Triomphe, Jean-François-Thèrése Chalgrin and Jean-Arnaud Raymond, begun 1806.

back into view. In 1806, Napoleon decided to build a temple to honor his Grand Armée. Before long, a Corinthian peripteral temple (surrounded on all sides by columns) became the focal point for the end of the rue Royal. After Napoleon's fall it was consecrated as the Church of St-Madeleine. The pagan style also dominates the interior, which was later "clothed" with a Christian decorative program. The sequence of three domed rooms refers to the architectural plans of Roman baths, and the colored marble-veneer interiors recall the Roman Pantheon. Roman-style triumphal arches are found throughout Paris. While the Arc du Caroussel copies its model, the Roman Arch of Constantine, very closely, the Arc du Triomphe at l'Etoile is already a freer adaptation of ancient art.

Theaters and Museums

During the Age of Enlightenment, cultural institutions, especially theaters and museums, became some of the most important architectural commissions. Boulée, Ledoux and the theoretician Jean-Nicolas-Louis Durand designed magnificent buildings, which, however, for the most part remained on paper.

Although court-based monarchial society continued into the nineteenth century, the general public in the form of the bourgeoisie penetrated further and further into the feudal sphere. These people demanded a new kind of

building. Theater design, in particular the layout of the audience area, was most influenced by classical models. Like amphitheaters, seating was organized in ascending tiers—including box seats for the wealthy—that were arranged in an oval or horseshoe. The stage area was outfitted with mechanical equipment, as it had been in a Greek or Roman theater. What had been stairways in ancient theaters were transformed into distinctive foyers.

Destructive fires were common. Often, entire districts full of traditional houses had to be rebuilt. In a slightly later period, this would lead to experiments with fire-safe building materials

▲ Milan, colored engraving of the stage and side box seating from the Teatro alla Scala, Giuseppe Piermarini, 1776–1778.

such as iron. In 1776, the Teatro alla Scala in Milan was rebuilt with funds paid by the box owners. Contemporaries considered the Grand Théâtre in Bordeaux (see p. 228), built a bit earlier, to be the most beautiful theater in the world. Its impressive exterior consisted of a broad, columned entry hall visually connected to the rest of the building by a continuous classical architrave. The elaborate grand stairway inside would serve as a model for the one in the

▶ Madrid, Prado Museum, Juan de Villanueva, 1785–1819, north facade.

neobaroque Paris Opera designed by Charles Garnier in 1860. An example of the process of rebuilding and renovation is the Dresden Opera House. The first one burned down in 1869 and was replaced in 1871–1878 (see p. 260) by one more in tune with the progress of nineteenth-century taste.

There was a similar increase in demand for museum buildings. What began as courtly cabinets of curiosities were transformed into systematically organized collections, now open to the general public (after some initial hesitation). The Fridericianum Museum in Kassel was one of the first buildings specifically commissioned for the exhibition of paintings. The Vatican Museum and Paris Louvre followed soon after. The Prado in Madrid, planned as a natural history museum, opened as a picture gallery in 1819 after the retreat of Napoleon's troops. It became a model for many future museums.

For a long time, ancient classical architecture was considered the most suitable model for museums and theaters. The Glyptothek in Munich by Leo von Klenz (see p. 241) and Karl

Friedrich Schinkel's Altes Museum in Berlin (see p. 243) are good illustrations of the neoclassical style. But as the nineteenth century progressed, architects devised other solutions. Heinrich Hübsch designed the Karlsruhe Kunsthalle, for instance, using rounded Roman arches and stylistic elements from the Renaissance.

▲ Kassel, Germany, Museum Fridericianum, Simon Louise du Rhy, 1769–1777.

◀ Bordeaux, Grand Théâtre, Victor Louis, 1772–1780, grand stairway.

▶ Karlsruhe, Kunsthalle, Heinrich Hübsch, 1837–1846.

◀ Würzburg, Women's Prison,
Peter Speeth, 1811–1827.

▶ Donaustauf near Regensburg, Walhalla,
Leo von Klenze, 1830–1842.

Neoclassicism in Southern Germany

By the turn of the nineteenth century, neoclassicism had made its way through all of Germany, inspired in part by utopian architectural movements that were based further west. New building commissions were formed.

The design of national monuments was significantly influenced by the work of French theoreticians, whose ideas were taken up eagerly. In addition to David and Friedrich Gilly, who worked for the Prussian court, Johann Heinrich Gentz, from Breslau, and Mannheim architect Peter Speeth were at the head of the movement.

Speeth's Women's Prison in Würzburg is a solid, cubic mass set on top of a heavily rusticated base. Its powerful, austere character is perfectly in tune with the concept of *architecture parlante*, which literally means "speaking architecture," i.e., buildings whose nature or purpose is self-evident.

The manifesto of the new style is embodied in the renovation of Munich that took place under Elector Maximillian IV Joseph and Crown Prince (later King) Ludwig I. The demolition of the fortifications around the city made possible a completely new, large-scale city plan. Karl von Fischer and Ludwig von Skell designed the English Garden, along with a wide range of public spaces and palaces. Their work gave the Bavarian royal residence city a classical-Mediterranean allure. Plans for the Glyptothek, Königsplatz and the Walhalla were begun in 1809. The buildings would not be constructed, however, until the second half of the nineteenth century. The layout of the Königsplatz, which included a Doric gateway (called the Propylon) flanked by two neoclassical museums (one Ionic, one Corinthian), was based on the king's desire that his architects build him "an Acropolis in a suburban meadow."

The Walhalla was intended to be the German Pantheon. After a number of different designs had been considered, Leo von Klenz' plans were selected. Set picturesquely at the peak of a rise and reached by a monumental, open-air staircase, the exterior of the Walhalla refers primarily to the Parthenon in Athens.

◀ Karlsruhe, Markplatz, Friedrich Weinbrenner, 1806–1826.

Leo von Klenze

Leo von Klenze is the most important architect of south German neoclassicism. Although his buildings have never enjoyed the level of attention generated by Schinkel's projects, von Klenze is largely responsible for the look of Munich and thereby for the visual appeal of the Bavarian cultural landscape.

Born in 1784 in Bockenem near Hildesheim, von Klenze studied at the Architecture Academy of Berlin with Aloys Hirt and David Gilly. In 1803 he traveled to Paris, where he became disillusioned with the utopian architecture he encountered in the teachings of Jean-Nicolas-Louis Durand. Between 1808 and 1813 von Klenze worked for the court in Kassler, at that time ruled by Jérome Bonaparte. In 1816 he entered the service of Crown Prince Ludwig of Bavaria. For Ludwig he designed his most significant Munich buildings: the Königsplatz, the Alte Pinakothek and the Odeon. Also spectacular are his monumental Walhalla on the Danube River, with its Doric peripteros, and the Befreiungshalle (Hall of Liberation) in Kelheim. After Prince Otto of Bavaria was

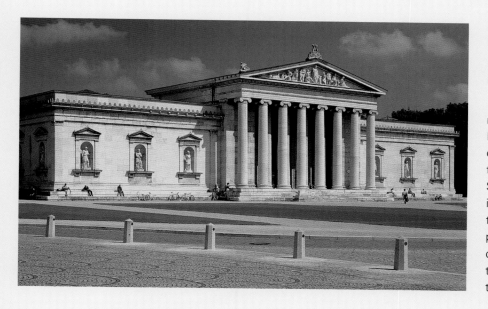

▲ Kelheim, Germany, Befreiungshalle, Leo von Klenze, 1836–1844.

◀ Munich, Königsplatz, Glyptothek, Leo von Klenze, 1815–1830.

named king of Greece in 1832, von Klenze drew up plans for a rebuilding of Athens. He was also involved in the design of the New Hermitage in St Petersburg. Von Klenze died in 1864 in Munich, a classicist through and through. In accordance with his patrons' desires, however, he also created designs with rounded forms that were rather more neorenaissance than neoclassical in style.

As time went on, antiquity and its motifs were increasingly linked to nationalistic self-identification. Romanticism and neoclassicism set off waves of archaeological investigation and sociopolitical theorizing. Following these trends, Kelheim's Befreiungshalle (Hall of Liberation), a small, circular building reminiscent of a Roman round temple or Greek tholos, was built in the picturesque landscape of the Danube valley. Its eighteen pilasters are crowned with statues personifying the Germanic tribes. City planning was adapted to the changing social and economic scene and now included industrial areas as well as residential districts. Nevertheless, planning remained closely bound to the royal residences, both in concept and execution. Thus, Friedrich Weinbrenner's detailed, radial city plan for Karlsruhe in 1797 incorporated new districts, but the center was still occupied by the palace, like a spider in its web.

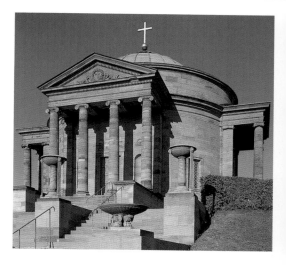

▶ Stuttgart, Chapel on the Rotenberg, Giovanni Salucci, 1819–1824.

Berlin

Berlin made great contributions to the golden age of neoclassicism—marked by Carl Gotthard Langhans' Brandenburger Tor, built in the late eighteenth century—as well as its later development. Brandenburg Gate is the terminus of Unter den Linden, a picture-perfect promenade. Its exterior resembles the propylaea of the Athenian Acropolis, bringing to mind the Greek polis. Langhan's students Friedrich Gilly and Johann Heinrich Gentz specialized in building precise copies of ancient models. Gilly, especially, reduced his designs to combinations of unadorned, symmetrical basic forms: spheres, cubes and pyramids.

The greatest figure in German neoclassicism is Karl Friedrich Schinkel. He traveled throughout Europe studying the great buildings of antiquity, but was also an enthusiastic student of medieval art. This combination led to his long career in service to the Prussian court. After early work as a painter, he was involved in all the major Prussian architectural projects from 1810 onward. In Berlin these included the Neue Wache (New Watchhouse), Schauspielhaus (a theater, now the Konzerthaus) and Altes (Old) Museum, originally the Royal Museum. Most of his designs are a combination of romantic and neoclassical ideas, with some designed completely in a medievalizing style. At the time, his interest in and use of both idioms was considered revolutionary, and his work did not always find favor with the crown princes.

The Altes Museum is one of Schinkel's crowning achievements. A free interpretation of many elements and

▲ Berlin, facade of the Altes Museum, formerly the Royal Museum, Karl Friedrich Schinkel, 1823–1830.

▼ Berlin, Schauspielhaus on Gendarmenmarkt, Karl Friedrich Schinkel, 1818–1821.

▲ Berlin, Brandenburger Tor, Carl Gotthard Langhans, 1789.

◄ Berlin, Neue Wache, Karl Friedrich Schinkel, 1816–1818.

styles, it incorporates colonnades, rotundas and a monumental double staircase. But it is also an innovative, functional public building, aesthetically exciting while fitting well within the Berlin cityscape. Schinkel's experiments with style and technical innovations in construction, including new uses for cast iron and brickwork, were a great influence on architecture of the later nineteenth century. His student, Ludwig Persius, later designed the Dampfmachinenhaus (Steam Pump House) in Potsdam—in Moorish style.

Eastern and Northern Europe

The Russian Empire had been involved in an active artistic exchange with Italy and France throughout the baroque period. These relationships would continue during the long reign of Catherine the Great, from 1762 to 1796, and those of her successors.

The most significant event contributing to Russia's adoption of the neoclassical architecture that still defines the look of St Petersburg and Moscow to this day was when French architect Jean Baptiste Vallin de la Mothe was called to St Petersburg to work on the Russian Academy of Art. The building Vallin de la Mothe designed for this revered institution was the foundation of the neoclassical movement in Russia. Additional projects followed, including the famed art galleries of the Small Hermitage and the Old Hermitage (later merged to become the renowned Hermitage Museum). The Marble Palace overlooking the Neva River, commissioned by Catherine the Great for Count Orlov, is another famous neoclassical building. It is the work of the Italian architect Antonio Rinaldi.

▲▲ Moscow, Kremlin, view from the Moskwa River (top); and the Grand Kremlin Palace by Constantine Thon, 1837–1851 (middle).

▲ St Petersburg, Kazan Cathedral, Andrei Voronichin, 1800–1811, north facade.

▶ Tsarskoe Selo (near St Petersburg), Achat Pavilion, part of the addition to Catherine the Great's summer palace known as the Cameron Gallery after its architect, Charles Cameron.

While the earliest neoclassical buildings were predominantly the work of foreigners, Russian architects, such as Ivan Starov, came along later. Nevertheless, Catherine the Great called the Italian Giacomo Quarenghi and Scotsman Charles Cameron to her court to design her palaces. Both were neopalladians, a style very much in evidence in the palaces that she had constructed. The large-scale renovation of the St Petersburg cityscape is largely the work of Andrei Woronichin and Carlo Rossi, who completely redesigned many of the city's most prestigious buildings.

Moscow, the "hometown" capital of Russia, was also entirely renovated under orders of Catherine and her successors. The Kremlin, and its important role in defining the image of the city, was a top priority.

In Scandinavia, neoclassicism took hold quickly in the last quarter of the eighteenth century. The tomb of Frederik IV in Roskilde Cathedral, completed in 1774, is already fully classical in style. In Sweden, the theater in Castle Gripsholm designed by Erik Palmstedt set a new standard. It became the model for what was known as Gustavian style after its patron, King Gustav III. In the nineteenth century, the Danish architect Frederik Hansen was most influential. His well-constructed buildings were based primarily on ancient Greek prototypes. The Thorvaldsen Museum in Copenhagen, designed by Gottlieb Bindesboll and built between 1839 and 1848, incorporates elements of neoclassical, neoegyptian and Greek Revival styles. Carl Ludwig Engel, a German architect who studied with Schinkel, created the neoclassical center of the Finnish capital city of Helsinki. His buildings there include the Senate, St Nikolaus Church (today's Helsinki Cathedral) and the University of Helsinki.

▲▲ Helsinki, Finland, St Nicholas Church (Helsinki Cathedral), Carl Ludwig Engel, begun 1826.

▲ Gran, Hungary, cathedral, Johann Packh and Joseph Hild, 1824–1845. This bishops' seat on the banks of the Danube is the high point of neoclassical church design in Hungary.

◀ Copenhagen, apse of Vor Frue Kirke (Church of Our Lady), Christian Frederik Hansen. The statue of Christ is by Bertel Thorvaldsen.

Federal Style in the United States

One of the earliest neoclassical buildings in the United States is the Redwood Library in Newport, Rhode Island, notable for its straightforward, temple-like facade. Its architect was Peter Harrison, an English sea captain and shipbuilder who had studied Palladio's designs. Most of the library's classical elements were carved from wood.

The buildings designed by Thomas Jefferson made the neoclassical style the mark of a newly independent America. Jefferson was also a follower of the English neopalladian style. In 1768 he began building the first version of Monticello on his estate in Virginia. In retrospect, this was one of the most important buildings in the development of what would be known as the federal style. Like the utopian architects in France, Jefferson used neoclassical elements as a means of expressing the ideals of the Enlightenment. At the same time, the monumentality of federal-style buildings and their relationship with the landscape took these ideals a step further. Jefferson's most important achievement is the University of Virginia in Charlottesville, one of the earliest college campuses. The buildings are grouped in a series of pavilions based on the quad system common in England, each visually tied to the surrounding landscape.

In 1790 Congress approved the founding of a city that would serve as the seat of the federal government. It was named Washington after the first president of the United States. French architect Pierre Charles L'Enfant was hired, on Jefferson's recommendation, to design the generously proportioned, grid-plan city. The first buildings completed were the United States Capitol and the White House. A design competition for the presidential mansion held in 1792 clearly stated that only American architects could apply. But their proposals did not meet with approval, and it was ultimately an Irishman, James Hoban, who designed the White House. His design was largely based on earlier plans for a country manor by English architect James Gibbs. The competition for the Capitol also seemed unlikely to produce an American winner until the physician and amateur architect William Thornton was finally selected.

▲ Newport, Rhode Island, Redwood Library, Peter Harrison, 1749–1758.

▼ Charlottesville, Virginia, Monticello, Thomas Jefferson, 1768–1775 and 1796–1809.

▶ Washington, D.C., United States Capitol, William Thornton, Benjamin Latrobe and Charles Bulfinch, 1792–1827. Significant rebuilding and renovation took place in the 1860s and early 20th century.

Historicism and Civil Engineering

The decades between 1820 and the beginning of the twentieth century were the age of historicism, which is the deliberate reproduction of the architectural styles of the past. Whereas classical art and architecture had been the subject of repeated rediscovery since the end of the eighteenth century, historicism was primarily interested in the architecture of other periods. The birth of the scholarly discipline of architectural history had increased interest not only in classical antiquity, but also in the medieval period, ancient Egypt and Islamic Spain. Over time, styles from other historical periods gained currency as well; inspiration was drawn from Romanesque, Renaissance or Early Christian periods. There was renewed interest in baroque in Europe in the late nineteenth century, when profits from industrialization led to rebuilding programs across the continent. The seemingly endless array of formal elements available under the heading of historicism posed a dilemma for architects. There was no unified stylistic direction, and no longer any visual language that belonged to the present. As early as 1828, Heinrich Hübsch, head architect for the German state of Baden, stimulated discussion with his essay *In What Style Should We Build?* The response was a deep uncertainty.

▲ Füssen, Germany, Schloss Neuschwanstein, Christian Rank, Eduard Riedel and Julius Hofmann, 1868–1892.

▼ Schwerin, Germany, Schweriner Schloss, Georg Adolph Demmler and Friedrich August Stüler, 1843–1857.

In addition, the growing need for new kinds of architecture posed challenges. The modern world needed factories, bridges, enormous exhibition halls, schools, department stores and public cemeteries. The need to develop new techniques and materials was urgent. Iron, glass and steel began to replace more traditional building materials, and architecture quickly became the realm of engineers as well as artists. Civil engineering would eventually make a stronger impression on the nineteenth century than historicism. Functional and rational, its practitioners offered a welcome alternative to architecture defined primarily by style. Although iron- and steel-frame structural

◀ Wörlitz, Germany, Gothic-style house, Friedrich Wilhelm von Erdmannsdorff, 1785–1786. One of the first buildings in the neogothic style, initiating the German romanticization of the Gothic period.

elements were also used in historical styles, these would eventually develop their own aesthetic, paving the way for twentieth-century architecture.

Viollet-le-Duc

The influence of the writings of Paris architect and scholar Eugène-Emmanuel Viollet-le-Duc (1814–1879) on scholarship, historical preservation and the progression of nineteenth-century architecture cannot be overestimated. His most influential works were a ten-volume dictionary of French architecture and the two volumes of *Entretiens sur l'architecture* (Discourses on Architecture) published in 1853–1868 and 1858–1872, respectively. While these are the key works in the historicist movement, Viollet-le-Duc's strict rationalism and support of new building materials make him a forerunner of modern architecture, too. Focusing his scholarly attention on Gothic art, Viollet-le-Duc concluded that the principles of rational architecture were embodied in the wood-framed masonry structure of the Gothic cathedral. The first cast iron and steel-framed buildings would be constructed using Gothic models. Throughout his life, Viollet-le-Duc would be a strong proponent of new techniques and modern materials.

Viollet-le-Duc also led numerous historic restoration campaigns. The abbey church of Vézelay, and Nôtre Dame and the Sainte Chapelle in Paris were comprehensively restored under his

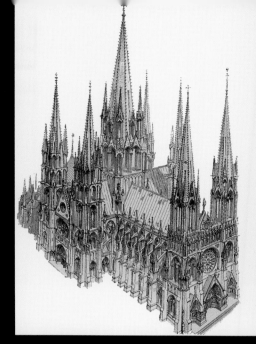

▲ Ideal Cathedral, woodcut by Viollet-le-Duc from his *Dictionnaire raisonné de l'architecture française du XIᵉ au XVIᵉ siècle* representing a synthesis of high Gothic cathedral architecture.

◀ Carcassonne, France, view of the medieval city with vineyards. Its nearly complete architectural restoration was supervised by Viollet-le-Duc.

supervision; the renovation of the medieval city of Carcassonne is mostly his work; and for Napoleon III he "rebuilt" the ruined late medieval castle at Pierrefonds in Picardy. Restoration, in the nineteenth-century sense of the word, was an extraordinarily free enterprise giving the architect a great deal of artistic license with what remained of the historic structures. Historical restoration proponents today would probably disapprove. Viollet-le-Duc's non-historicist work, including independently derived modern designs, such as those for the parish church of St-Denis-de-l'Estrée, received little attention.

◀ London, St Pancras Station, train shed and departure hall, William Harry Barlow, 1863–1865.

◀ Brighton, England, Royal Pavilion, John Nash, 1815–1822.

historical styles. The playful garden ambience welcomed unconventional—indeed, exotic—architectural forms, such as the Chinese Pagoda in Kew Gardens (see p. 230). But the orientalizing styles that were the specialty of its architect, John Nash, never quite caught the national imagination. The Royal Pavilion buildings that Nash built for George, the prince regent, in the seaside town of Brighton incorporated a wealth of details that were based on the architecture of Mogul India, but in all essentials they

Historicism in England

English architecture of the late eighteenth and early nineteenth century was extraordinarily imaginative and innovative. Just as neopalladianism recreated a Renaissance architectural style, an important (almost contemporary) neogothic building presaged a medieval revival. Horace Walpole's neogothic country house, Strawberry Hill was completed in 1750, long before the later romantic and historicist revivals of the style.

The culmination of neogothic style in England is without a doubt the emblematic silhouette of the Houses of Parliament in London. After a devastating fire in 1834 destroyed the original buildings, it was decided to rebuild quickly, using elements from medieval architecture. In contrast, the somewhat earlier Bank of England building by John Soane was fully neoclassical. Unfortunately, this spectacular building was torn down in 1920.

The English landscape garden continued to be an ideal field for experimentation with a variety of

▶ Twickenham, London, Strawberry Hill, Horace Walpole, 1749–1763, gallery.

▶ Westminster, London, Houses of Parliament, Charles Barry and Augustus Welby Northmore Pugin, 1835–1860.

varied little from the standard type of the neoclassical villa.

While more extreme experiments had clearly reached a stylistic cul-de-sac, the Royal Pavilion is a technically accomplished construction utilizing cast iron structural elements. The outer skin of the dome was made of a material similar to today's structural concrete.

New building materials were introduced experimentally from the late eighteenth century onward. Most could only be put into use with the coming of the machine age. Prefabricated pig iron, cast iron and wrought iron elements, as well as different mixes of cement and concrete, took on the task of providing structure and integral support. Mass production simplified the production of everything from bricks to pane glass.

A greenhouse—the Palm House in Kew Gardens—was the building that would revolutionize construction techniques in England and around the world. It was the first structure to use wrought iron supports in quantity and in structurally significant positions. This framework was then "closed" with glass panels. In 1850, this inno-

▲ Richmond, London, Palm House in Kew Gardens, Decimus Burton and Richard Turner, 1844–1848.

◀ London, bird's eye view of John Soane's Bank of England as a ruin, in a 1798 watercolor by Joseph Michael Gandy.

vative, functional and supremely economical construction method occupied center stage at the London Great Exhibition in the equally elegant, much larger, Crystal Palace. A new functional aesthetic, combining transparency and lightness, had been introduced.

The Neogothic

Neogothic is the most multi-faceted of the many stylistic movements in the architecture of the nineteenth century. It met both the romantic and antiquarian demands of the times, serving national interests while promoting both technological and aesthetic reform. In Germany, the recovery of the original plans for Cologne's largely unfinished cathedral led to a virtual outpouring of nationalistic sentiment. In 1814, journalist and scholar Joseph Görres called for the cathedral's completion: it had stood incomplete since 1560. Now, it would become a "symbol of the new empire." Work only began in earnest in

◀ Cologne Cathedral, facade of the south transept, Ernst Friedrich Zwirmer and Richard Voigtel, 1842–1880.

1842 under the direction of master cathedral builder Ernst Friedrich Zwirner. The transept was finished in 1861; by 1863 the interior had been renovated. In 1880, the final completion of the towers was celebrated with great ceremony. Three years prior to the beginning of work on the cathedral in Cologne, Ernst Friedrich Zwirner had laid the foundation stone for the Apollinaris Church in Remagen, yet another important neogothic building in the Rheinland. Here he could work with Gothic forms without the constraints of compliance with a pre-existing medieval building. Zwirner chose a Greek-cross plan, with two slender towers flanking the eastern choir in addition to the traditional pair of towers on the Gothic western facade.

The tendency toward central plan buildings as well as the architect's free interpretation of Gothic decorative ele-

▲ Florence Cathedral, facade between the Romanesque baptistery and Gothic campanile (bell tower), Emilo de Fabris, 1875–1887.

◀ Milan Cathedral, facade, Giuseppe Zanoia, Carlo Amati, et al., 1806–late 19th century.

◀◀ Remagen, Germany, exterior of the Apollinaris Church, Ernst Friedrich Zwirner, 1839–1843.

ments is reminiscent of the work of Karl Friedrich Schinkel, with whom Zwirner had spent some time as a student.

By the second half of the nineteenth century, neogothic architecture could be found all over Europe. Berlin, Vienna and Paris all sported picturesque neogothic churches. The neogothic style's Christian-nationalist associations made

it the preferred style for churches everywhere, including the New World. Unfinished medieval cathedrals were completed in Florence, Milan and Barcelona. As with Cologne Cathedral, the new additions were in part based on historical sources, and in part on fairly free interpretations of the nineteenth-century version of Gothic style.

▲ Sepia print showing a panorama of the expansion of the city of Vienna, Gustav Veith, ca. 1873.

▼ Vienna, Burgtheater, Gottfried Semper and Karl von Hasenauer, 1874–1888, grand stairway.

▼ Vienna, Kunsthistorisches Museum, Gottfried Semper and Karl Hasenauer, 1871–1891, facade detail.

The Vienna Ringstrasse

In the second half of the nineteenth century Vienna became the center of urban renewal and city planning by means of experimentation with historical architectural styles. Preceding Haussmann's work in Paris and Cerdá Suñer's "extension" of Barcelona, the redevelopment boom in Vienna was sparked by Emperor Franz Josef's 1857 decision to demolish Vienna's extensive medieval wall and fortification system. The wall that had limited the city's immediate growth was leveled, and an elegant boulevard, the Ringstrasse, lined with distinctive government and private buildings, bustling plazas and inviting green spaces, was to take its place. The entire architectural ensemble that lines the ring is both visually unified and functionally integrated.

Private and public buildings line up along the Ringstrasse like pearls on a chain. Parliament, the Rathaus (City Hall), the Opera and the Burgtheater are interspersed with noble residences of the aristocracy, elegant apartment buildings and distinctive retail shops. The only religious building is the Votivkirche (Votive Church), designed by Heinrich von Ferstel in 1856 in the neogothic style. The design for the imperial court complex, the Hofburg, was a separate project, directed by Gottfried Semper. In the end, the only parts of his ambitious plan to be realized were the museums of art (Kunsthistorisches Museum) and natural history (Naturhistorisches Museum), both constructed to house the extensive imperial collections.

The most important people involved in the design of the Ringstrasse and its buildings were Heinrich von Ferstel, Theophil Hansen, Friedrich von Schmidt, August Sicardsburg and Eduard van der Null, as well as Gottfried Semper and his worthy associate Karl von Hasenauer.

The buildings they designed form a remarkably unified visual landscape, an urban showplace with the individual buildings positioned like actors on a stage. A number of historical styles are represented, each according to function. Thus the church is, of course, neogothic, while the "late Gothic" Rathaus recalls Amsterdam during the

▲ Vienna, Votivkirche, Heinrich von Ferstel, 1856–1879, facade.

◄ Plan for expansion of the Hofburg (Imperial Court) in Vienna, Gottfried Semper and Karl von Hasenauer, 1869, Hof- und Staatsarchiv, Vienna.

Netherlands' golden age. The museums and cultural centers use Renaissance elements, while the Parliament is severely neoclassical. With Vienna as a vibrant model, the full range of historical styles would go on to conquer the world. But in Vienna itself, as early as 1890, the architect Otto Wagner was calling for a revolt against architecture that favored styles borrowed from earlier eras.

▲ Brussels, Royal Gallery at St Hubert, Jean-Pierre Cluysenaer, 1839–1846.

▲ Paris, facade of the Opera, Charles Garnier, 1862–1874.

▶ Brussels, Palais de Justice, Joseph Poelaert, 1866–1883, entrance hall.

Paris and Brussels

The urban landscape of Paris was deeply and irrevocably changed during the second half of the nineteenth century when Baron Georges-Eugène Haussmann, under orders from Napoleon III, supervised the demolition of some 30,000 buildings, some dating back to the medieval period. The cleared ground let Haussmann give Paris a network of broad boulevards lined with upper class houses. Buildings like the neobaroque Opera House provided a *point de vue*, or focal point, at the terminus of lengthy avenues. Haussmann's Paris was more than a city of prestigious buildings and dwellings: his city plan also included railway stations that took the wider transportation networks into account. Market halls, department stores, shopping arcades, hospitals, education facilities and prisons fulfilled a variety of needs for Paris's two million or so inhabitants. The largest and most original public building of this period is located, however, not in Paris, but in Brussels. Joseph Poelaert's 525 x 590 ft (160 x 180 m) Palais de Justice (Palace of Justice) plays with classical forms, taking familiar motives and monumentalizing them within a hierarchal format. Among the many new kinds of building, covered passageways and arcades played a special role. These enormously successful structures permitted a number of the elegances and comforts of urban life to be directly accessible via elegant shopping streets. Around the world, vaulted and domed glass roofs were built to provide atmospheric lighting and protection from the weather. Behind historicizing facades, covered arcades opened up on boutiques, cafés, theaters and (from their upper stories) offices and apartments.

◀ Aerial view of Paris showing Baron Haussmann's street plan, 1853–1891.

▲ Dresden, Semperoper, Gottfried Semper, rebuilt 1870–1878 after a fire in 1869.

Gottfried Semper

Gottfried Semper was the exception among historicist architects. Unlike most, Semper held that style alone was not reason enough to use an aesthetic from the past. As Louis Sullivan would conclude at the end of the nineteenth century, Semper recognized that a building's aesthetic should be based on a relationship between form and function.

Born in Hamburg in 1803, Semper studied in Munich and Paris, and visited Italy and Greece. The debate about whether or not ancient monuments had been brightly painted led him to develop the *bekleidungstheorie* (clothing theory), which presupposed surface decoration as archetypical, going back to the earliest human artistic expressions.

Semper's most important works are in Dresden, where he was professor of architecture at the Royal Academy. After the 1849 uprising he took a position in Zurich in 1855. He spent the last years of his life working on new plans for Vienna's imperial court buildings, including the famed Burgtheater. He died in 1879 in Rome. His two-volume work on practical aesthetics, published from 1861 to 1863, paved the way for a rationalist approach to architecture.

▶ Zurich, Swiss Polytechnic University, Gottfried Semper, 1861–1874.

Historicism in Germany

In addition to neoclassicism and neo-gothic, other historical styles became popular in Germany during the nineteenth century. Schinkel's late works have links to the Romanesque and Early Christian architecture of northern Italy. Schinkel's student Ludwig Persius developed the style known as *Rundbogen* (rounded arch), influenced by Moorish architecture, which was soon found throughout the country. Leo von Klenze and Friedrich von Gärtner designed an ensemble of historicizing buildings for King Ludwig of Bavaria, including St Ludwig's Church, the Staatsbibliothek (state library), the university, Feldherrenhalle (Field Marshall's Hall) and the Ludwigstrasse Siegestor (Victory Gate). All were more or less direct copies of Italian buildings dating from the Roman period to the early Renaissance quattrocento.

Gottfried Semper made use of a potpourri of High Renaissance and baroque elements in his first and second Dresden Opera houses. His Neues Museum (New Museum), also in Dresden, is an attempt at a unified design in harmony with the baroque Zwinger Palace, of which it is a part.

Typical of the late nineteenth century is a pathos-laden version of formal baroque style. Paul Wallot's Berlin Reichstag building and Raschdorff's Berlin Cathedral, both begun in 1884, fall into this category with their expressive, monumental stylistic gestures well in synch with the spirit of the early industrial revolution. Emperor Wilhelm II's favorite architectural style was a variation on the neoromantic movement recalling the Holy Roman Empire.

Imperial and state architecture were not the only buildings striving for bold, monumental gestures. Throughout Germany there was hardly a town hall that did not resemble a castle or palace.

▲ Kyffhauser, Germany, Kaiser Wilhelm Monument, Bruno Schmitz, Nikolaus Geiger and Emil Hundreiser, 1892–1898.

▼ Munich, Ludwigstrasse with historicizing buildings including St Ludwig's Church, Leo von Klenze and Friedrich von Gärtner, 1830–1840.

◀ Berlin, Reichstag, Paul Wallot, 1884–1894, with a new dome by Sir Norman Foster (see p. 327).

Civil Engineering

The industrial revolution that began in eighteenth-century England had a decisive effect on architecture. The leading innovators of civil engineering had to fight the prejudices of the time, by which they were not considered true architects. Advances in the mining and refining of iron ore set off an architectonic revolution. Iron structural framing and the liberal use of pane glass per-

▲ Bristol, England, Clifton Suspension Bridge, Isambard Kingdom Brunel, begun 1830.

▼ New York, Brooklyn Bridge, John Augustus Roebling, 1883.

▲ Hamburg, Speicherstadt (Warehouse District), begun 1883.

▼ Potsdam, Germany, Dampfmaschinenhaus, 1841–1843.

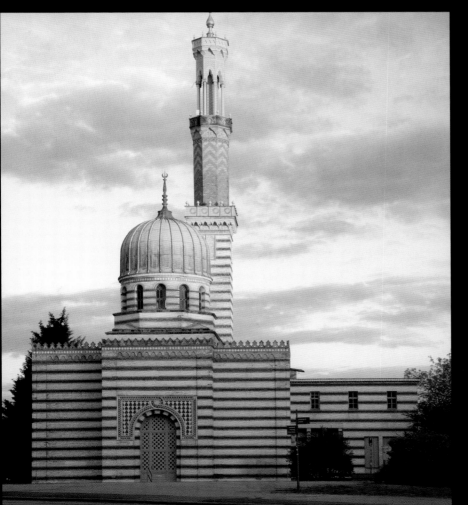

mitted experimentation with entirely new kinds of building. Spatial boundaries became transparent and support elements visible—and thus of interest in themselves. The focal point moved from the wall to its load-bearing structure. The development of reinforced concrete by François Hennebique at the end of the nineteenth century was the final prerequisite for the architecture of the modern age. Industrial production methods that facilitated serial reproduction of individual structural elements were crucial to the long-term success of the new techniques. Even a relatively unskilled construction worker could put together a building using prefabricated elements.

Bridge building was the first area to profit from the technical revolution. In 1779 a cast iron bridge was built across the Severn in southwest England. In 1830, the Clifton suspension bridge over the Avon Gorge in Bristol, England, was begun. Its central span was 702 ft (214 m) long, its filigree iron structure suspended between two neo-egyptian pylons. New York's Brooklyn Bridge spanned a distance of 5,989 ft (1,825 m), its central span rising 135 ft (41 m) above the East River.

Construction of railroad trestles, train stations, shipyards, warehouses, factories and manufacturing plants was also the domain of civil engineers. Urban train stations, in particular, symbolized progress and mobility. Their elaborate design called on historical styles, emphasizing their prestige. The Moorish-style Dampfmaschinenhaus (Steam Engine House) in Potsdam, designed by Ludwig Persius, is evidence that style-based architecture continued to play a significant part in functional architecture. Even the designers of Hamburg's extensive warehouse district, the Speicherstadt, where cast iron framing and modern storage techniques were the rule, clothed their buildings in brick facades with neo-gothic details.

CIVIL ENGINEERING   263

International Fairs and Expositions

The nineteenth century was the century of international fairs and expositions exhibiting the history of humankind while giving visitors the chance to learn about its achievements. The first of these was London's 1851 Great Exhibition of the Works of Industry of all Nations. Paxton's perfectly transparent Crystal Palace reflects the mid-century Victorian mindset. Built with prefabricated, reusable parts, the enormous exhibition hall generated great enthusiasm and vehement disapproval. In 1851 machines were the heroes, with the products of industry bearing witness to the spiritual and moral welfare of the British Empire. The structures built for these international expositions achieved iconic status. The main exhibition building of the Paris International Exposition of 1867 had an elliptical plan, after efforts to build a circular structure to symbolize the universe failed due to a lack of space. The 1889 Galerie des

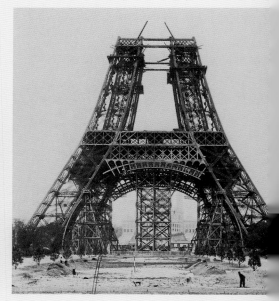

▲ Paris, Eiffel Tower, Gustave Eiffel, 1887–1889. The 986-ft (300.65-m) high tower was erected in just 26 months thanks to over 12,000 prefabricated parts, and almost as many detailed drawings. Over 1 million handmade iron rivets were used in its construction.

▲ Paris, Eiffel Tower under construction in June 1888. Its iron superstructure weighs over 8,000 tons (over 7,000 metric tons) and can withstand hurricane force winds.

▲ London, Crystal Palace, exhibition building for the 1851 Great Exhibition, Joseph Paxton, interior design by Owen Jones, 1850.

◀ Paris, historical photograph of the Galerie des Machines from the 1889 Paris World Exposition, Charles Louis Dutert and Victor Contamin, 1889.

Machines used an innovative system of supports involving arched and hinged trusses set on concrete pedestals, creating an illusion of lightness beneath the great weight of the glass and iron roof. The Eiffel Tower, also from the 1889 Paris Exposition, is in one sense the successful completion of the biblical Tower of Babel. The artistic worth of his bold construction was not immediately recognized: like most other exhibition buildings, the tower was scheduled for demolition at the end of the fair.

▲ ▼ New York, Public Library Main Branch Building on 5th Avenue, designed by the firm Carrère and Hastings, 1911, reading room (above) and exterior (below).

Historicism in the United States

Historic styles were as successful in the United States as they had been in England. Most obviously in the former colonies themselves, architectural references to classical and medieval styles served as a construct of traditions lost through the painful process of independence.

As in Europe, sacred architecture in America was dominated by the neo-gothic. Churches all over the country were remarkably true to their European models. John Upjohn, a British furniture maker who immigrated in 1829, became a pioneer of American Gothic revival architecture. He designed Trinity Church in New York City, among many others. James Renwick's St Patrick's Cathedral was once the tallest, mightiest building in New York. Today, this proud structure resembling Cologne Cathedral is almost completely overwhelmed by surrounding skyscrapers.

Romanticism also had its adherents. Henry Hobson designed Boston's Trinity Church with rounded entry portals and solid towers reminiscent of the Romanesque period in southern France. In 1911, the New York Public Library, a Beaux-Arts palace, opened its columned portico doors, inviting visitors into a towering vestibule with multiple grand stairways and interior courtyards flooded with light. The neoclassical Beaux-Arts style was also the architecture of choice for railway terminals, most of which were built in America in the early twentieth century. The style complemented the newly introduced iron and glass construction techniques well.

◀ New York, St Patrick's Cathedral, James Renwick, 1853–1889, view from a neighboring skyscraper.

▼ Boston, Trinity Church, Henry Hobson Richardson, 1873–1877, facade.

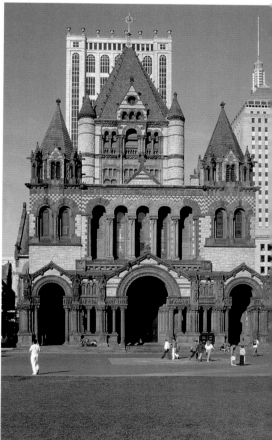

Chicago and the Birth of the Skyscraper

▲ Buffalo, New York, Guaranty Building, Adler and Sullivan, 1894–1895.

▲ Chicago, Carson Pirie Scott Building, Louis Sullivan, 1899–1906.

The Great Chicago Fire of 1871 led to a spectacular rebuilding of Chicago, which in turn led to the era of the skyscraper. With the city's building lots already divided and subdivided, growth could only be achieved by building upward, higher and higher. Modern technology made construction of tall buildings both quick and economical. The use of iron and steel made the new buildings fire-safe, while the prefabricated iron structure provided ample street frontage to be covered with brickwork veneer or decorative panels. Ultimately, though, it was the invention of the steam-powered safety elevator, able to convey passengers comfortably to the upper stories, that was most crucial to the skyscraper's success.

Buildings soared ever higher, bringing a number of aesthetic problems along with them. With classically proportioned, horizontal buildings no longer practical, the stylistic elements of neoclassicism and other historicizing styles were not easily adapted to the strongly vertical skyscraper. As a solution, Chicago architect Louis Sullivan, from the firm Adler and Sullivan, developed a decorative scheme that visually divided tall buildings into units derived from the column. With the vertical main floors of a building understood as a shaft, the skyscraper could accommodate as many floors as desired. The ground and lower floors (usually glassed-in shop fronts) were the base, while the overhanging moldings of the roof developed into a decorative zone comparable to a column's capital. Sullivan's late work, such as the Carson Pirie Scott Building, pushed structure further into the foreground. As Sullivan declared in his famous modernist mantra: "form ever follows function."

The Flatiron Building in New York is an interesting architectural curiosity. Occupying a sharply acute corner between Broadway and Fifth Avenue, the building really does resemble an old-fashioned flatiron, though one that has been finished with the ornate exterior decoration of a Renaissance palazzo. Built in 1902, at twenty-one stories tall, it was once the tallest building in New York.

▶ New York, Flatiron (Fuller) Building, Daniel Hudson Burnham & Co., 1902.

The Threshold of the Modern Age

In the last decades of the nineteenth century, artists' associations were forming all over Europe. They uniformly rejected the excesses of aesthetic eclecticism in favor of a visual culture that embraced all areas of life. In Glasgow, the Arts and Crafts Movement revived artisan cooperatives and promoted handmade, as opposed to industrial, production. In Vienna, the Secessionists declared themselves free from the smothering restrictions of academic art. In Darmstadt, Grand Duke Ernst Ludwig von Hessen founded the Matildenhöhe artists' colony. And in Barcelona, Antoni Gaudí's scurrilous, innovative buildings embodied the ideals of the Spanish Modernisme movement.

Rebellious artists debated ideas in magazines such as *Pan* and *Jugend* (Youth). In Paris, the owners of the Maison de l'Art Nouveau gallery committed to exhibiting only avant-garde art. The various groups had one thing in common: all were striving for a synthesis of the arts. In the late nineteenth and early twentieth centuries, artists and architects promoted the ideal of "total art" as a perfect interweaving of architecture, painting, sculpture and craft. The different genres had gone their separate ways since the end of the baroque period. Now they were called upon to reunite in service of the new culture of the middle class. In the process, a formal stylistic language uninfluenced by historicism would have to develop. After more than a century of clear, deliberate reference to the iconography of the past, a new design philosophy could finally emerge. It can be summed up as follows: a thing is either beautiful in itself, or due to the qualities of its materials. This set architecture on the path that would lead to the rational abstraction of International Style.

A few years later, a second wave of change moved through the international

◀ Amsterdam, Stock Market, Hendrik Petrus Berlage, 1898–1903.

◀ Wroclaw, Poland, formerly Breslau, Germany, Centennial Hall, Max Berg, 1911–1913, interior.

▼ Brussels, Palais Stoclet, 1905–1911, Josef Hoffman.

design community. A group of German artists, craftsmen and industrialists founded the *Deutscher Werkbund* (German Work Federation) in 1907 with the goal of improving the design quality of everyday objects. Hans Poelzig wrote of working toward the perfect "unembellished functional form" by means of utilitarian architecture endowed with a monumental, visually expressive functionality. In Vienna, architect Adolf Loos went so far as to call ornamentation a "crime." Engineer architects also had a role to play. Max Berg, among others, experimented with new technical advances in his design for the Centennial Hall in Wroclaw, Poland. San Francisco's Golden Gate Bridge, once the longest suspension bridge in the world, is another engineering marvel of the age.

On the eve of World War I, architecture began to move in a more visionary direction. The artists' group Gläserne Kette (Glass Chain), led by architect Bruno Taut, was one of the first to promote more socially responsible architecture. Taut's utopian city planning and worker housing design strove to create "a better world" through architecture, paving the way for the expressionist

▲ Potsdam, Germany, Einsteinturm (Einstein Tower), Erich Mendelsohn, 1920–1921.

◀ San Francisco, Golden Gate Bridge, initial planning by engineer James Wilkins in 1916, completed under the direction of Joseph B. Strauss 1933–1937.

movement, the ultimate result of architecture's new freedom from the restraints of the academic style. Erich Mendelsohn's Einsteinturm (Einstein Tower) in Potsdam is perhaps the most elegant expressionist work, with curves that look as if they were sculpted, and it is also perfectly functional. As its name suggests, it was designed as a station for astronomical observations to prove or disprove Einstein's theories

Vienna and Barcelona

Vienna and Barcelona are cities with many superb buildings marking the transition to the twentieth century. The Vienna Secession movement took the city by storm, demanding that art play a part in every aspect of daily life. Joseph Maria Olbrich designed the Secession Building as a symbol of this new start. Planned as a "temple of art," the somewhat archaic-looking plain white cube topped by a dome of brightly gilded laurel leaves is utterly unmistakable. Its reception was decidedly mixed. The work of Vienna architect Otto Wagner proved more influential. Once Wagner managed to free himself from the historicist restraints of the academy, he energetically promoted a more rationalistic approach to architecture. His firms' designs left their mark throughout early twentieth-century Vienna, and continue to impress today. Among his most famous works are the Postsparkasse (Postal Savings Bank) and St Leopold (*Kirche am Steinhof*), the latter a highly

▲ Vienna, dome of the Secession Building, Joseph Maria Olbrich, 1898.

▶ Barcelona, Palau de la Música Catalana, Lluis Domènich i Muntaner, begun in 1904.

functional design that reflects the church's location on the grounds of a psychiatric asylum. Wagner's student, Josef Hoffman, introduced the Vienna Secessionist style to the larger world.

His Palais Stoclet in Brussels is perhaps the era's most perfect example of a gesamtkunstwerk, or total work of art.

In 1888 Barcelona hosted the Universal Exposition, after which the city experienced an unprecedented building boom. Members of the Spanish and Catalan Modernisme movement on a "search for a national architecture" vowed to fight the overwhelming hegemony of the neogothic. For architects Lluis Domènich i Muntaner, Josep Puig and Antoni Gaudí, nature was the best inspiration for their revolutionary system of design that incorporated boldly sculptural techniques and forms. Gaudí's most important work in this style is the Sagrada Família (Holy Family) basilica, which he began in 1882.

◀ Vienna, Postsparkasse (Postal Savings Bank), today the Wagner Museum, Otto Wagner, 1904–1906, main room.

▶ Barcelona, Sagrada Família Basilica, Antoni Gaudí, initially planned in 1882, design completed as of 1906, construction ongoing.

▶▶ Barcelona, Casa Batlló, Antoni Gaudí, 1904–1907, facade.

▲ Paris, Abbesses Metro Station, originally part of the Hôtel de Ville Station, Hector Guimard, 1912.

▲ Glasgow, Glasgow School of Art, Charles Rennie Mackintosh, 1896.

▶ Weimar, Germany, Kunstschule (School of Art), Henry van de Velde, 1904–1911.

Other Reform Movements

There was an air of discontent in many European cities at the end of the nineteenth century. Several reform movements fought against the constraints imposed by academic art. Others condemned the coarsening of popular culture and taste in the wake of industrial mass production. In England and Scotland, the Arts and Crafts Movement aimed to transform decorative art and industrial design into crafts practiced "by the people, for the people." In 1899, Grand Duke Ernst Ludwig von Hessen initiated the paradigm known in German-speaking countries as *Jugendstil* (after the magazine *Jugend*), and elsewhere as Art Nouveau, by founding the artists' colony of Matildenhöhe in Darmstadt. Its buildings were deliberately designed to serve as a visual manifesto of the new style. Among the many who spent time at Matildenhöhe, Peter Behrens became one of the leading German architects of the early twentieth century. The Vienna Secessionist Joseph Maria Olbrich, a student of Otto Wagner, also spent time there. The Matildenhöhe Art Nouveau villas are complete works of art, from their plan and structure to interior and landscape design. They were intended as models for all buildings, everywhere. The jewels of the

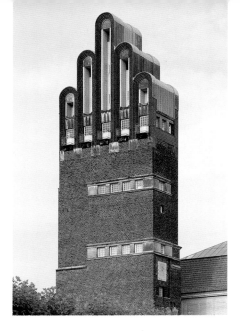

▲ ▶ Darmstadt, Germany, Hochzeitsturm at Matildenhöhe, 1908 (l), and main entry of the Ernst Ludwig Haus, 1901, both attributed to Joseph Maria Olbrich et al.

complex are Ernst Ludwig Haus, named for the colony's patron, and the Wedding Tower, erected after the grand duke's 1905 marriage. The idea of one or more buildings in a city as the embodiment of principles and formal vocabulary would reoccur in the expressionist concept of the *Stadtkrone* (city crown).

In Brussels, Victor Horta and Henry Van de Velde used Arts and Crafts ideas in their craftsman-like approach to architecture, furnishings and interior decor. Van de Velde moved to Weimar in 1902 and founded an influential art school.

▲ Alfeld, Germany, Fagus Factory, Walter Gropius, 1910–1911.

▼ Le Raincy, France, church of Notre-Dame, August and Gustave Perret, 1922.

▶ Berlin, AEG Turbine Hall, Peter Behrens, 1909, exterior (l) and facade detail (r).

The Objectification of Architecture

Form follows function. This revolutionary principle coined by the American Louis Sullivan was the starting point for a new architecture. According to Sullivan and his adherents, the structure of a building was much more than mere technical necessity. Instead, structure was the very essence of the building itself. Therefore, it went without saying that any building's exterior should reflect both its structure and its function. Vienna architect Adolf Loos was the first to carry this concept over into a European context. In addition to designing spare, elegant, highly functional urban buildings, Loos published the influential essay *Ornament and Crime*, in which he urged banning every kind of decorative embellishment.

Industrial architect and designer Peter Behrens prepared the way for functionalist design in his work for the German electric company AEG and his influence on the Deutscher Werkbund, of which he was an early member. The AEG turbine factory Behrens designed is a pioneering work of a new, expressive, monumental architecture. Measuring 680 x 84 ft (207 x 25.6 m), the

▲ Vienna, Goldman and Salatsch Building on Michaelerplatz, Adolf Loos, 1909–1911.

structure of the enormous factory hall was almost entirely steel and glass, "ennobled," as Behrens explained, by subtle details. Two massive, tapering concrete pylons support a broken pediment whose only ornamentation is the company insignia. With the AEG factory, Behrens achieved a near perfect synthesis of functional design and symbolic representation.

Behrens's student Walter Gropius took functionalism a step further with his 1911 Fagus Factory in Alfeld, a town on the Leine River in Germany. The Fagus Factory is a genuinely revolutionary building. The structural elements of the three-story factory cannot be misunderstood. The steel and glass facade boldly exposes the weight-bearing steel and glass wall. In the Fagus Factory, structure had finally become a genuine medium of expression.

Expressionist Architecture

It is no coincidence that a visionary architectural movement emerged around the time of World War I. In reaction to the brewing conflict, a group of utopian-minded architects led by Berlin architect and city planner Bruno Taut dedicated themselves to the creation of "a better world" through design. Their writings and projects demanded a new, expressively artistic architecture that made use of forms found in nature. Very few of their designs were built. Some, like the Glass Pavilion designed for the 1914 Deutsche Werkbund exhibition, were not technically possible at that time. Still, the Taut group paved the way for the style known as expressionism.

The high point of German expressionist architecture is the office building designed for saltpeter magnate Henry B. Sloman. It is better known as Chilehaus (Chile House), a reference to the country from which the commodity was imported. Completed in 1924, its architect was the relatively unknown Fritz Höger. The highly functional, steel-frame building makes formal reference to the traditional brick warehouses of northern Europe, but does so with grandiose, almost aggressive elements counterbalanced by subtle, sculptural details. Over time, Chilehaus' expressive urban dynamic has made it a beloved symbol of the city of Hamburg. In 1930–1933 Höger created a masterpiece with his design for the Hollenzollernplatz Church in Berlin. Its bold facade is both functional and visually appealing.

In the Netherlands, expressionist architecture had its greatest impact in urban planning. The Amsterdam expressionist group designed housing complexes like Het Schip (The Ship), Eigen Haard (Our Hearth) and De Dageraad (Dawn). Their goal was to provide the world with new, people-friendly housing by means of artistically unified, intelligible architecture.

▲ Hamburg, Chilehaus, Fritz Höger, 1922–1924.

▲ Amsterdam, Het Schip apartment building, Michel de Klerk, 1919–1920.

▲ Hilversum, the Netherlands, Dr. Bavinck School, Willem Marinus Dudok, 1921–1922.

▶ Berlin, Hohenzollernplatz Church, Fritz Höger, 1930–1933.

New York Becomes a Metropolis

At the end of the nineteenth century, New York City experienced a wave of foreign immigration like never before. Millions of immigrants from all over the world swarmed into America's metropolis. The end result was a dramatic rise in construction, accompanied by the proliferation of substandard housing and much social misery. In 1898, the five boroughs of Manhattan, the Bronx, Brooklyn, Queens and Staten Island were joined together to form Greater New York City, the largest city in the world.

Over the next few years, the face of New York City would undergo radical change. Fifth Avenue became a magnet for the wealthy upper reaches of society. What had been a simple thoroughfare was soon lined on both sides with palace-like residences. Elegant businesses, shops and office buildings would follow, and continue to define the character of Midtown Manhattan to this day.

The 1902 Flatiron Building (see p. 269) was New York's first skyscraper. It was followed by hundreds more, each one taller and more extravagantly imagined than the last. Before long, it was New York, not Chicago, that held the title of City of Skyscrapers. Even the great stock market crash of 1929 could not stop New York's precipitous rise. In the midst of economic despair, prestigious building complexes such as Rockefeller Center were planned so as to promote the city and increase investor confidence.

Among the pre-World War I skyscrapers of note, the 1913 Woolworth Building literally towered above the rest. Its facade is staggered as it rises until it is more a tower than a building, one capped by a copper-sheathed, pyramidal roof. The steel-clad, wheel-like motifs adorning the top of the 1930 Chrysler Building have made it one of New York's iconic structures. Like many New York skyscrapers, it is easily identifiable in the city's skyline. At 1,069 ft (319 m), this highly ornamented Art Deco building was the tallest building in the world until the Empire State Building surpassed it a few years later. At 1,250 ft (381 m)—1,472 ft (449 m) with its antenna—the Empire State Building is practically a vertical city. Its steel frame weighs well over 60,000 tons. At dusk, powerful lighting illuminates the upper thirty floors in a variety of colors. The 1897 Waldorf Astoria Hotel had to be demolished to make room for the Empire State Building, but in 1931, the new Waldorf Astoria was built across the street in full Art Deco style.

◀ New York, Empire State Building, Shreve, Lamb & Harmon, 1930–1931.

▲ New York, Woolworth Building, Cass Gilbert, 1911–1913.

▼ New York, Waldorf-Astoria Hotel, 1931, lobby.

▲ New York, Chrysler Building, William Van Alen, 1928–1930, detail of spire.

▲ Utrecht, Truus Schröder House, Gerrit Thomas Rietveld, 1924.

▼ Dessau, Bauhaus Building, Walter Gropius, 1926, interior.

◄ Rotterdam, Van Nelle Tobacco Factory, Joahnnes Brinkmann, Leendert van der Vlugt and Mart Stam, 1926–1930.

International Style Architecture

It took almost half a century for Louis Sullivan's mantra "form follows function" to make its way around the world. In 1911, Walter Gropius' Fagus Factory was already a sign of things to come. After World War I, modernism came to fruition in the International Style. In 1919, Gropius was named director of the School of Visual Arts and Industrial Design School in Weimar. Under his leadership, the two schools were subsumed into the Bauhaus, a studio workshop dedicated to improving the industrial design of everything from buildings to wallpaper. Internal conflicts led to dissolution of the Weimar Bauhaus, which Gropius then refounded in the city of Dessau. The Dessau Bauhaus Building was designed by Gropius himself to serve as a visual manifesto of his ideas. He deliberately divided the building into formally distinct sections based on the kind of work that would be carried out there. In the Netherlands, De Stijl (The Style) formed around similar principles. De Stijl architects specialized in modular apartment houses. Not unlike a painting by Dutch artist Piet Mondrian, the individual rectilinear elements were visually distinguished using line and color. "Transparency" was the idea behind the design of the glass-fronted Van Nelle Tobacco Factory in Rotterdam, an influential industrial building of this period.

Architecture soon became a vehicle for the sociocultural upheaval of the times, with each building intended as a model for the future. One of the most impressive of these exemplary buildings was Mies van der Rohe's Pavilion at the 1929 Barcelona World's Fair. Its all-inclusive design program ensured that everything, from the structure itself

▲ Barcelona, reconstruction of the Pavilion for the 1929 World's Fair, Mies van der Rohe, 1929.

▼ Chandigarh, India, Parliament Building, Le Corbusier, 1955.

to the interior furnishings, was visually and functionally integrated into the whole. Demolished at the end of the fair, the pavilion was eventually rebuilt from the original plans.

The Congrès Internationaux d'Architecture Moderne (International Congress on Modern Architecture) was formed in 1928 to promote modern architecture internationally. While the congress succeeded in popularizing rationalistic design as a sensible alternative to traditionalist approaches, its push for the creation of new architectural utopias proved more problematic. An example of the pitfalls encountered in such an enterprise is Le Corbusier's only moderately successful planned city of Chandigarh in Indian Punjab.

Urban Housing Complexes

Building more and better housing was a main focus of architecture between the World Wars. Urban growth and expansion had led to serious social problems that many architects perceived as their next great challenge. New buildings, they claimed, would make the best use of industrial products in the service of society. Given the shortage of urban land available for building and growing populations, optimal use of the smallest possible area was a formal principle of nearly all architects of the time.

New designs for housing complexes led the way, based on the ideal of the Garden City, first described in late nineteenth-century England. Bruno Taut's Berlin Hufeisensiedlung (Horseshoe Estate) was a late 1920s interpretation of the Garden City. The community housing of Red Vienna—"red" is a reference to the city's socialist government between the wars—addressed the need for increased access to affordable, quality housing at all levels of society.

The Weissenhofsiedlung, several blocks of housing in Stuttgart, Germany, was one of the earliest of what its instigator, Mies van der Rohe, dubbed "pattern settlements." These were designed to display the principles of the new style by showcasing its application in a wide range of housing options. Mies managed to involve the avant-garde of European architecture in his project, giving Hans Scharoun, Bruno and Max Taut, Walter Gropius, Le Corbusier and Peter Oud each the task of designing the prototypical house of the future. The result is one of the earliest examples of what would be called the International Style. The general public, however, was less enthusiastic. Most of the housing was uninhabited until after World War II.

▶ Vienna, Karl-Marx-Hof housing complex, Karl Ehn, 1926–1930.

▲ Stuttgart, Weissenhofsiedlung, housing units by Mies van der Rohe (above) and Peter Oud (below), 1927.

▶ Marseille, France, Unité d'Habitation (Housing Units), 1953–1955.

Designing Space

The experience of space in all its variability and interaction with the outside world was another preoccupation of the International Style architects. As early as 1914, Le Corbusier's *Domino* construction system of interchangeable, mass-produced structural design elements made it possible for a building's walls, ceiling, supports and facade to be considered separately, as relatively independent and easily manipulated units. This cleared the way for the open floor plan. Non-supporting walls for the division of a living space into rooms could now be placed just about anywhere.

The concept was taken up with the greatest enthusiasm in the design of freestanding houses and villas. Within a flexible living space, glass walls were used to provide stunning views of the surrounding landscape. Sliding doors blurred the difference between inside and outside, and space became fluid. Le Corbusier brought this trend to a head with his concept of a *promenade architecturale*. He describes moving through a building as a transitional, though definitive, experience. As one moves through a building, a physical awareness of space unfolds architecturally; one's point of view is in constant flux as one moves along the path to awareness.

The Villa Savoye in the Parisian suburb of Poissy stands on *pilotis*, Le Corbusier's term for steel-reinforced concrete pillars. The living area is set atop a glassed-in base unit that houses the garage and servant's quarters. The curving walls of the building's attic anticipate the extraordinary plasticity of Le Corbusier's late period buildings.

Mies van der Rohe's Villa Tugendhat in Brünn and Hans Scharoun's Villa Schminke in Löbau, both from the 1930s, also provide residents and visitors alike with architectural direction through the living spaces and into the

▲ Cologne, St Engelbert, Dominikus Böhm, 1930–1932, interior.

garden. Ramps and staircases were used increasingly as an elegant means of passing through space. The color white began to predominate, and concrete surfaces became increasingly sculptural.

The design options made possible by new construction techniques and improvements in building materials, together with the spiritual freedom of directed space, helped the International Style conquer sacred architecture as well. Architect Dominikus Böhm, using steel-reinforced concrete, designed a parabola-shaped altar room for St Englebert's Church in Cologne. The towering space shimmers in glistening light that dissipates into deep shadows on either side of the altar.

◄ Löbau, Germany, Villa Schminke, Hans Scharoun, 1930–1933.

▼ Poissey near Paris, Villa Savoye, Le Corbusier and Pierre Jeanneret, 1929–1931.

Houses in the American Landscape

Frank Lloyd Wright was one of many Chicago School architects who once worked for Louis Sullivan. But his interests did not lie solely with skyscrapers. Frank Lloyd Wright wanted to build houses. It is the urban houses he built in his singular Prairie Style, as well as his later modular and sculptural works, for which he is most famous. Prairie Style houses are low and broad, with cantilevered terraces and projecting rooflines. While local forms and materials predominate, Wright also found inspiration in Asian architecture, particularly in Eastern conceptions of space. In Wright's later work, the influence of Le Corbusier and Mies van der Rohe's International Style is unmistakable.

▲ Chicago, Frederick C. Robie House, Frank Lloyd Wright, 1910.

▼ Bear Run, Pennsylvania, Fallingwater (Kaufmann House), Frank Lloyd Wright, 1935.

The Kaufmann House, better known as Fallingwater, is a series of compact, buff-ivory concrete terraces projecting dramatically over a waterfall. A towering chimney made of local fieldstone is the focal point of the interior.

Austrian architects Rudolf Schindler and Richard Neutra took Wright's ideas—they both had briefly worked in his studio—and built their own modern houses ideally integrated into the landscape of southern California. In the 1940s, the glass wall became a formal statement. Philip Johnson's 1949 Glass House is an almost completely transparent rectilinear structure built on his own heavily wooded estate. Only the bathroom is completely surrounded by solid wall. Mies van der Rohe's 1951 Farnsworth House is similarly glass-walled. Designed as a weekend retreat, it is a single room set on steel pillars.

▲ New Caanan, Connecticut, Glass House, Philip Johnson, 1949.

▼ Palm Springs, California, Kaufmann Desert House, Richard Neutra, 1946–1947.

Architecture and Dictatorship

Twentieth-century dictatorships consciously used architecture as a tool for propaganda. Neoclassical styles were overwhelmingly the choice for prestige buildings because they provided a reference point to thousands of years of tradition. Residential architecture became decidedly regional. Fake thatched roofs and faux half-timbering served as proof that a house's inhabitants were, as fascist philosophy defined patriotism, "rooted in the soil."

▼ Moscow State University, Lev Rudnev, et al., begun in 1947.

During the Third Reich in Germany, as well as in other dictatorships, what was called neoclassical art and architecture was deeply lacking in classical spirit. The monumental buildings designed by Nazi architects Albert Speer and Paul Ludwig lacked the steady harmony of proportions that define classical architecture. Instead, they rely on the visually tiring devices of endless arcades and massively columned facades. Their party government buildings, People's Assembly Halls (*Volkshalle*), regional centers (*Gauforen*) and parade grounds were uniformly gigantic and intimidating. Ornament was largely absent, and when present was limited to heroic relief sculpture, imperial eagles and swastikas. The Haus der Kunst (House of Art) in

Munich is an early iconic building in Nazi architecture. Adolf Hitler praised the "noble German tectonics" of this perfectly neo-Egyptian building. Albert Speer's megalomaniac Nazi Party Rally Grounds in Nuremburg are fully in the spirit of "renovation" Hitler deemed necessary for German cities. Speer's plan for the imperial capital of Berlin fell victim to a rain of allied bombs. Delusions of grandeur were apparent in the architecture of other dictator-led countries, as well. Moscow State University was designed to serve as a colossal Stalinist prestige project. Somewhat surprisingly, the Case del Fascio (House

▼ Munich, Haus der Kunst, Paul Ludwig Troost, 1934–1937.

of Fascism) in Como, Italy, is an utterly modern building with elegant, harmonious proportions. Also initiated under Mussolini, the EUR (Esposizione Universale Roma), a Roman suburb built for the aborted World's Fair of 1942, shares this structure-focused, compelling, thoroughly urban quality. In Franco's Spain, architects were first ordered to make frequent reference to Spain's golden age in the design of ministerial buildings. By the late 1940s and 1950s, Spanish architecture had developed its own version of modernism, one that could hold its own with the best that International Style could offer. Many Spanish architects emigrated to the United States, Latin America, Turkey and Israel, taking the ideals of modernism along.

▲ Nuremburg, Congress Hall of the Nazi Party Rallying Grounds, Ludwig and Franz Ruff, 1934–1941.

▼ Como, Italy, Casa del Fascio, today Casa del Popolo (House of the People), Giuseppe Terragni, 1932–1936.

▲ New York, World Trade Center, destroyed in 2001, Minoru Yamasaki & Associates, 1970–1975.

The Postwar Period to the Present

World War II brought the eager optimism of the modern age to a crashing halt. In Europe and the United States, the immediate post-war years were relatively unproductive and little progress was made. Happily, that was not so in Latin America, where what was called the International Style (after a 1932 exhibition of that name at the Museum of Modern Art in New York) flourished more or less unhindered. Though its roots lay largely elsewhere, it received an enthusiastic reception in Central and South America.

In the United States, postwar architecture was influenced by new immigrants Ludwig Mies van der Rohe and Walter Gropius, as well as the New York mega-firm of Skidmore, Owings and Merrill (SOM). American architecture took on many of the urban social challenges first raised by the Congrès Internationaux d'Architecture Moderne (CIAM) in the 1920s and 1930s. Van der

▲ Frankfurt, Messe Torhaus (Gatehouse), Oswald Mathias Ungers, 1984.

◄ New York, United Nations Headquarters, Wallace K. Harrison et al., 1949–1950

▲ Säynätsalo, Finland, Town Hall, Alvar Aalto, 1949–1952

Rohe's design mantra of "less is more" motivated architects to create rationalist, function-oriented buildings free of historical ballast. As a result, minimalist monuments such as the United Nations Headquarters in New York predominated the early days of American postwar architecture. Derided at first as a "Miesian Box," that design influenced the architecture of office buildings all over the world.

Over time, rationalism made its way back to Germany via the USA. As of 1960, architectural innovation was back on familiar soil. This second wave of European modern architecture arrived in the form of organic buildings, designed such that the form of a building evolved naturally from its interior functional areas, to be expressed on an exterior that was in harmony with its surroundings. This principle is embodied by Le Corbusier's Chapelle Notre-Dame-du-Haut in Ronchamp, France (see p. 304). At the same time, some crossfertilization is evident in Finnish architect Alvar Aalto's Säynätsalo Town Hall and Hans Scharoun's stately Berlin Philharmonic. Both are organic buildings influenced by the earlier expressionist movement, as well. The long reign of International Style modern architecture came to an end in the 1970s. Rapid advances in technology and alternating waves of avant-garde and conservative design movements led to hi-tech architecture, which existed side by side with the overwhelming historicizing detail characteristic of postmodernism. Civil engineering was revived, largely as a result of Santiago Calatravas's breathtakingly innovative bridge design.

The deconstructivists ruled the 1990s. Their exploding designs and lively use of color introduced a wealth of original ideas into late twentieth-century architecture. The popularity of deconstructivist architects including Zaha Hadid and Rem Koolhaas continued into the new millennium.

▶ Seville, Bridge over the Alamillo, Santiago Calatrava, 1987–1992.

▲ Paris, Grande Arche, Johan von Spreckelsen, et al., 1989.

▼ Berlin, Philharmonic, Hans Scharoun, 1960–1963.

Modern Architecture in Latin America

Modern architecture took off in Latin America in the 1940s, a time when much of the world was focused on World War II and its aftermath. As early as 1935, Le Corbusier and Lucio Costa collaborated on the design of the Ministry of Education and Health (MEH) in Rio de Janeiro, aided by a young Brazilian architect, Oscar Niemayer. The MEH Building put Brazil at the forefront of modern architecture. The box-like block of offices stands on Le Corbusier's characteristic reinforced concrete *pilotis*. The north side has a projecting *brise-soleil* (sunshade) wall, another of his inventions. Sculptures and subtle decorative details, enhanced by Roberto Burle Marx's landscape design, ensured that

▶ Mexico City, Main Library of the City University, Juan O'Gorman, 1950–1952.

▶▶ Rio de Janeiro, Ministry of Education and Health (MEH) building, Lucio Costa, Le Corbusier and Oscar Niemeyer, 1935.

the MEH Building retained an unmistakably Brazilian character. Niemayer later designed some of the most revolutionary concrete buildings ever, including the parabola-form Church of San Francisco in Pampulhla. Meanwhile, in Mexico, Félix Candela was experimenting with thin

concrete shells. His results made construction of buildings like Jørn Utzon's Sydney Opera House possible.

Back in Brazil, a progressive new president, Juscelino Kubitschek, made modern architecture the national style when he commissioned the new capital city of Brasilia. Costa and Niemayer had a daunting task: design an urban utopia in the Amazon tropical savanna in the undeveloped state of Goías. Costa devised the famous Pilot Plan Brasilia, which schematically resembles a bird with outstretched wings. Government buildings occupy the long axis; the cross axis has apartment blocks and leisure facilities. The Praca dos Tres Poderes (Plaza of the Three Powers) is the heart of the city, as well as its architectural showpiece. Three magnificent concrete and steel buildings occupy the spacious open area: the Congresso National (National Congress), Palacio do Planalto (Presidential Palace) and Palacio de Justica (Palace of the Judiciary). Oscar Niemeyer designed all three, as well as

▲ Mexico City, Torres de Satélite, Luis Barragán and Mathias Goeritz, 1957–1958.

▶ Brasilia, Congresso National on the Plaza of the Three Powers, Oscar Niemeyer, 1958–1960.

the parabolic National Cathedral, between 1956 and 1960.

The nationalist stamp of modern architecture in Mexico is crystallized in the design of Ciudad Universitaria (City University) in Mexico City, the largest university in Latin America. The Main Library Building is covered in mosaics illustrating events from Mexican history made from local stone. Imposing education buildings are also typical of the Venezuelan capital, Caracas. The Alexander Calder mobile *Clouds* is permanently displayed in the Aula Magna (auditorium) of Caracas University.

Luis Barragán designed the multicolored Torres de Satélite (Satellite Towers) in the northern part of Mexico City. The 98–170 ft (30–52 m) prisms are the focal point of a 1950s planned urban development.

Postwar Movements

Ludwig Mies van der Rohe dominated architecture in the postwar period. Having already worked with steel and glass in his prewar expressionist buildings, Mies was well-equipped to lead the International Style that would define the postwar period. In 1938, Mies emigrated to Chicago, where his pioneering glass, concrete and steel-frame office and apartment buildings, including the famous Lake Shore Drive Apartments, revolutionized the urban landscape. The 38-floor Seagram Building in New York is his masterpiece. A perfectly proportioned, rectilinear slab of glass, the Seagram Building has a timeless elegance. Its simple, block-like appearance and complete lack of embellishment are a radical departure from the splendid detailing of Art Deco. Yet these "Miesian boxes" are far from ugly. Louis Sullivan's classical divisions

▲ La Jolla, California, Jonas Salk Institute, 1962–1963.

of base and attic are subtly preserved and visually distinguished.

Lever House, designed by Gordon Bunshaft in collaboration with the firm of Skidmore, Owings and Merrill (SOM), is another milestone in the design of modern office towers. Lever House is a green-shimmering glass box

resting on a flat, elongated base. The two intersecting masses are visually and structurally integrated by means of a steel-profiled facade. The German architect Helmut Hentrich came up with another solution in his design for the Thyssen Haus in Düsseldorf. Three parallel narrow, rectilinear slabs of glass and steel appear to have randomly slid across the ground into their final overlapping positions.

The reduction of formal elements in favor of straightforward design and structural transparency reached its apex in office buildings. Contemporary with these developments, architect Louis Kahn experimented with unconventional massing and the aesthetics of concrete surfaces. His Jonas Salk Institute is an assembly of open-plan workspaces designed to promote collaboration between the scientists working there. The individual units are constructed of finely finished concrete lacking any trace of traditional ornamentation. Instead, their archaic monumentality radiates a sublime strength.

▲ New York, Lever House, Gordon Bunshaft with Skimore, Owings and Merrill, 1951–1952.

▲ New York, Seagram Building, Mies van der Rohe, 1957–1958.

▶ Düsseldorf, Thyssen Haus, Helmut Hentrich and Hubert Petschnigg, 1957–1960.

Chicago

From the dawn of the modern age, Chicago has been a city of skyscrapers. The decisive steps in the technical design of very tall buildings were made here, in the late nineteenth century, in the offices of Louis Sullivan and the firm Holabird & Roche. Their pioneering work in developing steel-framed buildings and the use of fire-resistant materials made today's cities possible. With the arrival of Mies van der Rohe at the end of the 1930s, Chicago was ready to join the world's leading architectural cities. It was soon a showcase of the International Style in America. In addition, the renowned architecture firm of Skidmore, Owings and Merrill (SOM) developed a new steel frame system in Chicago that let tall buildings soar ever higher.

Mies was head of the School of Architecture at the Illinois Institute of Technology in the 1950s and 1960s. Among his many works are two apartment towers on Lake Shore Drive that are among the most significant International Style buildings in the USA. Struc-

▲ Chicago, Sears Tower, Bruce Graham and SOM, 1971–1974.

▼ The Chicago skyline.

▲ Chicago, John Hancock Center, Bruce Graham and SOM, 1969–1970.

▶ Chicago, James R. Thompson Center (formerly the State of Illinois Center), Helmut Jahn, 1979–1984.

turally, they consist of concrete laid over a double-T steel girder frame. Their facades are almost entirely aluminum-framed glass.

The late 1960s and early 1970s were the era of very tall skyscrapers in Chicago. In 1969, the John Hancock Tower was built, followed by the Sears Tower in 1974. Both were designed by Bruce Graham in collaboration with SOM. Very tall buildings required innovative support structures. The floors of the Sears Tower are suspended from nine structurally separate vertical units of varying heights. The grouping or "bundling" of these units permitted the construction of a tall, narrow building rising in steps to a single tower. With a height of 1,451 ft (442 m), Sears Tower was the tallest building in the world until 1998.

The steel-frame skeleton of the John Hancock Center makes use of x-braced steel beams visible through the glass curtain wall facade. The building's characteristic black anodized aluminum facing was at first heavily criticized. Today, the Hancock Center is a beloved Chicago emblem.

German architect Helmut Jahn's State of Illinois Center, recently renamed the James R. Thompson Center, consists of a breathtakingly tall atrium surrounded by galleries of offices. The glass and steel used in its construction are not only visible, but accentuated with color. In 2010 a further architectonic highlight will be completed along Chicago's lakefront: the Chicago Spire. Designed by Spanish architect Santiago Calatrava, it will be the tallest freestanding structure in North America, standing 2,000 ft (610 m) high.

Buildings as Sculpture

As early as the beginning of the twentieth century, architects working in the spirit of total art were trying to give their buildings a sculptural quality. Both Mies van der Rohe and Le Corbusier designed organic buildings that were expressively sculptural, but also in tune with the rationalist doctrine of functionalism. Both sculptural-expressive and rational-technical approaches continued throughout the early phase of International Style and into the postwar period. Technical advances and experimentation with new materials played no small role in artistic design. The perfecting of structural concrete and improved casting methods made swooping facades and flying rooflines possible. In the 1950s, Le Corbusier moved toward more sculptural design. His pilgrimage church of Notre-Dame-du-Haut in Ronchamp was revolutionary. Projecting like the bow of a ship, the interior and exterior of the church are still very functional. Curved walls embrace an interior space dappled with colored light filtered through stained-glass windows. Some of the walls consist of local stone with a thin skin of white concrete; others are entirely concrete, some of which was cast in place. The overhanging roof, its concrete stained light brown, recalls the heavy thatching of the indigenous village architecture. Frank Lloyd Wright's abstractly sculptural Guggenheim Museum was built about the same time. The main exhibition space is conceived as a ramp spiraling upward, with the spiral dramatically articulated in the museum's exterior.

Danish architect Jørn Utzon won the competition to build a new opera house in Sydney, Australia, with a design of breathtaking audacity. The precast concrete roof of the theater and concert hall is formed from thin concrete shells up to 198 ft (60 m) high. From a distance, they look like wind-filled sails. Despite the design's many detractors,

▲ New York, lobby of the Solomon R. Guggenheim Museum, Frank Lloyd Wright, 1956–1960.

▼ Ronchamp, France, pilgrimage church of Notre-Dame-du-Haut, Le Corbusier, 1950–1955.

▼ Sydney, Australia, Opera House, Jørn Utzon, 1957–1973.

▲ New York, TWA Terminal at John F. Kennedy Airport, Eero Saarinen, 1962.

▼ Brussels, Atomium, André Waterkeyn, 1958.

and financial and engineering problems exacerbated by the long design and construction period, the Sydney Opera House has survived to become the very symbol of Australia.

One of the most functional sculptural buildings of its time is Eero Saarinen's former TWA Terminal (currently out of service) at John F. Kennedy airport near New York City. Compact, Y-shaped pylons support four arced concrete shells resembling the wings of a bird that just happened to alight in the middle of the departure hall. This futuristic monument became a symbol of modern travel. The steel-clad Atomium in Brussels was designed as the emblem of the 1958 World's Fair. The 335-ft (102-m) tall accessible sculpture is an accurate model of an iron crystal molecule, enlarged 165 million times.

▲ ▼ Berlin, Kaiser Wilhelm Memorial Church, Egon Eiermann, 1961–1963, interior (above) and exterior (below).

Berlin in the 1950s and 1960s

After 1945, the primary task of German architects was to quickly rebuild the infrastructure and cities so as to establish a new, democratic Federal Republic of Germany. Egon Eiermann's Kaiser Wilhelm Gedächtniskirche (Memorial Church) in Berlin came to symbolize the rebuilding process. An artfully provocative, almost brutalist octagon forms the main church building, which is paired with a freestanding prismatic bell tower. The new church is side-by-side with the bombed-out ruins of its neo-romantic predecessor, left standing as a reminder. Eiermann's uncompromising building is most effective from within. The concrete and steel facade is pierced by thousands of small squares of blue glass, creating an

almost mystically intense atmosphere. Hans Scharoun's nearly contemporary Berlin Philharmonic (see p. 297) took a different direction. Influenced by the expressionism of the 1920s, the Philharmonic is a more organic interpretation. In every way, its vibrant exterior expresses the building's function as a center for musical performance.

After a detour in America, the progressive ideas of International Style began to make their way back to Germany around 1960. Mies van der Rohe himself designed the 1965–1968 Neue Nationalgalerie (New National Gallery), the very quintessence of his genius as well as his most deliberate reduction of the rationalist principles of International Style. The glassed-in exhibition hall is interrupted only by short intervals of vertical steel framing supporting a flat, overhanging roof. The effect is transparent and nearly weightless. While an

architect of the Mies's stature was able to see his designs through to completion, the reality was often different elsewhere, particularly when rapid urban reconstruction was prioritized at the expense of design quality. A lack of informed city planning transformed the residential areas of many postwar German cities into concrete jungles.

In the former German Democratic Republic (GDR), neoclassical symmetry and axial city planning were the rule. The street named Stalin Allee (today Karl Marx Allee and Frankfurter Allee) was the prestige address for buildings of the socialist state. Despite a certain formal conservatism, city planning in the former GDR pointed to the future. Mixed housing and retail complexes complete with integrated leisure facilities meant there were no "dead" quarters in most East German cities, neither during the day nor at night.

▲ Berlin, Neue Nationalgalerie, Mies van der Rohe, 1965–1968, exterior.

▼ Berlin, Stalin Allee (today Karl-Marx-Allee and Frankfurter Allee), Hermann Henselmann et al., 1952–1958.

Hi-Tech Architecture

Groundbreaking changes took place in architecture in the early 1970s, eventually leading to the renunciation of the International Style in favor of postmodernism. Hi-tech architecture took over the mantle of functionalism. As technological advances developed, hi-tech architects freely experimented with new materials and construction methods while still trying to maintain structural transparency according to modernist principles. A pioneer work in the hi-tech genre is the Centre Pompidou in Paris by Richard Rogers and Renzo Piano. This exhibition building in the heart of the city is nearly exhibitionist in the extent to which it exposes its technical equipment. The exterior facade features heating pipes, stairways and elevators, all on view for anyone to see. With the mechanical and circulation elements attached to the outside of the building, maximal space was left open and free for exhibition space.

Sir Norman Foster's administration building for the Hongkong & Shanghai Bank Corporation (HSBC) literally "hangs" from four giant steel girder towers, which are visually articulated in each of the building's main facades. The girder towers gain lateral support from the addition of angled steel frame elements attached to the vertical girders at multiple levels.

In Germany, Günter Behnisch and Frei Otto designed a tent-like roof made of tensile materials for the 1972 Munich Olympic Stadium. Thin pylons support a lightweight, arcing steel net covered with a thin skin of transparent acrylic. When viewed from above, the flexible skin tent becomes a high design, urban monument that seems to grow naturally out of the landscape.

▲ Munich, roof of the Olympic Stadium, Günter Behnisch and Frei Otto, 1972.

▼ Paris, Centre Pompidou, Richard Rogers and Renzo Piano, 1971–1977.

▶ Hong Kong, HSBC (Hongkong & Shanghai Bank Corporation) Main Building, Sir Norman Foster, 1983–1986.

Postmodernism

▲ New Orleans, Piazza d'Italia,
Charles Moore, 1976–1979.

▲ Vienna, shop front, formerly the
Retti candle store, Hans Hollein, 1964.

Mies van der Rohe's "less is more" had defined the aesthetic of modern architecture for more than half a century. In 1966, a young American architect, Robert Venturi, dared to counter the master with the words "less is a bore."

Venturi promoted a complex, multi-faceted, even contradictory architectural language to counteract the purism of postwar modernism. The new trend would be christened postmodernism, a name imported from literary theory.

Postmodernism's initial success was assured by the reception of New York's AT&T Building, a veritable architectural compendium of the style. The 37-story corporate headquarters has a classic structure with a crowning broken pediment, a visual quote from mid-eighteenth-century neoclassicism. The AT&T Building cleared the way for a more ornamental, pictorial architectural style. Its architects Philip Johnson and John Burgee debated bitterly with proponents of International Style over the legitimacy of postmodernism, which purists saw as kitsch rather than aesthetically-motivated design. Postmodernists responded that their incorporation of historical elements, particularly of motifs that had long been out of circulation, was part of a conscious design process carried out in full knowledge of their content, symbolism and figurative interpretations.

◄ Philadelphia, Guild House, John Rauch and Robert Venturi, 1960–1963.

► New York, the former AT&T Building, today the Sony Building, Philip Johnson and John Burgee, 1984.

Deconstructivism

Deconstructivism was the magic word at the end of the 1980s. Finally, it was the buildings themselves, instead of the architects, that were in a continuous state of unrest. Shattered forms, wildly slanting walls and precariously tipped rooflines gave the impression of an explosion-like process underway, one that has sent the substance of the building into a perpetual state of disorder. Philip Johnson, the man who had already launched postmodernism, was also a protagonist of the deconstructivist movement. Deconstructivism broke through internationally with the work of Zaha Hadid, Peter Eisenman, Frank Gehry, Daniel Liebeskind, Rem

▲ Stuttgart, Germany, Hysolar Institute, Günter Behnisch & Partner, 1987.

▼ Den Haag, Dance Theater, Rem Koolhaas, 1984–1987.

Koolhaas and the Vienna design studio COOP Himmelblau.

In 1987, Günter Behnisch & Partner designed the Hysolar Institute in Stuttgart with slanted glass surfaces, brushed aluminum details, and structural elements that seem to crash into one another. The building is practically a satire of technological precision.

In Weil am Rhein, also in Germany and home of the furniture company Vitra, the 1993 Factory Firehouse designed by Zaha Hadid is a spectacularly realized project. The seemingly support-free concrete hall resembles an arrow soaring through space. Smooth surfaces of concrete and glass boldly intersect with shining aluminum edges. Angles and seemingly arbitrary fractures define the facade.

▲ Weil am Rhein, Germany, Vitra Design Museum Factory Firehouse, Zaha Hadid, 1993.

▼ Dresden, Germany, UFA Cinema Center, COOP Himmelblau, 1998.

Japanese Architects and Architecture in Japan

Japan has long been inspired by Western arts. The International Style of the postwar period excited an ongoing interest in modern architecture. The metabolist movement founded in Tokyo in 1959 sought to generate buildings that responded to the needs of massed society: flexible, adaptable and technologically innovative design was the goal. Their urban planning projects, such as "City Swimming in the Sea" (Kikutake Unabara, 1960) or "Helix City" (Kisho Kurikawa, 1961) received considerable attention among specialists for their utopian yet decidedly urban expression of grandeur, but for the most part they remained on paper. Architect Kenzo Tange experimented with futuristic urban design in his expansion plan for Tokyo. The plan calls for islands of cell-like mega-structures occupying an 11-mile (18-km) long axis extending across Tokyo Bay. Tange's internationally acclaimed Yoyogi National Gymnasium, built for the 1964 Olympics, as well as with his 1970 World's Fair buildings in Osaka, drew international attention to Japanese modern architecture. Tange next tried to take traditional Japanese building elements and transform them into functionalistic architecture, an effort that moved his later work ever closer to prevailing international trends. His 1991 Tokyo City Hall with its double-towered facade is a functional, modernist building that brings to mind a giant European cathedral.

A younger generation of architects led by Tadao Ando brought the aesthetic principles of Japanese culture to a wider audience. Ando's rooms are constructed of finely finished concrete that has been cast in place. Each piece has the same area as a typical tatami mat that might be hung on the wall of

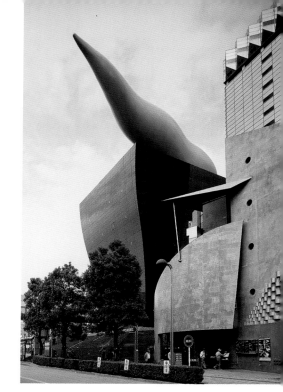

▲ Tokyo, Asahi Beer Hall, Philippe Starck, 1988–1990.

▼ Weil am Rhein, Germany, Vitra Design Museum Seminar House, Tadao Ando, 1993.

▲ Tokyo, City Hall, Kenzo Tange, 1986–1991.

a traditional Japanese house. Ando's spare, peaceful, evocative spaces are as suitable for meditation as they are for assembly. Subtle lighting effects created by filtering natural light through narrow slits in the ceiling enhances the mystical, contemplative atmosphere. In Weil am Rhein, Ando designed the conference center for the Vitra furniture company. His plan established an area of peace and calm between the ecstatically deconstructivist Vitra buildings by Zaha Hadid and Frank Gehry located nearby. It is no surprise that Ando is a museum architect par excellence, with commissions around the world.

Internationally famed designers like Philippe Starck have also worked in Japan. A mysterious golden flame crowns his monolithic Asahi Beer Hall in Tokyo. Uruguayan architect Rafael Viñoly designed the Tokyo International Forum, which resembles a nineteenth-century glass exhibition palace.

▶ Tokyo, International Forum, Rafael Viñoly, 1989–1997.

New Museums in Europe

Museums were some of the most important commissions of the late twentieth century. Austrian architect Hans Hollein's museum complex in Mönchengladbach, Germany, nestles into the slopes of a hill. The different elements are grouped in combinations that produce collage-like effects, offering a new view with every change of position. Each exhibit has its own unique space.

"A house is a house" might well be the guiding idea behind Oswald Mathias Unger's 1984 German Architecture Museum in Frankfurt. The design had to integrate a pre-existing building, as was the case for Richard Meier's neighboring Frankfurt Museum of Art. Unger's take on the situation is that of a vivid comedy of errors that plays with the topic of what is and what is not constructed space. This is itself a deeper, subtle visualization of the building's function as a museum of architecture. One of the most acclaimed museums

of the late twentieth century is James Stirling's Neue Staatsgalerie (New State Gallery) in Stuttgart, famous as the work that brought postmodernism to Germany. Stirling plays with historicist motifs, which he combines with modern elements. A fantastic outdoor, C-shaped rotunda elegantly directs visitors to the exhibition wings. Traditional elements like triangular pediments, triumphal arches and the occasional Roman aedi-

▲ Mönchengladbach, Germany, City Museum on the Abteiberg, Hans Hollein, 1972–1978.

cule are given new life by their seamless integration into surfaces shot through with lively bursts of color.

Architect Rafael Moneo plays with history in his Museum of Roman Art in Mérida, Spain. Moneo paraphrases the city's architectural heritage by housing

▼ Stuttgart, Neue Staatsgalerie, James Stirling, 1977–1984.

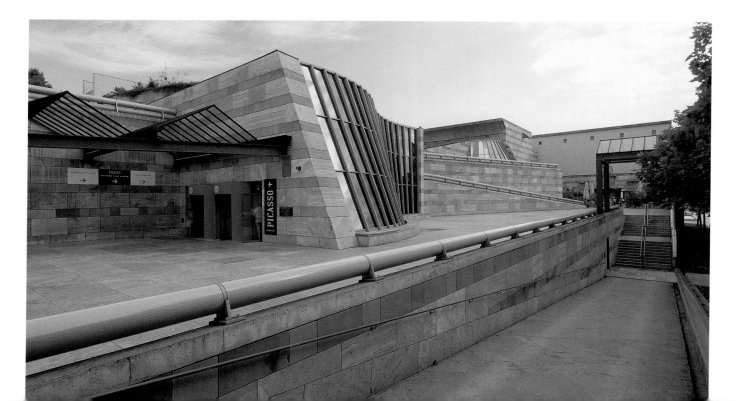

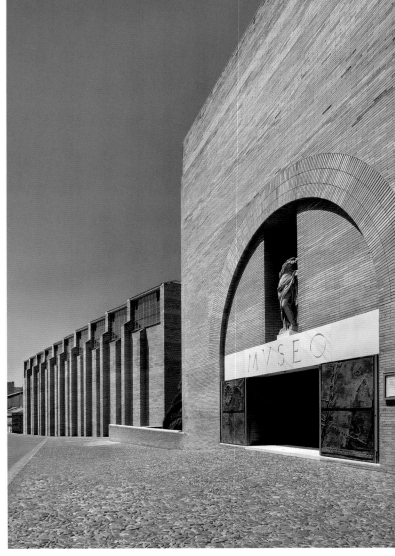

▲▲ Mérida, Spain, Museum of Roman Art, exhibition room (l) and exterior (r), Rafael Moneo, 1980–1985.

◀ Bregenz, Austria, Kunsthalle, Peter Zumthor, 1997.

the archaeological collection in an antique-style brick building.

Peter Zurnthor's Kunsthaus in Bregenz, Austria, represents a rejection of postmodernism and a return to the International Style. The museum is an unembellished rectilinear block sheathed in matte glass. After dark, colorful lighting brings the building to life. The boldest late twentieth-century museum is without doubt Frank Gehry's Guggenheim Museum Bilbao (see p. 328).

Museums in the United States

▲ Washington D.C., East Wing of the National Gallery, I.M. Pei, 1978.

▲ Los Angeles, Getty Center, Richard Meier, 1996–1997.

I. M. Pei's addition to the National Gallery in Washington, D.C. set a new standard for museum design in America. Built of marble-clad concrete on an irregular, roughly trapezoidal lot, Pei's bold H-facade welcomes visitors to the new East Wing. The entire complex is defined by precise, sharp angles, giving the building the visual weight of an archaic sculpture.

Much like Pei, architect Richard Meier remained within the International Style. His High Museum of Art in Atlanta was the prototype for small urban museums of the type that has since spread to cities all over the world. Like all of his buildings, the High Museum is a gleaming white composition that uses a range of modular elements. Glass facades admit abundant natural light, illuminating the individually designed galleries. Ramps are used freely throughout the interior to permit a variety of views of any

space. In his design for California's Getty Center, Meier had the chance to try out his collage-like architectonic massing on a 124-acre lot. The resulting culture and research center perches like a crown above Los Angeles. In New York City, the Museum of Modern Art has been expanded many times. In 1974, Philip Johnson designed the East Wing extension to the core building,

which dates from 1939, and in 1979 Cesar Pelli renovated the exhibition galleries. A comprehensive renovation and expansion took place between 1997 and 2004 under the direction of Japanese architect Yoshio Taniguchi. His work greatly improved the museum's aesthetics, at the same time providing additional exhibition space for contemporary art.

▶ ▶ Atlanta, High Museum of Art, exterior (r) and interior (opposite), Richard Meier, 1980–1983.

Paris in the Mitterand Era

While he was president of France, François Mitterand gave Paris an avant-garde look by commissioning monuments to himself and his grand nation. In 1989, the bicentennial of the French Revolution, American architect I. M. Pei completed the light-filled glass pyramid in the courtyard of the Louvre Museum. The crystalline edifice, along with several smaller pyramids, sits atop the now underground entrance to the museum. The formal aspects of this controversial monument played with several historical associations, including the revolutionary period idea that the Egyptian pyramid represented the ideal architectonic form. Paris's new La Grande Arche (see p. 297) was a much more pretentious enterprise, an oversized triumphal arch along the historical axis that runs between the Louvre and the Palace of St-Germain-en-Laye. Danish architect Johan von Spreckelson designed the arch as a kind of gigantic, 361-ft (110-m) high "window" for La Défense, an area of mostly new buildings from the 1950s. Symbolically, the arch's opening indicates Paris and France opening up to the world and to the future. In 1996, the four massive L-shaped book towers of the Bibliothèque de France, designed by the firm Dominique Perrault, were finally opened to the public.

Architecture could also take a light-hearted tone in the Mitterand era. In 1985, Bernard Tschumi designed a number of follies for Parc de la Villette, structures intended only to amuse. Christian de Portzamparc created a colorful culture center in his nearby Cité de Musique (Music City). Jean Nouvel's Institut du Monde Arabe (Arab World Institute) is resplendent with its hi-tech facade of metal screening that reacts to light, functioning as a *brise-soleil*.

▲ Paris, folly in Parc de la Villette, Bernard Tschumi, 1982–1985.

▼ Paris, Louvre Pyramid, I. M. Pei, completed in 1989.

▲ Paris, Cité de la Musique,
Christian de Portzamparc, 1990.

▼ Paris, Institut du Monde Arabe,
Jean Nouvel, 1987.

The Scene in Asia

New York and Chicago no longer boast the tallest buildings in the world. Increasingly, Asian cities are taking the lead in the architectonic avant-garde behind the creation of these immense edifices. The drive to erect taller and taller buildings has turned the construction of towering skyscrapers into a competitive sport, with cities and countries striving to build higher than anyone else.

In addition to skyscraper megalomania, Asian boomtowns present architects with a number of serious environ-

◄ Bangkok, Suvarnabhumi International Airport, Helmut Jahn, 1994–2006.

► Kuala Lumpur, Petronas Towers, Cesar Pelli, 1992–1999.

▼ Shanghai's futuristic skyline.

mental challenges. In return, the opportunities to build something completely new make overcoming the challenges worthwhile. Similar to the situation during the first Industrial Age in the West, there is a desperate need to house and otherwise organize the countless people who move to Asian cities every day in search of work. In addition to the

need to accommodate the massive local populations, earthquakes and seasonal typhoons make exceptional demands on construction materials, technology and structural engineering.

At 1,482 ft (451 m) tall, the 1999 Petronas Towers in Kuala Lumpur, Malaysia, are no longer the tallest buildings in the world. Even without the record, Cesar Pelli's design invoking the elegant silhouettes of oriental sacred architecture breaks new aesthetic ground. Helmut Jahn's gigantic Bangkok Airport boasts what is probably the longest continuous glass facade ever constructed. There is no lack of investment in prestige buildings in Asia. Hong Kong and Shanghai and their futuristic skylines have long been a mecca for architecture fans. Other mega-cities, like Beijing, Singapore or Tokyo, are already hard at work trying to catch up.

▲ Marco de Canveses, Portugal, Santa Maria, Álvaro Siza, 1995.

▼ Vaals, Netherlands, Abbey on Benedictusberg, plan by Dominikus Böhm (1922), expansion by Hans van der Laan completed in 1986.

Places of Worship

There were no revolutionary developments in the design of sacred spaces during the 1970s and 1980s. The trend was for multifunctional religious buildings that for the most part avoided specific ritual furnishings or characteristic décor. This tendency is pronounced in the abbey of St. Benedict in the Dutch city of Vaals. Portuguese architect Álvaro Siza selected utterly unembellished International Style cubic forms for his church of St. Maria in Marco de Canaveses. A similarly straightforward baptistery and bell tower flank the main building. It was only toward the end of the twentieth century that things began to change, with a movement toward the "reconsecration" of religious architecture.

In 1998, the architectural firm Allmann Sattler Wappner designed the Herz-Jesu-Kirche (Sacred Heart Church) in the Neuhausen section of Munich in a boldly avant-garde style that nonetheless retains its spiritual power. Herz-Jesu consists of a glass cube that delicately filters natural light through to a second, interior wooden shell enclosing the altar. Enormous blue glass double doors, as tall as a house, open like wings to welcome visitors. The open doors are inscribed like the pages of a book with an etched motif of nails that develops into a script with passages from the Passion in the Gospel of John. Contemporary architectural details and multimedia art combine with the extraordinary architectural effects to make the church a satisfying artistic synthesis.

The oval-plan Kapelle der Versöhnung (Reconciliation Chapel) is within what was once no-man's-land between the eastern and western halves of Berlin. The simple, thought-provoking structure is surrounded by a shell of wooden louvres, and a bed of gravel marks the former east-west border.

◄ ▼ Munich, Herz-Jesu-Kirche, Allmann Sattler Wappner, interior (l) and exterior (below), 1998.

▲ Berlin, Kapelle der Versöhnung, Peter Sassenroth and Rudolf Reitemann, 2000.

The New Face of Berlin

The reunification of Germany and transfer of the capital from Bonn to Berlin sparked a new urban architectural movement in Germany. Bucking the prevailing trend toward downsized city centers and urban decentralization, in Berlin there was a sudden, urgent call for monumental prestige architecture. Berlin needed government offices, lots of them, and soon. Sir Norman Foster's transparent Reichstag dome and the expressionist-style Jewish Museum by Daniel Liebeskind are the most spectacular examples of Berlin's architectural revival. Axel Schultes' impressive plan for the administrative complex known as the Band des Bundes (government strip) included a new Chancellor's Building, and on Potsdamer Platz, several world-renowned architects created a new urban center from the ground up.

▲ Berlin, DG (now DZ) Bank Conference Hall, Frank Gehry, 1996–1999.

▼ Berlin, Potsdamer Platz ca. 1990 with the Daimler Chrysler Quarter (Renzo Piano and Hans Kollhoff) and Sony Center (Helmut Jahn).

▲ Berlin, the "void" of the Jewish Museum, Daniel Liebeskind, completed 1999.

▲ Berlin, dome of the Reichstag,
Sir Norman Foster, 1999.

▼ Berlin, Bundeskanzleramt (Chancellor's
Building), 1997–2001.

▼ Berlin, Marie Elisabeth Lüders Haus an
der Spree, Stephan Braunfels, part of the
Bundespressestrand project, 1998–2003.

On Pariser Platz, Frank Gehry's fish-like conference hall for the former DG (now DZ) Bank is also of note. The newly completed Berlin Hauptbahnhof (main railway station) by Meinhard von Gerkan displays a bold, urban quality. Finally, the Bundespressestrand is a creative bar and restaurant complex on the banks of the Spree River that represents a first effort to make Berlin's riverfront accessible to the public.

New Shapes and Colors

The transition into the third millennium came with a wealth of new shapes and forms. The visually exhausting faux-columns and pediments of postmodernism were finally passé. Instead, one stared ecstatically at Frank Gehry's glimmering colossus built in the harbor district of Bilbao. The Guggenheim Museum Bilbao, completed in 1997, resembles a gigantic sculpture composed of enormous, shining, dramatically arranged curving pieces of metal. The building has a glistening skin of titanium plates; based on Gehry's sketches, their curvature was precisely calculated by a computer. The imposing, expressive structure has become a pilgrimage site for architecture lovers from all over the world. In the meantime, Spain's Basque country has

gained a second jewel of a bu Rafale Moneo's Kursaal (Spa) Sebastián. The leisure comple of two monumental glass cub described by the architect as "rocks stranded on the shore."

With Jean Nouvel's Torre Agbar, Barcelona, already an avant-garde city, gained a new emblem. The layered aluminum-and-glass skin of the bullet-shaped office tower radiates color.

The combination of technology with colorful accents also defines the new Allianz Arena in Munich, constructed from 2,760 inflated hi-tech polymer panels. The colors vary depending on which teams are playing on any given day. The sinuous design for the fantastic Ministry for the Environment in Dessau testifies to an increased interest in the dialogue between form and color, and sets a new standard for German government buildings.

▲ Barcelona, Torre Agbar, Jean Nouvel, 2005.

▼ San Sebastián, Spain, Kursaal Center, Rafael Moneo, 1999.

▼ Bilbao, Spain, Guggenheim Museum, Frank Gehry, 1993–1997.

▲ Berlin, dome of the Reichstag,
Sir Norman Foster, 1999.

▼ Berlin, Bundeskanzleramt (Chancellor's
Building), 1997–2001.

▼ Berlin, Marie Elisabeth Lüders Haus an
der Spree, Stephan Braunfels, part of the
Bundespressestrand project, 1998–2003.

On Pariser Platz, Frank Gehry's fish-like conference hall for the former DG (now DZ) Bank is also of note. The newly completed Berlin Hauptbahnhof (main railway station) by Meinhard von Gerkan displays a bold, urban quality. Finally, the Bundespressestrand is a creative bar and restaurant complex on the banks of the Spree River that represents a first effort to make Berlin's riverfront accessible to the public.

New Shapes and Colors

The transition into the third millennium came with a wealth of new shapes and forms. The visually exhausting faux-columns and pediments of postmodernism were finally passé. Instead, one stared ecstatically at Frank Gehry's glimmering colossus built in the harbor district of Bilbao. The Guggenheim Museum Bilbao, completed in 1997, resembles a gigantic sculpture composed of enormous, shining, dramatically arranged curving pieces of metal. The building has a glistening skin of titanium plates; based on Gehry's sketches, their curvature was precisely calculated by a computer. The imposing, expressive structure has become a pilgrimage site for architecture lovers from all over the world. In the meantime, Spain's Basque country has gained a second jewel of a building: Rafale Moneo's Kursaal (Spa) in San Sebastián. The leisure complex consists of two monumental glass cubes, described by the architect as "rocks stranded on the shore."

With Jean Nouvel's Torre Agbar, Barcelona, already an avant-garde city, gained a new emblem. The layered aluminum-and-glass skin of the bullet-shaped office tower radiates color.

The combination of technology with colorful accents also defines the new Allianz Arena in Munich, constructed from 2,760 inflated hi-tech polymer panels. The colors vary depending on which teams are playing on any given day. The sinuous design for the fantastic Ministry for the Environment in Dessau testifies to an increased interest in the dialogue between form and color, and sets a new standard for German government buildings.

▲ Barcelona, Torre Agbar, Jean Nouvel, 2005.

▼ San Sebastián, Spain, Kursaal Center, Rafael Moneo, 1999.

▼ Bilbao, Spain, Guggenheim Museum, Frank Gehry, 1993–1997.

▲ Dessau, Germany, Bundesumweltamt, Matthias Sauerbruch and Louisa Hutton, 2005.

▼ Munich, Allianz Arena, Herzog & de Meuron, 2005.

▲ Beijing, Olympic Stadium, Herzog & de Meuron, to be completed in 2008.

▼ Nouméa, New Caledonia, Jean-Marie Tjibaou Cultural Center, Renzo Piano, 1991–1998.

The Globalization of Architecture

Globalization has long been a factor in the world of architecture. For over half a century, skyscrapers designed by SOM have towered over cities around the planet. Richard Meier's white cubes have become part of Europe's museum landscape, and Tadao Ando's Japanese aesthetic has found its way into everyday life. The new Scottish Parliament Building was designed by a Catalonian, Englishman Richard Rogers designs for the European Union, and the Swiss firm Herzog & de Meuron is responsible for the Olympic Stadium in Beijing.

That architectural styles travel and take root in different places is certainly nothing new. Cistercian monks carried their conceptualization of the ideal monastery to every region of Europe. The Jesuits had a strictly supervised "building committee" that made sure the precepts of their architectural canon were followed wherever a Jesuit church was built, even in far away colonies. In the nineteenth century, the neogothic cathedral became a worldwide symbol of faith, while the International Style of the twentieth century dotted the planet with rationalist buildings.

Today, the works of internationally famous architects can be found in every part of the world, often to the detriment of the local building style. In this context, the solution arrived at by Renzo Piano for the Jean-Marie Tijibaou Cultural Center on the island of New Caledonia seems eminently sensible. Their design blends the most up-to-date technology with thousand-year-old architectural forms. The result is a magnificent synthesis of both.

◄ Strasbourg, European Court of Human Rights, Richard Rogers, 1995.

► Wolfsburg, Germany, Phaeno Science Center, Zaha Hadid, 2005.

Index of Illustrated Buildings

Aachen Cathedral, palatine chapel 75
Aegina, Temple of Aphaia 14
Alcalá de Henares, Spain, university, paranito, 65
Alfeld, Germany, Fagus Factory 278
Amiens, France, Nôtre-Dame Cathedral 118
Amsterdam, Stock Market 272
— Het Scheep 280
— Noorderkerk 195
Anet, France, château 177
Annaberg, Germany, St Anna 139
Antwerp, City Hall 178
— Grote Markt with guild houses 179
Aranjuez, Spain, Casa del Labrador 230
— Round Temple in castle gardens 230
Arc-et-Senans, France, Saline Royale 229
Arles, St-Trophîme 84
Arras, France, Town Hall 134
— St-Vaast 235
Assisi, San Francesco 128
Athens, Acropolis with Parthenon 20
— Acropolis, Erechtheion 20/21
— Acropolis, reconstruction 19
— Monument of Lysicrates 16
Atlanta, High Museum of Art 318, 319
Augsburg, Fugger Chapel 180
Augustusburg (near Chemnitz), Schloss 180
Autun Cathedral 90
Auxerre, St-Étienne Cathedral 121
Avignon, Papal Palace 133
Ávila, Spain, city wall 106/107
Azay-le-Rideau, France, château 175

Bagnaia, Italy, Villa Lante 174
Bangkok, Suvarnabhumi International Airport 322
Barcelona, Casa Batlló 275
— Palau de la Generalitat 135
— Palau de la Música Catalana 275
— Pavilion for 1929 World's Fair 285
— Sagrada Famiglia Basilica 275
— Santa Maria del Mar 125
— Torre Agbar 328
Basel Münster 141
Batalha, Spain, Santa Maria da Vitória Monastery 135
Bath, England, The Circus, 185
— Roman baths 35
Bear Run, Pennsylvania, Fallingwater
   (Kaufmann House) 290
Beaune, France, Hôtel-Dieu 137
Beauvais, France, St-Pierre Cathedral 119
Beijing, Olympic Stadium 330
Belém (near Lisbon), Jerónimos Monastery 138
Bergama, Turkey, see Pergamon
Berlin, AEG Turbine Hall 279
— Altes Museum 243
— Brandenburger Tor 242
— Bundeskanzleramt 327
— DZ (formerly DG) Bank 326
— Hohenzollernplatz Church 281
— Jewish Museum 326
— Kaiser Wilhelm Memorial Church 306
— Kapelle der Versöhnung 325
— Marie E. Lüders Haus 327
— Neue Nationalgalerie 307
— Neue Wache 242
— Philharmonic 297
— Potsdamer Platz 326
— Reichstag Building 261
— Reichstag (dome) 327
— Schauspielhaus on Gendarmenmarkt, 243
— Stalin Allee 307
— Pergamon Museum with Zeus Altar 19
Besalú, Catalonia, medieval bridge 109

Bilbao, Spain, Guggenheim Museum 328
Birnau, Germany, Liebfrauenkirche 214
Blois, France, château 149, 172
Bordeaux, Grand Théâtre 228, 239
Borgund, Norway, stave church 101
Boston, Trinity Church 267
Bourg-en-Bresse, France, Brou monastic church 145
Bourges, France, Palais Jacques-Cœur 144
— St-Étienne Cathedral 118
Brasília, Congresso National 299
Bregenz, Austria, Kunsthalle 317
Brighton, England, Royal Pavilion 252
Bristol, England, Clifton Suspension Bridge 262
Brühl, Schloss Augustusburg 203
Brussels, Atomium 305
– Palais de Justice 259
– Palais Stoclet 272
– Royal Gallery at St Hubert 258
Buffalo, New York, Guaranty Building 268
Burg Eltz, Germany 113
Burgos, Spain, cathedral 65
Bury St Edmunds, abbey 88

Caen, France, St-Étienne 88
Cambridge, England, King's College Chapel 123
Caprarola, Italy, Palazzo Farnese 149
Caracas, Venezuela, Aula Magna at the university 298
Carcassonne, France, medieval city 251
Cardona, Catalonia, St Vicenç 81
Careggi (near Florence), Villa Medici 158
Caserta, Italy, La Reggia 206
Castel del Monte, Italy 113
Castile, Spain (near) Gómaz Castle 58
Catalonia, St Pere de Rodes, 80
— Santa Maria de Poblet, 92
Chambord, France, château 172, 173
Chandigarh, India, Parliament Building 285
Charlottesville, Virginia, Monticello 246
Chartres, Nôtre-Dame Cathedral 116
Château de Blois see Blois
Chenonceaux, France, château 173
Chepren and Cheops Pyramids 10
Chicago, Carson Pirie Scott Building 268
— Frederick C. Robie House 290
— John Hancock Center 302
— Sears Tower 302
— James R. Thompson Center (State of Illinois
   Center) 303
Chorin, Germany, former abbey church 127
Cividale, Italy, Santa Maria della Valle 69
Cluny, model of third abbey church 90
Cologne, cathedral 113, 254
— St Aposteln 98
— St Engelbert 288
— St Maria im Kapitol 93, 98
— St Pantaleon 79
Como, Italy, Casa del Fascio (Casa del Populo) 293
Constantinople, see Istanbul
Conques, France, Ste-Foy 95, 96
Copenhagen, Vor Frue Kirke 245
Córdoba, Great Mosque (Mezquita) 60, 61
Corvey, Germany, former abbey church 77
Coutances, France, Nôtre-Dame Cathedral 120

Darmstadt, Mathildenhöhe 276, 277
Delphi, Tholos Temple of Atena Pronaia 15
Den Haag, Dance Theater 312
Dessau, Bauhaus Building 270/271, 284
— Bundesumweltamt 329
Donaustauf, Germany, Walhalla 228, 240
Dresden, Semperoper (Hoftheater) 260
— UFA Cinema Center 313
— Zwinger 214
Durham, England, cathedral 88
Düsseldorf, Thyssen Haus 301

Einsiedeln, Switzerland, Benedictine abbey 218
Ely Cathedral, England 89
Ephesos, Temple of Artemis 11
Epidauros, Theater 16/17

Florence, Baptistery of St John 102, 151
— campanile 129
— cathedral 150, 255
— Ospedale degli Innocenti 148
— Palazzo Pitti 174
— Palazzo Rucellai 156
— Palazzo Strozzi 156
— Palazzo Vecchio 130
— Santa Croce, Pazzi Chapel 151
— San Lorenzo 152, 153
— San Lorenzo, Biblioteca Laurenziana 167
— San Lorenzo, Medici Chapel 166
— San Miniato al Monte 102
— Santa Maria Novella 128, 153
— Santo Spirito 152
— Uffizi Corridor 176
— (near) Villa Cafaggiolo (painting) 159
Fontenay, France, Cistercian abbey 90, 91
Frankfurt, Messe Torhaus 296
Freiberg, Germany, cathedral and Tulip Pulpit 134
Freiburg Münster 141
Fulda, Germany, cathedral 222
— St Michael 76
Füssen, Germany, Schloss Neuschwanstein 250

Gdánsk, Poland, St Mary's Church 138
Gelnhausen, Germany, imperial palace 108
Germiny-des-Prés, France, oratory of Bishop Theodulf
   of Orléans, 68
Gernrode, Germany, St Cyriacus 79
Girona, Spain, Santa Maria Cathedral 124
Glasgow, Glasgow School of Art 276
Goslar, Germany, imperial palace (reconstruction) 108
Gran, Hungary, cathedral 245
Granada, Alhambra 59, 62, 63
— La Cartuja Monastery 224
Greenwich, The Queen's House 210

Haarlem, Fleischhalle 178
Halicarnassos, mausoleum (reconstruction) 11
Hamburg, Chilehaus 280
— Speicherstadt 263
Hameln, Germany, Leisthaus 181
Hampton Court Palace 211
Hannoversch-Münden, Germany, Town Hall 176
Heidelberg, castle 180
Helsinki, cathedral, St Nicholas 245
Herculaneum, House of Neptune and Amphitrite 27
— Women's Baths 27
Hildesheim, St Michael 78
Hilversum, Netherlands, Dr Bavinck School 280
Hong Kong, HSBC building 309
Hosios Lukas Monastery, Greece 54
Huesca, Spain, Loarre Castle 109

Istanbul, Basilica Cistern 53
— Hagia Sophia 40/41, 52
— Kariye Camii (form. St Savior in Chora) 50
— Sts Sergios and Bacchus 50
— Suleimaniye 59
— Theodosian land walls 53

Jericho, former Premonstratensian church 100
Jerusalem, Church of the Holy Sepulcher 46
— Dome of the Rock 46
— (near) Sabbas Monastery 47
Jouarre, France, Crypt of St Paul 66/67
Jülich, Germany, citadel 212
Jumièges, France, Nôtre-Dame 86

Kalundborg, Denmark, Vor Frue Kirke 101
Karlsruhe, Kunsthalle 239
— Marktplatz 240
Kassel, Löwenburg at Schloss Wilhelmshöhe 230
— Museum Fridericianum 239
Kelheim, Germany, Befreiungshalle 241
Knossos, palace complex 12
Koblenz (near), Schloss Stolzenfels 228
Kuala Lumpur, Petronas Towers 323
Kyffhäuser, Germany, Kaiser Wilhelm Monument 261

La Jolla, California, Jonas Salk Institute 300
Landshut, Germany, St Martin 140
Laon, France, Nôtre-Dame Cathedral, 114
Le Raincy, France, Nôtre-Dame 278
Léon, Spain, cathedral 124
— (near) San Miguel de Escalada 70
Leuven, Belgium, town hall 136
Limburg an der Lahn, Germany, cathedral 100
Lincoln Cathedral 123
Lisbon, Church of Divine Providence (cross section) 196
Löbau, Germany, Villa Schminke 289
London, Crystal Palace, 1851 Great Exhibition 265
— Kew Gardens, Chinese Pagoda 230
— Kew Gardens, Palm House 253
— St Pancras 233, 251
— St Paul's Cathedral 195
— Twickenham, Strawberry Hill 252
— Westminster, Houses of Parliament 253
Lorsch, Germany, gatehouse 74
Los Angeles, Getty Center 318
Lübeck, Germany, Marienkirche 127

Madinat az-Zahra, near Cordoba, former palace city 61
— Salón Rico 56/57
Madrid, Prado Museum 239
Mainz, cathedral 97
Mantua, Italy, Palazzo del Te 177
— San Andrea 148, 155
Marburg, Germany, St Elisabeth 126
Marco de Canaveses, Portugal, Santa Maria 324
Maria Laach, Germany, abbey church 99
Marseille, Unité d'Habitation (housing) 287
Meissen, Germany, Albrechtsburg 144
Melk, Austria, Benedictine abbey 219
Mérida, Spain, Museum of Roman Art 317
— Roman theater 31
Mexico City, Torres de Satélite 299
— University, Main Library 298
Middlesex, Chiswick House 232
Milan, cathedral 254
— Palazzo della Ragione 106
— San Ambrogio 104
— San Lorenzo 42
— Teatro alla Scala 238
Miletus, city plan 18
Millau, France, Viaduc de Millau 6
Modena, San Geminiano 104
Moissac, France, St-Pierre 92
Mönchengladbach,Germany, Abteiberg Museum 316
Monkwearmouth, England, abbey church 73
Monreale, Italy, cathedral 104
Monte Naranco, Spain, palace pavilion 70
Montepulciano (near), Madonna di San Biagio 155
Moscow, Kremlin 244
— State University 292
Mostar, Bosnia and Herzegovina, Old Bridge 212
Mount Athos, Greece, Chilandariou Monastery 51
Munich, Allianz Arena 329
— Amalienburg in Schloss Nymphenburg Park 217
— Asamkirche 223
— Haus der Kunst 292
— Herz-Jesu-Kirche 325

— Königsplatz with Glyptothek 241
— Ludwigstraße 261
— Olympic Stadium 308
— Residence, antiquarium 149
— St Johann Nepomuk 223
— St Michael's Church 194
Münster, Germany, Erbdrostenhof 215
Müstair, Switzerland, St John 74
Mycenae, Lion Gate 12
— Treasury of Atreus 12

Nancy, France, Place Royal (Place Stanislas) 215
Neresheim, Germany, abbey church 218
Neuf-Breisach, France, model 213
New Canaan, Connecticut, Glass House 291
New Orleans, Piazza d'Italia 310
Newport, Rhode Island, Redwood Library 246
New York, A.T. & T. Building (former) 311
— Brooklyn Bridge 262
— Chrysler Building 283
— Empire State Building 282
— Flatiron (Fuller) Building 269
— Lever House 300
— Public Library Main Branch 266
— Seagram Building 300
— Solomon R. Guggenheim Museum 304
— St Patrick's Cathedral 267
— TWA Terminal, John F. Kennedy Airport 305
— United Nations Headquarters 296
— Waldorf-Astoria Hotel 283
— Woolworth Building 283
— World Trade Center 296
Nîmes, France, Pont du Gard 25
— Maison Carrée 31
Nouméa, New Caledonia, cultural center 330
Noyon, France, Nôtre-Dame Cathedral 114
Nuremberg, Congress Hall of the Nazi Party Rallying Grounds 293

Olympia, Temple of Hera 13
— Stadium 16
Orange, France, Roman theater 30
— Monumental gate 36
Osnabruck, Germany, Willmansches Haus 181
Ottmarsheim, Alsace, former monastic church 69
Oxford, Radcliff Camera 208
Oxfordshire, Blenheim Palace 211

Paestum, Italy, Temple of Athena 8/9
Palm Springs, California, Kaufmann Desert House 291
Palma de Mallorca, Bellver Castle 133
— cathedral 110/111
— Llotja (bourse) 137
Paray-le-Monial, France, priory church 90
Paris, Abesses Metro Station 276
— Arc-de-Triomphe 237
— Centre Pompidou 308
— Church of the Sorbonne 198
— Cité de la Musique 321
— Eiffel Tower 264
— Galerie des Machines (1889 photograph) 265
— Grande Arche 297
— Haussmann's street plan 258
— Hôtel Beauharnais 236
— Hôtel de Rohan-Soubise 216
— Institut du Monde Arabe 321
— La Sainte Chapelle 112
— Les Invalides, 199
— Louvre 173, 197,198
— Louvre, glass pyramid 2, 320
— Nôtre-Dame Cathedral 112
— Opera 258
— Pantheon 236
— Parc de la Vilette, follies 320

— St-Denis (near) 114
— St-Étienne-du-Mont 177
— St-Madeleine 237
Pergamon, Turkey, plan of ancient city 19
— Zeus Altar of Pergamon 19
Périgueux, France, St-Front 87
Persepolis, palace complex 13
Philadelphia, Guild House 310
Pienza, Italy, city center 160
Pisa, Campo del Miracoli 103
— Santa Maria della Spina 129
Pistoia, Italy, San Giovanni Fuorcivitas 103
Poggio a Caiano, Italy, Villa Medici 158
Poissy (near Paris), Villa Savoye 289
Poitiers, France, baptistery 68
— St-Pierre Cathedral 121
Pompeii, ancient street 26
— city plan 26
— House of the Dioscuri 27
— Villa of the Mysteries 27
Pont du Gard (near Nîmes, France) 25
Pontigny, France, former abbey church 112
Potsdam, Dampfmaschinenhaus 263
— Einsteinturm 273
— Schloss Sanssouci 215, 217
— Tee Pavilion at Sanssouci 215
Prague, St Margaret's 222
— St Vitus Cathedral 143
— Villa Amerika 222
— Vladislav Hall, Prague Castle 144
Prenzlau, Germany, Marienkirche 127
Provence, Le Thoronet, former abbey 93

Qalaat Seman, Syria, Monastery of Simeon 47
Quedlinburg, Germany, St Servatius 93

Ratzeburg, Germany, cathedral 100
Ravenna, Italy, Mausoleum of Galla Placidia 48
— Mausoleum of Theoderic 48
— San Vitale 43, 49
Reichenau, Germany, St Georg 73
Reims, France, Nôtre-Dame Cathedral 117
Remagen, Germany, Apollinaris Church 254
Ribeauvillé, Alsace, Château St-Ulrich 108
Rievaulx Abbey, England 88
Rimini, Italy, San Francesco (Tempio Malatestiano) 148
Rio de Janeiro, Ministry of Education and Health 298
Rohr, Germany, monastery church 223
Rome, Arch of Constantine 22
— Aurelian city walls 25
— Baths of Caracalla 34
— Basilica of Maxentius 43
— Belvedere Court in Vatican 162
— Capitoline Hill, design 161
— Castel Sant'Angelo 37
— Colosseum 33
— Domus Aurea 39
— Early Christian catacomb 42
— Eurysaces tomb 37
— Fontana di Trevi 192
— Forum of Augustus 29
— Forum Romanum 22, 28, 29
— Il Gesù 186
— Mausoleum of Emperor Hadrian (Castel Sant'Angelo) 37
— Old St Peter's 44
— Palazzo della Cancelleria 162
— Palazzo dei Conservatori 162
— Pantheon 32
— Piazza del Popolo 192
— Piazza Navona 192
— Pyramid tomb of Cestius 37
— Round temple in Forum Boarium 23
— San Andrea al Quirinale 190

— San Carlo alle Quattro Fontane 190
— San Ivo alla Sapienza 191
— San Pietro in Montorio 163
— Santa Constanza 45
— Santa Sabina 45
— Santa Susanna 187
— Santi Luca e Martina 187
— Spanish Steps 193
— St Peter's 164, 165, 188, 189
— St Peter's Square 185
— Temple of Vesta 28
— Trajan's Market 23
— Trajan's Column 36
Ronchamp, France, Notre-Dame-du-Haut 304
Rotterdam, Van Nelle Tobacco Factory 284

Salamanca, New Cathedral 138
— Plaza Mayor 225
Salem, Germany, former abbey church 139
Salisbury Cathedral, England 122
Salzburg, cathedral 194
— collegiate church 184
San Francisco, Golden Gate Bridge 273
— Transamerica Pyramid 7
San Gimignano, Italy, patrician towers 107
San Lorenzo del Escorial (near Madrid) 184
San Sebastián, Spain, Kursaal 328
Santa Cristina de Lena (Spain) 71
Santiago de Copostela, cathedral 94, 225
Säynätsalo, Finland, Town Hall 296
Schloss Clemenswerth (near Sögel, Germany) 216
Schloss Weißenstein (near Pommersfelden) 203
Schwäbisch-Gmünd, Germany, Heiligkreuzkirche 140
Schwarzrheindorf (near Bonn), chapel 98
Schwerin, Germany, Schweriner Schloss 250
Segesta, Italy, Temple 14
Sens Cathedral, France 139
Serrabone, France, Nôtre-Dame 93
Seville, Bridge over the Alamillo 297
— Casa de Pilatos 64
— Cathedral with Patio de los Naranjos 64
— Torre del Oro 58
Shanghai, Skyline 322/323
Siena, Campo with Palazzo Pubblico 131
— cathedral 129
Silos, Spain, Santo Domingo, 82/83, 93
Sintra, Portugal, Palácio da Pena 248/249
Sirmione, Italy, Scaliger Castle 132
Soissons, France, St-Gervais-et-Protais 114
Speyer, Germany, cathedral 96, 97
St-Antonin, France, Granolhet mansion (plan) 107
Staffelstein, Germany, Vierzehnheiligen 220, 221
St Blasien, Germany, St Blaise 226/227, 234
St-Denis (Paris), former abbey church 115

Steingaden (near Bamberg), Wieskirche 220
Steinhausen, Germany, St Peter and Paul 220
St Gall (Switzerland) Abbey, library 209
— monastic plan 72
St-Nectaire, France, former abbey church 87
Stowe, England, Palladian bridge 231
St Pere de Rodes, see Catalonia
St Petersburg, Kazan Cathedral 244
Strasbourg, European Court of Human Rights 330
— Münster 126
St-Rémy-de-Provence, France, triumphal arch, 37
St-Savin sur Gartempe, France, former priory church 84
Stuttgart, Chapel on the Rotenberg 241
— Hysolar Institute 312
— Neue Staatsgalerie 316
— Weissenhofsiedlung 286
Sydney, Opera House 305

Teruel, Spain, Santa Maria Cathedral 65
Timgad, Algeria, ancient theater 22
Tivoli, Italy, Hadrian's Villa 38, 39
Todi, Italy, San Fortunato 128
— Santa Maria della Consolazione 154
Tokyo, Asahi Beer Hall 314
— International Forum 315
— City Hall 315
Toledo, Spain, cathedral 124, 224
— San Cristo de la Luz 64
— Santa María la Bianca 65
Tomar, Portugal, Templar church 85
Torgau, Germany, Schloss Hartenfels 180
Toulouse, Dominican church 134
— St-Sernin 95
Tournus, France, St-Philibert 86
Trani, Italy, San Nicola Pellegrino 105
Trier, Germany, Aula Palatina 23
— Liebfrauenkirche 126
— Porta Nigra 24
Tsarskoe Selo (near St Petersburg), Achat Pavillon 244
Turin, Basilica di Superga 207
— Chapel of the Most Holy Shroud 206
— Palazzina di Stupinigi (near) 207

Ulm, Münster 141
Urbino, Italy, Palazzo Ducale 157
Utrecht, Truus Schröder House 284

Vaals, Netherlands, Abbey on Benedictusberg 324
Valencia, Spain, Museo de las Ciencias 294/295
Vatican, see Rome
Vaux-le-Vicomte, France, château 182/183
Venice, Doges Palace 131
— Il Redentore 168
— Palazzo Grimani 169

— San Giorgio Maggiore 146/147
— San Marco 55
Verona, Italy, San Zeno Maggiore 104
Versailles, palace 185, 200, 201
— palace garden, Hameau de la Reine 236
— palace garden, Petit Trianon 236
Vézelay, France, Ste-Madeleine 85
Vicenza, Italy, basilica (plan) 171
— Teatro Olimpico 168
— Villa Capra (La Rotonda) 169
Vienna, Burgtheater 256
— Goldman and Salatsch Building, Michaelerplatz 279
— Hofbibliothek 205
— Hofburg, plan for expansion 257
— Karlskirche 204
— Karl-Marx-Hof (housing) 286
— Kunsthistorisches Museum 256
— Maria am Gestade 141
— panorama of city expansion 256
— Postsparkasse (Wagner Museum) 274
— Retti candle store (former) 310
— Schloss Schönbrunn 205
— Secession Building 274
— St Stephan's Cathedral 142
— Upper Belvedere 184, 204
— Votivkirche 257
Villandry, France, château 175

Warwickshire, Packington Hall 233
Washington, D.C., Capitol Building 247
— National Gallery 318
Weil am Rhein, Germany, Vitra Design Museum
— Factory Firehouse 313
— Seminar House 314
Weimar, Germany, Kunstschule 276
Wells Cathedral, England 122
Wiblingen (near Ulm, Germany), library 209
Wiltshire, landscape garden 231
— Wilton House 211
Wolfsburg, Germany, Phaeno Science Center 331
Wörlitz, Germany, castle and landscape garden 234
— Gothic-style house 250
Worms, Germany, cathedral 84
Wroclaw, Poland, Centennial Hall 272
Würzburg, Residence 202
— Women's prison 240

Yorkshire, Castle Howard 211

Zamora, Spain, cathedral 85
Zaragoza, Spain, Aljaferia 65
Zurich, Polytechnic University 260

Index of Architects

Aalto, Alvar 296–297
Adler, Dankmar 268
Álava, Juan de 138
Alberti, Leone Battista 148, 150, 153, 155, 156, 158, 160, 170
Alen, William van 282–283
Amati, Carlo 255
Ammanati, Bartolomeo 175
Ando, Tadao 314–315
Anthemius of Tralles 53
Apollodorus 23
Arras, Matthias von 142
Asam, Cosmas Damian and Egid Quirin 223
Averlino, Antonio, see Filarete

Barlow, William Harry 251

Barragán, Luís 299
Barry, Charles 253
Bartolomeo, Michelozzo di 158–159
Behnisch, Günter 308, 312–313
Behrens, Peter 276, 279
Benckert, Johann Peter 215
Berg, Max 272–273
Berlage, Hendrik Petrus 272
Bernini, Gianlorenzo 185, 188–191, 197
Blondel, François 196
Boccador, see Cortona, Domenico da
Boffrand, Germain 216
Bofill, Guillem 124
Böhm, Dominikus 288–289, 324
Bondone, Giotto di 129
Bononi, Joseph 233
Borromini, Francesco 190–191

Boullée, Étienne-Louis 229
Boytac, Diogo 138
Bramante, Donato 162–164
Braunfels, Stephan 327
Brinkmann, Johannes Andreas 284
Bruant, Libéral 198
Brunel, Isambard Kingdom 262–263
Brunelleschi, Filippo 148, 150, 151, 152
Bulfinch, Charles 246
Bunshaft, Gordon 300
Burgee, John 310–311
Burghausen, Hans von 140
Burnham, Daniel Hudson 268
Burton, Decimus 253

Calatrava, Santiago 297, 303
Cameron, Charles 244

Campbell, Colen 232
Caprarola, Cola da 155
Castilho, João de 138
Cesarino, Cesare 171
Chalgrin, Jean-François-Thérèse 237
Chambers, William, 230
Chambiges, Martin 139
Churriguera, Alberto de 224–225
Clysenaer, Jean-Pierre 258
Contamin, Victor 265
COOP Himmelblau 312–313
Corny, Emmanuel Héré de 215
Cortona, Domenico da, 149, 172–173
Cortona, Pietro da 187
Costa, Lúcio 298–99
Cotte, Robert de 201
Cuvilliés, François de 217

Demmler, Georg Adolph 250
Despuig, Ramon 124
Dientzenhofer, Georg, Christoph and
    Kilian Ignaz 222–223
Dientzenhofer, Johann 203, 222
Domènech i Montaner, Lluis 274–275
Dudok, Willem Marinus 280
Dutert, Charles Louis Ferdinand 265

Egkl, Wilhelm 149
Ehn, Karl 286
Eiermann, Egon 306
Eiffel, Gustave 264–265
Eisenman, Peter 312
Engel, Carl Ludwig 245
Ensingen, Ulrich von 141
Erdmannsdorff, Friedrich Wilhelm von 234, 250

Fabris, Emilio de 255
Fauran, Henri und Jacques de 124
Ferstel, Heinrich von 257
Filarete (Antonio Averlino) 160, 170
Fischer von Erlach, Johann Bernhard 184, 196,
    204–205
Fischer von Erlach, Joseph Emmanuel 205
Floris, Cornelis 178
Foster, Sir Norman 6, 308–309, 326–327

Gabriel, Jacques-Ange 236
Galli Bibiena, Giuseppe 197
Garnier, Charles 258
Gaudí, Antoní 274–275
Gehry, Frank O. 6, 312, 326, 328
Geiger, Nikolaus 261
Gibbs, James 208, 231
Gilbert, Cass 282–283
Giorgio, Francesco di 157
Goeritz, Mathias 299
Graham, Bruce 302–303
Gropius, Walter 278–279, 284
Guarini, Guarino 196, 206
Guimard, Hector 276

Hadid, Zaha 312–313, 330–331
Hansen, Christian Frederik 245
Hanson, Theophil 257
Hardouin-Mansart, Jules 185, 198, 200–201
Harrison, Peter 246
Harrison, Wallace K. 296–297
Hasenauer, Karl von 256–257
Hawksmoore, Nicholas 210–211
Heilmann, Jakob 139
Henselmann, Hermann 307
Hentrich, Helmut 300–301
Herrera, Juan de 184
Herzog & de Meuron, 328–329, 330

Heymüller, Gottlieb 215
Hild, Joseph 245
Hildebrandt, Johann Lukas von 184, 203–204
Hippodamus of Miletus 18
Hoffmann, Josef 272, 274
Hofmann, Julius 250
Höger, Fritz 280–281
Hollein, Hans 310, 316
Hontañón, Rodrigo Gil de 138
Horta, Victor 276
Hübsch, Heinrich 239
Hundrieser, Emil 261
Hurtado Izquierdo, Francisco de 224
Hutton, Louisa 328–329
Huvé, Jacques-Marie 237

Iktinos 20
Inwood, William und Henry William, 233
Isidore of Miletus 53
Ivry, Pierre Contant d' 234
Ixnard, Pierre-Michel d' 234

Jahn, Helmut 303, 323, 326
Jank, Christian 250
Jefferson, Thomas 246
Johnson, Philip 291, 310–311, 318
Jones, Inigo 210–211
Jussow, Heinrich 230
Juvarra, Filippo 197, 207

Kahn, Louis I. 300
Kallikrates 20
Kent, William 232
Key, Lieven de 178
Keyser, Hendrick de 195
Klenze, Leo von 228, 240–241
Klerk, Michel de 280
Knab, Michael 141
Knobelsdorff, Georg Wenzeslaus von 217
Kollhoff, Hans 326
Koolhaas, Rem 312
Kuen, Hans Georg 218
Kurikawa, Kisho 314

Laan, Hans van der 324
Langhaus, Carl Gotthard 243
Latrobe, Benjamin 246
Laurana, Luciano 157
Layens, Matheus de 137
Le Corbusier 285, 288–289, 297, 298, 304
Le Roy, Philibert 200
Le Vau, Louis 185, 200
Ledoux, Claude-Nicolas 229
Lemercier, Jacques 198
Leonardo da Vinci 170
Lescot, Pierre 173
Liebeskind, Daniel 312, 326
Loos, Adolf 273, 279
Loser, Gabriel 208
Louis, Victor 228, 239

Mackintosh, Charles Rennie 276
Maderno, Carlo 187, 188
Maiano, Benedetto da 156
Mansart, François 201
Mantagut, Berenguer de 124
Meier, Richard 318–319
Mendelsohn, Erich 273
Michelangelo 153, 161, 164–167, 176
Mies van der Rohe, Ludwig 284–85, 286, 288,
    292, 300, 306–07
Mignon, Alexandre 237
Mique, Richard 236–237
Moneo, Rafael 316–317, 328

Moore, Charles 310
Moosbrugger, Kaspar 218
Mungenast, Joseph 218

Nash, John 252
Natoire, Charles Joseph 216
Neumann, Balthasar 203, 218, 220
Neutra, Richard 291
Niemeyer, Oscar 298–299
Nouvel, Jean 320–321, 328

O'Gorman, Juan 298–299
Olbrich, Joseph Maria 274, 276–277
Ordish, Rowland 251
Orme, Philibert de l' 177
Otto, Frei 308
Oud, Pieter 286

Pacassi, Nikolaus 205
Packh, Johann 245
Palladio, Andrea 168–171
Parler, family of architects and builders 140
Parler, Peter 142
Pasqualini, Alessandro 212
Paxton, Joseph 265
Pei, I.M. 2, 318, 319
Pelli, Cesar 318, 323
Pereira, William 7
Perrault, Claude 198
Perret, Auguste and Gustave 278
Persius, Ludwig 263
Peruzzi, Baldassare 174–175
Petschnigg, Hubert 300–301
Pflüger, Konrad 139
Piagge, Nicolas de 234
Piano, Renzo 308, 326, 330
Piermarini, Giuseppe 238
Pilgram, Anton 142
Pisano, Andrea 129
Poelaert, Joseph 258
Poelzig, Hans 273, 286
Polykleitos the Younger 16
Pöppelmann, Matthäus Daniel 214
Porta, Giacomo della 161, 186
Portzamparc, Christian de 320–321
Prandtauer, Jakob 218
Pugin, August Welby Northmore 253
Puig i Cadafalch, Josep 274

Quinones, Andrés Garcia de 225

Raffael 162, 164, 174
Rateau, Jean 137
Rauch, John 310
Raymond, Jean-Arnaud 237
Reitermann, Rudolf 324–325
Renwick, James 267
Rhy, Simon Louis du 239
Richardson, Henry Hobson 267
Ried, Benedikt 145
Riedel, Eduard 250
Rietveld, Gerrit Thomas 284
Roebling, John Augustus 262–263
Rogers, Richard 308, 330
Romano, Giulio 176–177
Rosselino, Bernardo 156, 160
Rudnew, Lew 292
Ruff, Ludwig und Franz 293

Saarinen, Eero 305
Safont, Marc 135
Sagrera, Guillem 137
Salucci, Giovanni 241
Salvá, Pere 133

Salvi, Nicola 192
Sangallo, Antonio da 155, 162, 164, 175
Sangallo, Giuliano da 156, 158–159, 164
Sanmicheli, Michele 168–169
Sassenroth, Peter 324–325
Sauerbruch, Matthias 328–329
Scharoun, Hans 286, 288–289, 297
Schinkel, Karl Friedrich 228, 243
Schlaun, Johann Conrad 215, 216
Schmidt, Friedrich von 257
Schmitz, Bruno 261
Schultes, Axel 326–327
Semper, Gottfried 256–257, 260–261
Serlio, Sebastiano 171, 173
Shreve, Lamb & Harmon 282
Sicardsburg, August, 257
Sinan 59
Siza, Alvaro 324
Soane, Sir John 252–253
Solari, Santino 194
SOM (Skidmore, Owens & Merrill) 300, 302–303
Soufflot, Jacques Germain 236
Specchi, Alessandro 192
Speer, Albert 292
Speeth, Peter 240
Spreckelsen, Johann von 297, 320
Stam, Mart 284
Starck, Philip 314–315
Stirling, James 316
Strada, Jacopo 149
Strauss, Joseph B. 273
Stuler, August 228

Stüler, Friedrich August 250
Sullivan, Louis Henry 268, 279

Talenti, Francesco 129
Tange, Kenzo 314–315
Taut, Bruno 273, 280
Terragni, Giuseppe 293
Thon, Constantine 244
Thornton, William 246
Thumb, Peter 214
Tjibaou, Jean-Marie 330
Toledo, Juan Bautista 184
Tomé, Narciso 224
Troost, Paul Ludwig 292
Tschumi, Bernard 320
Turner, Richard 253

Ulrich, Peter 139
Unabara, Kikutake 314
Ungers, Oswald Maria 296, 316
Upjohn, John 267
Utzon, Jørn 304–305

Vanbrugh, Sir John 210–211
Vanvitelli, Luigi 206
Vasari, Giorgio 176
Vauban, Sébastien le Prestre de 213
Velázquez, Isidro Gonzáles 230
Velde, Henry van de 276
Venturi, Robert 310
Vignola, Giacomo Barozzi da 149, 171, 175, 186
Villanueva, Carlos Raúl de 298–299

Villanueva, Juan de 239
Vinoly, Rafael 315
Viollet-le-Duc, Eugène-Emmanuel 251
Virlogeux, Michel 6
Vitruvius 148, 158, 160, 170–171
Vlugt, Leendert Cornelius van der 284
Voigtel, Richard 254
Voronichin, Andrei 244–245
Vorst, Sulpitius van 137
Vries, Vredeman de 177, 178

Wagner, Otto 274
Wallot, Paul 261
Walpole, Horace 252
Waterkeyn, André 305
Weinbrenner, Friedrich 240
Welsch, Maximilian 203
Wiedemann, Christian and Johann Rudolf 208
Witten, Hans 134
Wood, John 185
Wren, Sir Christopher 195, 210–211
Wright, Frank Lloyd 290, 304

Yamasaki, Minoru 296

Zanoia, Giuseppe 255
Zimmermann, Dominikus 220
Zumthor, Peter 317
Zwirner, Ernst Friedrich 254–255

Picture Credits

The editor-in-chief and publisher have made every effort to trace the ownership of all copyrighted material included in this book. Any errors that may have occurred are inadvertent. Individuals or institutions who claim the rights to illustrations therein and have not been contacted are kindly requested to contact the publisher.

© Corbis 7, 10, 13 t., 14 b., 22 b., 35, 46 t., 46 b., 60 b.r., 212 b., 238, 244 t., 245 t., 245 m., 246 b., 247, 258 t.r., 258 b., 262 b., 266 t., 266 b., 267 l., 267 r., 268 l., 268 r., 269, 273 b., 276 m., 282, 283 t.l., 283 l., 283 b., 285 b., 290 t., 291 t., 291 b., 292 b.l., 296 l.t., 296 l.b., 298 b.r., 299 l., 300 t., 300 b.l., 300 b.r., 302 t.l., 302 t.r. 302/303 b., 303 t., 304 t., 305 t., 305 b.l., 309, 314 t., 315 l., 315 r., 318 t.l., 318 t.r., 318 b., 319, 322 t., 323 r., 330 t., 330 m.
© Barragan Foundation, Switzerland/Salas, Portugal/ VG Bild-Kunst, Bonn 2008: 299 t.
© Markus Bollen, Bergisch-Gladbach: 47 t.
© Bridgeman Art Library/Berlin: 19 b., 166, 298 b.l.
© Burkatovski Fine Art Images, Rheinböllen: 244 m., 244 b.
© A. F. Kersting, London: 195 t., 232 t.
© Bildarchiv Monheim, Krefeld: 173 b., 230 t.r., 231 t., 231 m., 233 t., 233 b., 252 t., 252 b., 253 t., 253 m.,
© Scala, Florence: 42 b., 44 b., 128 t., 156 b., 206 t.
© VG Bild-Kunst, Bonn 2008: Walter Gropius (284 M), Ludwig Mies van der Rohe (285 t.), Frank Lloyd Wright (290 b., 304 t.), Le Corbusier (304 b.)
© R.M.N., Paris: 213 t., 269 t., 229 b.
© Vitra (http://www.vitra.com): 313 t., 314 b.

Illustrations on page 2 and chapter opening pages

p. 2   Paris, Louvre, glass pyramid, I.M. Pei, 1882–1889.
p. 8–9   Paestum, Italy, Temple of Athena, ca. 500 BCE.
p. 40–41   Constantinopel/Istanbul, Turkey, Hagia Sophia, Anthemius of Tralles and Isidore of Miletus, 532–537.
p. 56–57   Madinat az-Zahra, Spain, Califs' Residence, 936–976.
p. 66–67   Jouarre, France, Crypt of St Paul, 7th century.
p. 82–83   Santo Domingo de Silos, Spain, transept, 12th century.
p. 110–111 Palma de Mallorca, Spain, Cathedral, begun ca. 1300.
p. 146–147 Venice, Italy, San Giorgio Maggiore, Andrea Palladio, begun 1566.
p. 182–183 Vaux-le-Vicomte, France, Louis Le Vau (architecture) and André Le Nôtre (garden design), begun 1656.
p. 226–227 St Blasien, Germany, former Benedictine abbey church, Pierre-Michel d'Ixnard and Nicolas De Pigage, 1768–1783.
p. 248–249 Sintra, Portugal, Palácio da Pena, Wilhelm Freiherr von Eschwege, 1839–1885.
p. 270–271 Dessau, Germany, Bauhaus Building, Walter Gropius, 1926.
p. 294–295 Valencia, Spain, Ciudad de las Artes y de las Ciencias, Santiago Calatrava, 2000.

This is a Parragon Publishing book
This edition published in 2013

Copyright © Parragon Books Ltd 2008
Parragon Books Ltd
Chartist House
15-17 Trim Street
Bath, BA1 1HA, UK

Original edition production: Thomas Paffen

Editor-in-chief: Rolf Toman
Text: Barbara Borngässer
Photography: Achim Bednorz

All rights reserved.
No part of this publication may be reproduced or transmitted in any form or by any means, electronic or mechanical, including photocopying, recording, or any information storage and retrieval system, without express written permission from the copyright holders.

Copyright © 2008 for the English edition
English edition produced by: APE Int'l. Richmond, VA
Translation from German: Dr. Maureen Basedow, Mary Dobrian, Linda Marianiello and Sally Schreiber for APE Int'l
Editing: Dr. Pippin Michelli and Tammi Reichel

ISBN 978-1-4075-4311-6

Printed in China